DATE DUE			

The Philosophy of W. V. Quine

Willard Van Orman Quine

The Philosophy of W. V. Quine
An Expository Essay

Roger F. Gibson, Jr.

with a foreword by
W. V. Quine

A University of South Florida Book

University Presses of Florida
Tampa / St. Petersburg / Sarasota

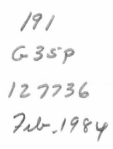

University Presses of Florida is the central agency for scholarly publishing of the State of Florida's university system. Its offices are located at 15 NW 15th Street, Gainesville, Fl 32603. Works published by University Presses of Florida are evaluated and selected for publication by a faculty committee of any one of Florida's nine public universities: Florida A&M University (Tallahassee), Florida Atlantic University (Boca Raton), Florida International University (Miami), Florida State University (Tallahassee), University of Central Florida (Orlando), University of Florida (Gainesville), University of North Florida (Jacksonville), University of South Florida (Tampa), University of West Florida (Pensacola).

The author and publisher of *The Philosophy of W. V. Quine: An Expository Essay* are grateful to the following for permission to reprint copyrighted materials:

The Roots of Reference by W. V. O. Quine: copyright © 1974 by Open Court Publishing Co. All rights reserved.

Essays on the Philosophy of W. V. Quine, edited by Robert S. Shahan and Chris Swoyer: copyright 1979 by the University of Oklahoma Press, Norman, Publishing Division of the University.

Library of Congress Cataloging in Publication Data

Gibson, Roger F.
  The Philosophy of W. V. Quine.

  "A University of South Florida Book."
  Bibliography: p.
  Includes index.
  1. Quine, W. V. (Willard Van Orman)   I. Title.
B945.Q54G5   191   81–16338
ISBN 0–8130–0707–0   AACR2

Contents

List of Abbreviations
Works by W. V. Quine

EES   "On Empirically Equivalent Systems of the World." *Erkenntnis* 9 (1975):313–28.

EN   "Epistemology Naturalized." In *Ontological Relativity and Other Essays*, pp. 69–90. New York: Columbia University Press, 1969.

FM   "Facts of the Matter." In *Essays on the Philosophy of W. V. Quine*, edited by Robert S. Shahan and Chris Swoyer, pp. 155–69. Norman: University of Oklahoma Press, 1979.

IR   "Intensions Revisited." *Midwest Studies in Philosophy* 2 (1977):5–11.

LK   "The Limits of Knowledge." In *The Ways of Paradox and Other Essays*, revised and enlarged edition, pp. 59–67. Cambridge, Mass.: Harvard University Press, 1976.

LP   "Linguistics and Philosophy." In *The Ways of Paradox and Other Essays*, revised and enlarged edition, pp. 56–58. Cambridge, Mass.: Harvard University Press, 1976.

MRCLT   "Methodological Reflections on Current Linguistic Theory." In *On Noam Chomsky: Critical Essays*, edited by Gilbert Harman, pp. 104–17. Garden City, N.Y.: Anchor Press/Doubleday, 1974.

MVD   "Mind and Verbal Dispositions." In *Mind and Language*, edited by Samuel Guttenplan, pp. 83–95. Oxford: Clarendon Press, 1975.

NNK   "The Nature of Natural Knowledge." In *Mind and Language*, edited by Samuel Guttenplan, pp. 67–81. Oxford: Clarendon Press, 1975.

OME   "On Mental Entities." In *The Ways of Paradox and Other Essays*, revised and enlarged edition, pp. 221–27. Cambridge, Mass.: Harvard University Press, 1976.

OR   "Ontological Relativity." In *Ontological Relativity and Other Essays*, pp. 26–68. New York: Columbia University Press, 1969.

PL   *Philosophy of Logic*. Englewood Cliffs, N.J.: Prentice-Hall, Inc., 1970.

PPLT   "Philosophical Progress in Language Theory." *Metaphilosophy* 1 (1970):2–19.

PR   "Posits and Reality." In *The Ways of Paradox and Other Essays*, revised and enlarged edition, pp. 246–54. Cambridge, Mass.: Harvard University Press, 1976.

QPA   "Quantifiers and Propositional Attitudes." In *The Ways of Paradox and Other Essays*, revised and enlarged edition, pp. 185–96. Cambridge, Mass.: Harvard University Press, 1976.

RC   "Reply to Chomsky." In *Words and Objections, Essays on the Work of W. V. Quine*, edited by D. Davidson and J. Hintikka, pp. 302–11. Dordrecht-Holland: D. Reidel Publishing Company, 1969.

RH   "Reply to Harman." In *Words and Objections, Essays on the Work of W. V. Quine*, edited by D. Davidson and J. Hintikka, pp. 295–97. Dordrecht-Holland: D. Reidel Publishing Company, 1969.

RIT   "On the Reasons for Indeterminacy of Translation." *The Journal of Philosophy* 67 (1970):179–83.

RM   "Reference and Modality." In *From a Logical Point of View*, pp. 139–59. New York: Harper and Row, 1963.

RPM   "Reply to Professor Marcus." In *The Ways of Paradox and Other Essays*, revised and enlarged edition, pp. 177–84. Cambridge, Mass.: Harvard University Press, 1976.

RR   *The Roots of Reference*. La Salle, Ill.: Open Court, 1974.

RS   "Reply to Smart." In *Words and Objections, Essays on the Work of W. V. Quine*, edited by D. Davidson and J. Hintikka, pp. 292–94. Dordrecht-Holland: D. Reidel Publishing Company, 1969.

TDE   "Two Dogmas of Empiricism." In *From a Logical Point of View*, pp. 20–46. New York: Harper and Row, 1963.

UPM   "Use and Its Place in Meaning." *Erkenntnis* 13 (1978): 1–8.

WB   (with J. S. Ullian). *The Web of Belief*, 2d edition. New York: Random House, Inc., 1978.

WO   *Word and Object*. Fifth paperback printing. Cambridge, Mass.: The M.I.T. Press, 1970.

WPO   "Whither Physical Objects." In *Essays in Memory of Imre Lakatos*. Edited by R. S. Cohen et al., pp. 497–504. Dordrecht-Holland: D. Reidel Publishing Company, 1976.

WTI   "On What There Is." In *From a Logical Point of View*, pp. 1–19. New York: Harper and Row, 1963.

To Joyce and Georgia

Foreword

It was in 1975, when he was studying at the University of Missouri, that I first heard from Roger Gibson. He had written on my philosophy earlier for his master's degree, and was now outlining a doctoral dissertation on the same flattering subject. If he could make his way to Harvard for a few weeks, could he attend my lectures and ask questions? He came, all business, and his questions were brisk and to the point. Answers sparked further questions, ever more searching, and discussion throve. I sensed before his weeks ran out that my views were in very good hands. His dissertation fulfilled these high expectations, and in his three post-doctoral years he has worked it over into the book that is now before us.

It is a rare pleasure to read someone who understands my position so fully, presents it so clearly, defends it so cogently, and relates it so illuminatingly to earlier doctrines and rival schools. In reading Gibson I gain a welcome perspective on my own work. Fussing with the structure from my cramped position within it, I do not easily gain a proportionate overall view of what I am up to. Roger Gibson, surveying the scene from his external vantage point, does much to fill that need.

W. V. Quine

Cambridge, Massachusetts
June 1980

Preface

In a rather straightforward sense the history of Western philosophy has been dialectical: philosophical ideas have been put forth and subjected to critical evaluation. In modern times the institutionalized study of philosophy has perpetuated this tradition insofar as students are required to learn the ideas of various philosophers and to criticize them. This is how philosophers are trained, and I, for one, know of no better method.

The method is not, however, foolproof. The student who acquires knowledge of a variety of philosophies but neglects to develop the skills necessary for evaluating them risks becoming a dogmatist, or, alternatively, risks becoming merely confused when it comes to taking a stand on some philosophical issue. On the other hand, the student who develops his critical skills but fails to comprehend his subject matter is destined to waste much of his time sparring with phantoms. Thus it would seem that proper training in philosophy requires a balance between comprehension and criticism.

For some years now, it seems to me, in the institutionalized study of philosophy there has been an imbalance between comprehension and criticism: comprehension has waned while criticism has waxed. Students of philosophy have been encouraged to sharpen their critical skills to the detriment of improving their comprehension. Fortunately, things seem to be righting themselves again. The slogan 'Philosophy is an activity' does not have quite the nihilistic ring it had some few years ago, nor is it any longer fashionable—at least in most places—to act as though the history of philosophy began and ended with Wittgenstein's *Philosophical Investigations*.

In this light, I prefer to see the following *expository* essay on Quine's philosophy as contributing to the movement toward regaining equilibrium between comprehension and criticism in the arena of philosophical instruction, for the essay was written primarily with an audience of undergraduate and graduate students of philosophy in mind. It is my hope that students and professionals in disciplines related to philosophy (particularly psychology and linguistics) as well as interested nonstudents may find something of value in it.

Acknowledgments

Although any errors and misinterpretations of Quine's views that are contained in the following essay are entirely my doing, I want to acknowledge other persons who had some role in the production of this book: they are Professor Henry Smits, who first introduced me, some years back, to Quine's writings; Professor John Kultgen, who directed the dissertation out of which this book grew; Professor William Wilcox, who instructed me in Quine's writings and whose many suggestions have made this book better than it would otherwise have been; Professor G. N. Georgacarakos, with whom I have had numerous instructive discussions concerning Quine's philosophy; and Professor W. V. Quine, who has been exceedingly generous to me with his time, materials, and comments. I also would like to express my gratitude to Professor W. Maurice Nielsen for taking charge of seeing that the final version of this manuscript got typed, and to Ms. Jean Livermore, who most expertly carried out that task.

I am also indebted to Professor Stephen P. Turner for the encouragement he gave to me in connection with publishing this book. And I am indebted to the staff of University Presses of Florida for their conscientious assistance which regularly contributed significant improvements to the logic and grammar of the book.

R. F. G.

The author and publisher of *The Philosophy of W. V. Quine: An Expository Essay* are grateful to the following publishers who have granted permission to reprint copyrighted material:

D. Reidel Publishing Company, Dordrecht, Holland: "Use and Its Place in Meaning" by W. V. Quine, *Erkenntnis* 13 (1978): 1–8; "On Empirically Equivalent Systems of the World" by W. V. Quine, *Er-*

kenntnis 9 (1975): 313–28; "Are There Really Two Quines?" by Roger F. Gibson, Jr., *Erkenntnis* 15 (1980): 349–70; "Reply to Harman," "Reply to Chomsky," and "Reply to Smart" by W. V. Quine, and "Quine's Empirical Assumptions" by Noam Chomsky, from *Words and Objections, Essays on the Work of W. V. Quine*, ed. D. Davidson and J. Hintikka (1969); "Whither Physical Objects" by W. V. Quine, from *Essays in Memory of Imre Lakatos*, ed. R. S. Cohen et al. (1976).

Oxford University Press: "Mind and Verbal Dispositions" and "The Nature of Natural Knowledge" by W. V. Quine, from *Mind and Language*, ed. Samuel Guttenplan (1975).

Random House, Inc.: *The Web of Belief* by W. V. Quine and J. S. Ullian (1970, 1978), 2d ed. paper.

Pantheon Books (a division of Random House, Inc.): *Reflections on Language* by Noam Chomsky (1975), 1st ed., paper.

Open Court Publishing Company, La Salle, Illinois: *The Roots of Reference* by W. V. Quine (1974).

W. V. Quine, copyright holder: "Epistemology Naturalized" and "Ontological Relativity" by W. V. Quine, from *Ontological Relativity and Other Essays* by W. V. Quine (1969, 1971), 2d printing.

University of Oklahoma Press, Norman: "Facts of the Matter" by W. V. Quine, from *Essays on the Philosophy of W. V. Quine*, ed. Robert S. Shahan and Chris Swoyer (1979).

Harvard University Press, Cambridge: "Linguistics and Philosophy," "On Mental Entities," "Posits and Reality," and "Reply to Professor Marcus" by W. V. Quine, from *The Ways of Paradox and Other Essays* by W. V. Quine (1966, 1976), rev. and enlarged ed., paper; "Reference and Modality" and "Two Dogmas of Empiricism" by W. V. Quine, from *From a Logical Point of View* by W. V. Quine (1953, 1961, 1963), Harper Torchbook (1963), paper.

The M.I.T. Press, Cambridge: *Word and Object* by W. V. Quine (1960), 5th paper printing, 1970.

W. V. Quine and the editor of *Metaphilosophy*, Hyde Park, New York: "Philosophical Progress in Language Theory" by W. V. Quine, *Metaphilosophy* 1 (1970): 2–19.

We see, then, a strategy for investigating the relation of evidential support, between observation and scientific theory. We can adopt a genetic approach, studying how theoretical language is learned. For the evidential relation is virtually enacted, it would seem, in the learning. This genetic strategy is attractive because the learning of language goes on in the world and is open to scientific study. It is a strategy for the scientific study of scientific method and evidence. We have here a good reason to regard the theory of language as vital to the theory of knowledge.

—W. V. Quine, "The Nature of Natural Knowledge"

Introduction

Not long ago Professor Stuart Hampshire referred to Willard Van Orman Quine (b. 1908) as "the most distinguished living systematic philosopher."[1] Professor Hampshire's remark is both surprising and instructive. Surprising not because he regards Quine to be a distinguished philosopher; most philosophers would go along with that. The surprising thing is to be told that Quine is a system builder, and for at least two reasons: first, because of the generally acknowledged fact that in the twentieth century systematic philosophers are almost as rare as dinosaurs, especially in the Anglo-American strain of which Quine is a significant member; second, because it seems contrary to the generally accepted image of Quine as a philosopher who has focused his *analytic* talents on a multiplicity of apparently disparate doctrines and theses—for example, the doctrine of inscrutability of reference, the thesis of indeterminacy of translation, the doctrine of empirical slack (with its dual aspects—holism, or revisibility, and underdetermination of theory), and the doctrine of ontological relativity. Professor Hampshire's claim is instructive just because it corrects this misconception of Quine's philosophy. For these various philosophical doctrines and theses, which are associated with Quine's name, are not simply a collection of Quine's thoughts on a variety of more or less unrelated topics. They are, on the contrary, related to one another so as to form a systematic whole.

1. Bryan Magee, "Conversations with Stuart Hampshire," in *Modern British Philosophy*, ed. Bryan Magee (New York: St. Martin's Press, 1971), p. 27.

The importance of recognizing the systematic character of Quine's philosophy cannot be overemphasized, for if it is overlooked or ignored, the chances of misunderstanding Quine's position regarding any of various topics are increased. For example, Quine's position on the question of the intelligibility of the notion of synonymy when confronted as a doctrine isolated from the rest of Quine's philosophical system is bound to appear trivial or even ad hoc and dogmatic. But when Quine's position on synonymy is put in perspective by incorporating it into the larger picture of his philosophical system, it appears quite otherwise. Consequently, one of my chief concerns in this expository essay is to convey to the reader an appreciation of the systematic character of Quine's philosophy.

If I had to characterize Quine's philosophy beyond merely saying with Hampshire that it is systematic, and yet at the same time had to restrict myself to a single sentence, I would say the following: *Quine's philosophy is a systematic attempt to answer, from a uniquely empiricistic point of view, what he takes to be the central question of epistemology, namely, 'How do we acquire our theory of the world?'* Indeed, I use this general characterization of Quine's philosophy, centered as it is around a single question of epistemology, as the focus of my entire essay. In so doing, I have found it useful to divide my presentation of Quine's philosophy into four stages.

In the first stage (Chapter 1, The foundation), I introduce certain doctrines and concepts which provide the *foundation* for understanding Quine's account of how we acquire our theory of the world. The doctrines and concepts that I deal with at this stage of my presentation are "foundational" only in the sense that an understanding of them is presupposed by, and will facilitate the understanding of, what I say in the second and third stages. Furthermore, this is the *only* rationale I used in assembling Chapter 1, so that apart from this rationale the topics I consider there, namely the nature of Quine's brand of empiricism (§1.1), his views on perceiving and learning (§1.2), and his grammatical analysis of English (§1.3), may appear to be rather strange bedfellows. Because of the technical terms introduced in Chapter 1, it may seem unusually demanding to some readers. But the price of learning Quine's technical vocabulary must be paid somewhere along the line if one wants to understand him, and it is just as well, or better, to make a big down payment at the start.

In the second stage of my presentation (Chapter 2, The framework), I explain how Quine reformulates the question of how we acquire our theory of the world as the question of how we acquire our *theoretical talk* about the world, or, more generally, how we acquire our talk about the world (§2.1). I also explain Quine's naturalistic-behavioristic conception of language (§2.2), that is, his views on linguistic meaning (semantics) (§2.2.1) and on language learning (§2.2.2). Quine's behavioristic conception of language is especially germane to the question of how we acquire our theory of the world because he regards theories, from first to last, to be linguistic structures. So, it is quite natural for him to reformulate the question of how we acquire our theory of the world as the question of how we acquire our theoretical *talk* about the world. Any answer to this question that is going to be acceptable to Quine must be propounded within the parameters of his general, behavioristic theory of perceiving and learning and, more particularly, within the *framework* of his behavioristic conception of language. Such is the restrictive role that behaviorism plays in Quine's philosophical enterprise.

In the third stage of my presentation (Chapter 3, The edifice), I present in some detail the various doctrines and theses that comprise Quine's philosophy in such a way as to reveal, so far as I can, their interrelations and their connection with Quine's naturalistic-behavioristic conception of language. I have made an effort to be comprehensive in my inclusion of topics, but I am sure readers who are familiar with Quine's writings will discover that I have omitted some important topic(s). Most notably I have omitted a detailed account of Quine's views on logic. I do, however, discuss his criterion of ontic commitment, his program of regimentation, and his position regarding modal logic. The reader who is interested in Quine's logic could do no better than to consult Quine's works that deal specifically with that topic. (Also in this regard, and in others, Alex Orenstein's *Willard Van Orman Quine* is very informative.)

I have also attempted to make my account of Quine's philosophy as current as possible. Consequently, I have relied heavily on essays which Quine published after *Word and Object* (1960) and even after *The Roots of Reference* (1974). As a rule, I have made no attempt to indicate the historical development of Quine's thinking on particular topics, nor in general. Anyway, so far as I can see (logic aside), he has refined his views greatly but changed them only slightly since he began to write philosophy. One notable exception is, perhaps, his change in attitude toward phenomenalism, and this I do point out in my discussion of his physicalism (§3.5.2).

My presentation of Quine's philosophy is conditioned in large part by my perception of the central role which behaviorism plays in his philosophy. As I see it, Quine's behaviorism prescribes the content of almost all of his more important doctrines and theses by restricting, ahead of time, what are to count as acceptable answers to a multitude of philosophical questions. Quine's behaviorism also serves to unite these doctrines and theses into a systematic philosophy. From within this behavioristic framework Quine can argue, for example, that meaning is indeterminate, that reference is inscrutable, that ontology is relative, that theories are underdetermined by experience in principle, that the truth value of *any* sentence or statement can be revised, that there are no meanings, no propositions, no attributes, no relations, no numbers, no synonymity, no facts, no analytic truths, and so forth.

It would appear from this catalogue of negative findings (issuing from Quine's behavioristic orientation) that Quine is in danger of suffering Bishop Berkeley's unjust fate, namely, that of becoming famous (or infamous) more for what he denies than for what he affirms! I doubt that things will go that badly for Quine, but these separate, negative conclusions have doubtlessly obscured the fact that Quine's philosophy forms a systematic whole. A more interesting speculation of a historical sort is that Quine's commitment to behaviorism may very well prove to be his Achilles' heel; for if, at some time in the future, behaviorism (in Quine's sense of term) is abandoned, say, in favor of some form of mentalism, then an overwhelming majority of Quine's cardinal doctrines and theses would be left without any obvious firm support and, therefore, cast into doubt.

However, it is one thing to say that much of what is important in Quine's philosophical system hinges on his behavioristic orientation. It is quite another thing to say *just how much* of his system would remain intact if that orientation were eschewed, for nonbehavioristic bases of support might well be discovered for these same doctrines and theses. Such, indeed, is one possible scenario for the historical development of empiricism in the twenty-first century.

In the fourth stage of my presentation (Chapter 4, The defense), I sketch a defense of Quine's theory of language learning, and I attempt to clarify further the nature of his particular brand of behaviorism. I conclude there merely that he has been consistent over the years in his advocacy of behaviorism and that his theory of language learning, though incomplete in important respects, remains nevertheless a viable theory.

The Philosophy of W. V. Quine

Chapter 1. The foundation

§1.1. *Enlightened empiricism*

From a historical point of view, Quine's philosophy, as a whole, is an attempt to salvage and to reorient an empiricism that had its beginnings at least as far back as John Locke's *Essay* and its most recent stage before Quine in Rudolf Carnap's *Aufbau*. This statement is not intended to detract from the originality of Quine's contribution but to underscore the importance of his place in modern empiricism.

Over the centuries since Locke, empiricism has enjoyed (or suffered) a more or less programmatic continuity of seeking to reduce knowledge of the world, in one way or another, to sense experience. This program reached its zenith in the writings of Carnap and others of the Vienna Circle. The goals of such empiricism, which Quine calls *radical empiricism*, were twofold: to *deduce* the truths of nature from sensory evidence, and to *translate* (or *define*) those truths in terms of observation and logico-mathematical auxiliaries. Quine has identified the former ambition with what he calls the *doctrinal* side of epistemology and the latter with what he calls the *conceptual* side of epistemology. On the doctrinal side the primary concern is with justifying our knowledge of the truths of nature in sensory terms; on the conceptual side the primary concern is with explaining the notion of body in sensory terms.

The chief motivation behind these ambitions, namely, the desire to attain absolute certainty in our knowledge about the world, was something empiricism had inherited from the seventeenth-century rational-

1

ist René Descartes. Empiricistic philosophers after Descartes sought a theory of knowledge that would establish the rationale for indubitable propositions of sense and would prescribe techniques for constructing (or deducing) from these the other propositions of scientific knowledge. In short, what these philosophers sought was a first philosophy, or metaphysics. Furthermore, they thought that such a first philosophy must stand outside the body of scientific knowledge whose acquisition it made possible, for they thought it would be viciously circular to use the findings of science as data for justifying scientific knowledge itself.

What was sought by these empiricists was not forthcoming: there was no successful first philosophy. On the doctrinal side of epistemology, radical empiricism had not gotten beyond the position of David Hume. Since (on the conceptual side of epistemology) Hume had identified bodies with sense impressions, he was able to maintain (on the doctrinal side of his epistemology) that some singular statements about bodies, namely, statements about impressions immediately present, were, indeed, indubitable. But neither general statements of existence nor statements about the future gained any degree of certitude as a result of Hume's identifying bodies with sense impressions. For even modest generalizations about observable traits (such as 'Grass is green') will cover more cases than the person making the generalization could ever have actually observed. Consequently the hopelessness of justifying our knowledge of the truths of nature in terms of immediate experience in a firmly logical way must be acknowledged. As Quine notes epigrammatically, the Humean predicament is the human predicament. One of the primary ambitions of radical empiricism must therefore be abandoned: there will be no deducing the truths of science from indubitable truths of sense experience, and the Cartesian motivation—the desire to establish all truths of nature with a certitude comparable to the certitude of truths of immediate experience—must be denied.

On the conceptual side of epistemology the story is equally grim but more complex. Even though Carnap recognized the impossibility of deducing science from immediate experience, he nevertheless kept pursuing the other primary aim of radical empiricism: the defining of the concepts of science in sensory and logico-mathematical terms. Quine points out two reasons for Carnap's persistence:

> One was that such constructions could be expected to elicit and clarify the sensory evidence for science, even if the inferential steps between sensory evidence and scientific doctrine must

fall short of certainty. The other reason was that such constructions would deepen our understanding of our discourse about
the world, even apart from questions of evidence; it would
make all cognitive discourse as clear as observation terms and
logic and . . . set theory. (EN, 74–75)

If Carnap's program had succeeded, it would have been a great epistemological achievement, for it would have provided the means for
translating science into logic, observation terms, and set theory, thereby showing that the rest of the concepts of science were theoretically
superfluous.

Despite Carnap's best efforts, however, no such *rational reconstruction* of scientific discourse in observation terms and logico-mathematical auxiliaries was forthcoming. Carnap's failure was not due to
any personal shortcomings; rather, if Quine is right, he failed because
not every statement about the world to be found in scientific theories
has a fund of empirical implications it can call its own. In other words,
it is not the case that each and every sentence of scientific theories has
a unique empirical meaning, given one account of meaning (namely
the verificationists' account). Hence, there is no hope of translating
each of the sentences, taken individually, into an equivalent sentence
expressed in observational terms and logico-mathematical auxiliaries.
Consequently, hope of attaining the second primary aim of radical empiricism must also be abandoned.

I should like to emphasize in passing that the claim that *a statement
about the world does not always or usually have a separate fund of
empirical consequences (or meaning) that it can call its own* is the
most important single statement that occurs in Quine's writings. It is
the discovery of this truth, if it be a truth, that allows Quine to salvage
and to reorient modern empiricism. I shall have occasion later (in
Chapter 3) to say much more not only about the consequences of
Quine's insight but also about its origins. For if one understands why
Quine makes this claim and what the consequences of the claim are,
then one understands a sizable part of Quine's philosophy.

Certainly the failure of radical empiricism, with its despairing of
deducing science from immediate experience and also of rationally
reconstructing scientific discourse from observation terms and logico-
mathematical auxiliaries, is a failure for empiricism in general. However, there are still two cardinal tenets of empiricism that Quine thinks
remain intact: "One is that whatever evidence there *is* for science *is*

sensory evidence. The other . . . is that all inculcation of meanings of words must rest ultimately on sensory evidence" (EN, 75). In a modest way these two statements are, respectively, the *doctrinal* and *conceptual* sides of the new empiricism Quine is forging.

Now that the basic tenets of empiricism have been chopped down to size, Quine thinks that we should reassess the ultimate goal of empiricism and also the means of pursuing it. In the old epistemology the goal was to start from self-evident, nonscientific truths about sensory experience and deduce (by self-evident steps) or construct (by means of logic and set theory) all of the truths of natural science. In such a program, as noted earlier, it would be impermissible to use the findings of scientific theories as part of the initial data. The idea was that our theory of knowledge, our first philosophy, should somehow contain, but not be contained in, science. Now, however, amidst the wreckage of radical empiricism, Quine is suggesting that the goal for the emerging empiricism is much the same as, if not identical to, that of the old empiricism. *The goal of the new empiricism is to provide an account of how, given only the evidence of our senses, we construct (but do not deduce) our theory of the world.*

But how does this differ from Carnap's program of rational reconstruction? It differs in that the account now sought of the link between observation and theory is not to be one of translation or of definition but one of empirical fact. That is, Carnap was content to rationally reconstruct physical discourse from observation and logico-mathematical auxiliaries by any (within certain general parameters) workable set of constructions. Any reconstruction of theoretical discourse in sensory terms and logico-mathematical auxiliaries would be counted as acceptable if it made the theoretical discourse come out right. "But why all this creative reconstruction, all this make-believe? The stimulation of his sensory receptors is all the evidence anybody has had to go on, ultimately, in arriving at his picture of the world. Why not just see how this construction really proceeds? Why not settle for psychology?" (EN, 75).

Indeed, since it is now widely recognized that the rational reconstruction of scientific discourse along the lines advocated by Carnap is an impossibility, and, as a consequence, that it is also impossible to show by translating science into sensory terms and logico-mathematical auxiliaries that many of the concepts of science are theoretically superfluous, there is no longer any reason for preferring rational reconstruction over psychology. To be sure, psychology, in attempting to provide a factual account of the link between observation and scientific theory, cannot supply the desired translations either, since no one grows up learning scientific language in terms of a prior language of set theory, logic, and observation. Nevertheless, Quine believes that it would be "better to discover how science is in fact developed and learned than to fabricate a fictitious structure to a similar effect" (EN, 78).

Thus Quine's proposal is that the primary goal of epistemology is to provide a *factual account* of the link between observation and theory, or, as he has so graphically phrased it, "between the meager input and the torrential output" (EN, 83). Furthermore, this factual account is to be pursued within the framework of natural science itself, that is, within the framework of empirical (behavioristic) psychology.

> Such a study could still include, even, something like the old rational reconstruction, to whatever degree such reconstruction is practicable; for imaginative constructions can afford hints of actual psychological processes, in much the way that mechanical simulations can. But a conspicious difference between old epistemology and the epistemological enterprise in this new psychological setting is that we can now make free use of empirical psychology. (EN, 83)

It is this methodological shift to naturalism that signals Quine's departure from and reorientation of traditional, empiricistic epistemology. Quine's naturalism is a departure from the old epistemology because it constitutes an abandonment of the latter's quest for a first philosophy upon which to construct scientific theory; it is a reorientation of the old epistemology in the sense that it relocates epistemology within the confines of scientific theory itself.

But what of the charge of circularity? How can the new epistemologist legitimately use the findings of natural science to validate the institution of scientific knowledge itself? The answer to this question lies, Quine thinks, in the nature of the skeptical challenge to our knowledge of the external world. For centuries philosophers have recognized that knowledge is the offspring of doubt: it is skepticism that prompts us to try to develop a theory of knowledge. But, it is equally true, even if less frequently noted, that doubt is the offspring of knowledge. The basis for skeptical doubt is the awareness of illusion. Mirages, straight sticks seemingly bent by water, rainbows, afterimages, double images, and dreams are all familiar illusions cited by skeptics intent on showing the fallibility of our senses. But such illusions are recognizable *as illusions* only because they are known to be other than they appear—they appear to be material objects, but they are not.

Hence, illusions are illusions only relative to a prior acceptance of genuine bodies with which to contrast them: "Rudimentary physical science, that is, common sense about bodies, is thus needed as a springboard for scepticism" (NNK, 67–68).

Under the influence of a more sophisticated science the skeptical challenge takes on a more precise form. The challenge to the modern epistemologist runs as follows:

> Science itself teaches that there is no clairvoyance; that the only information that can reach our sensory surfaces from external objects must be limited to two-dimensional optical projections and various impacts of air waves on the eardrums and some gaseous reactions in the nasal passages and a few kindred odds and ends. How, the challenge proceeds, could one hope to find out about that external world from such meager traces? (RR, 2)

According to Quine, the epistemologist's problem is that of finding ways, in keeping with natural science, whereby the human animal can have projected this same science from the sensory information that could reach him according to that science. "A far cry, this, from old epistemology. Yet it is no gratuitous change of subject matter, but an enlightened persistence rather in the original epistemological problem" (RR, 3). The new epistemologist's undertaking is *enlightened* because he recognizes that the skeptical challenge springs from within science itself and that in coping with it he is free to use whatever scientific knowledge is available.

Hence, the new epistemologist no longer dreams of a first philosophy, firmer than science, on which science can be based. Rather, he is out to defend science from within, against its own self doubts. But the epistemologist's project, even apart from any concern with the skeptical challenge to science, is one of major philosophical interest; for we can grant the truth of natural science and persist in raising the question, within natural science, how it is that man can have arrived at his scientific theories of the world on the meager evidence of the impingements that are available to his sensory surfaces.

> This is a question of empirical psychology, but it may be pursued at one or more removes from the laboratory, one or another level of speculativity. Its philosophical interest is evident. If we were to get to the bottom of it, we ought to be able to see

just to what extent science is man's free creation; to what extent, in Eddington's phrase, it is a put-up job. And we ought to be able to see whatever there is to see about the evidence relation, the relation borne to theory by the observations that support it. (RR, 3–4)

Such is Quine's program for the new epistemologist of enlightened empiricism. In Chapter 2 we shall see how Quine's enlightened empiricism takes a *genetic approach* to the central question of epistemology, but for now we must direct our attention toward Quine's general theory of learning.

§1.2 *Perceiving and learning*

In the previous section we saw that Quine views the central problem of epistemology to be one of providing a factual, scientific account of how man arrives at his theory of the world from impingements upon his sensory receptors. The problem is, according to Quine, merely part of the general problem of explaining how man learns anything at all. Epistemology thus seen is a chapter of empirical psychology, and empirical psychology for Quine means behavioristic psychology. Such psychology is ultimately mechanistic and physicalistic and does not acquiesce in talk of ideas and other mental entities. Thus the behavioral psychologist talks of learning in terms of stimuli, responses, dispositions, and the like.

Quine has developed in some detail such a general behavioristic theory of learning. Furthermore, his theory of language learning, which will be discussed in Chapter 2, is based on this general behavioristic theory of learning. Consequently, we might do well to survey this general theory before confronting his theory of language learning itself.

One might suspect that learning, for Quine, as for any good empiricist, begins with perception. This suspicion finds confirmation in Quine's writings, but Quine's account of learning begins with a more physical concept: *reception*. To say that a subject is in a (physical) state of reception—which he always is, unless he is dead—is to say that his nerve endings are receiving stimulation. Such a state is what Quine calls an *episode*.

The episodes of a single subject's life are related in various important ways. One of these relations is what Quine calls *receptual similarity*. The receptual similarity of a subject's episodes is the mere physical similarity of impact on the subject's sensory surface, regardless of his behavior. Receptual similarity is, of course, a matter of degree: "Episodes are receptually similar to the degree that the total set of sensory receptors that are triggered on the one occasion approximates the set triggered on the other occasion" (RR, 16).

By utilizing the mathematical notion of a neighborhood, Quine generalizes the concept of receptual similarity beyond simply relating individual, dated, concrete occasions in a subject's life. Such generalization is important inasmuch as conditioning requires repeatable types of occasions and each episode is a unique event. Also, the generalized notion of receptual similarity will serve later to help characterize another relation of episodes, namely, the relation of *perceptual similarity*.

A *mathematical neighborhood* can be characterized as a collection of points *all* of which are closer to some point *p*, than is some other point *q*; in other words, all the points closer to *p* than *q* is constitute a mathematical neighborhood—the neighborhood of *p*. Further, when we predicate a property of all the points in the neighborhood of *p*, we mean that all the points nearer to *p* than *q* is have that property. Now, applying this idea to episodes rather than to points, we can say that a *receptual neighborhood* is a collection of a subject's episodes *all* of which are receptually more similar to some one episode *a* than is some other episode *d*; in other words, all the episodes receptually more similar to *a* than *d* is constitute a receptual neighborhood—the neighborhood of *a*. Further, when we predicate a property of all the episodes in the neighborhood of *a*, we mean that all the episodes receptually more similar to *a* than *d* is have that property.

Unlike reception, perception does involve the subject's awareness, as the Gestalt psychologists have demonstrated. Nevertheless, perception is accessible to a behavioral criterion. Thus, suppose we provide an animal with both a screen to look at and a lever to press. If he presses the lever when the screen shows a circular stripe, a pellet of food is delivered. If he presses the lever when the screen shows four spots spread in a semicircular arc, a shock is delivered. Suppose that on a subsequent occasion the screen shows those same four spots arranged as before but supplemented with four more spots, suggesting the complementary semicircle. If the animal now presses the lever, he may be said to have perceived the circular Gestalt rather than the component spots. Approached in this behavioral way "the notion of perception belongs to the psychology of learning: to the theory of conditioning, or of habit formation. Habits, inculcated by conditioning, are *dispositions*" (RR, 4; *my emphasis*).

Behavioristic philosophers, like Quine, are disposed to use the term 'disposition' and it is a fair question to ask what they could possibly mean by it. For Quine, the general dispositional idiom (i.e., the term 'disposition', and the general technique of applying suffixes like '-ble' to verb stems, e.g., 'breakable', and the corresponding intensional conditional, e.g., 'would break if struck') is programmatic; it plays a regulative role rather than a constitutive role. "It forms families of terms on the basis not of structural or causal affinities among the physical states or mechanisms that the terms refer to, but on the basis only of a sameness of style on our part in earmarking those states or mechanisms" (RR, 11). In other words, when we say that something *x* 'has the disposition to dissolve', or 'is soluble', or 'would dissolve if placed in water', and that something *y* 'has the disposition to break', or 'is breakable', or 'would break if struck', we are not thereby, for Quine, asserting anything about the physical structures of the objects *x* and *y*, let alone that their structures have anything in common. The only thing in common denoted by our dispositional talk about *x* and our dispositional talk about *y* is that by means of such talk we can refer to a hypothetical state or mechanism that we do not yet understand while merely specifying one of its characteristic effects, such as dissolving when immersed in water, or breaking when struck.

The general dispositional idiom is useful, then, in referring to hypothetical states or mechanisms that we do not understand, by specifying some characteristic effect such as dissolving in water. As such, the general dispositional idiom is indispensable to developing theory. On the other hand, a very developed theory, once the relevant underlying mechanisms have been discovered, can do without disposition-talk: "As theory progresses, some of these terms can be paraphrased, like 'water soluble', into terms of the mechanics of small bodies. Others, like 'intelligent', may stay on as uneliminable components of a few theoretical statements" (RR, 11).

Quine's theory of perception makes use of the general dispositional idiom because it could not be stated without it. Perception is dispositional for Quine just because the neurophysiological mechanisms of perception are so little understood. His hope is, of course, to keep his functional specifications, i.e., his disposition-talk, as simple and specific as possible in order to hasten the day when their physical mode of operation may be understood.

Returning now to the animal experiment and the elucidation of a behavioral criterion of perception, we noted that when the animal was confronted with a circular stripe and pressed the lever it was rewarded with food; and when it was confronted with the four spots placed in a semicircle and it pressed the lever it received a shock. By these means the animal is inhibited from pressing the lever when the four spots are presented and is habituated to press the lever when the circular stripe is presented. Granting this, when confronted with eight spots arranged in a circle, if the animal then presses the lever, it could be said to have perceived the circular Gestalt rather than the component spots.

Some flexibility is gained if, instead of speaking merely of what is or is not perceived, we speak in a way that allows for differences of degree. Thus we could say that the configuration of the eight spots proves to be perceptually more similar to the circular stripe (for this animal) than to the configuration of the four spots. Even better, we can take *perceptual similarity* as relating episodes in the animal's life.

> This shift from perceptions to perceptual similarity brings not only flexibility but also a certain gain in ontological clarity, by dismissing the percepts or perceptions. Ontologically the episodes that are related by perceptual similarity may be understood simply as brief stages or temporal segments of the perceiving subject's body. They are times in his life. Thus they are global episodes, including all irrelevancies. But the perceptual similarity that relates them is no overall point-by-point similarity. It can be as partial as you please, focussing on where the action is. (RR, 16)

By making use of the earlier notions of receptual similarity and receptual neighborhood, we can now state the behavioral conditions for perceptual similarity thus: a is shown to be perceptually more similar to b than to c when the subject has been conditioned to respond in some way to all episodes in the receptual neighborhood of b, and to withhold that response from all episodes in the receptual neighborhood of c, and is then found to so respond to those in the neighborhood of a. This formulation of the criterion can be expanded to a polyadic form— a is perceptually more similar to $b_1, \ldots, b_n$ than to $c_1, \ldots, c_n$— where the learning situation demands. Take, for example, the situation where a certain response is reinforced in the presence of a red block and is penalized in the presence of a yellow rose. A red rose, then, will perhaps not elicit the response, since it has a favorable color but an unfavorable shape. But if the response had been reinforced also in the presence of a red handkerchief, thereby eliminating shape from the similarity basis of the association, the red rose will elicit it. So we do not want to say in such situations that the episode of the red rose was perceptually more similar to that of the red block than to that of the yellow rose, but we do want to say that it was perceptually more similar jointly to the episodes of the red ball and the red handkerchief than to the episode of the yellow rose.

Perceptual similarity is thus an indication of a subject's disposition to submit to conditioning, of his disposition to acquire and to change his habits of response. These habits, also, are dispositions to behavior, and it is thus that perceptual similarity is a bundle of second-order dispositions to behavior.

For Quine these bundles of second-order dispositions, behaviorally detectable as the relations of perceptual similarity of episodes, are of two kinds: innate and acquired. This dichotomy is, strictly speaking, not Quine's, because he thinks that some perceptual similarity standards are acquired *in utero* and he calls these innate too. Hence it would be more accurate to say that Quine thinks the two kinds of second-order dispositions are prenatal and postnatal. Even so, among the prenatal kind there must be, he thinks, some implicit standards, however provisional, for ordering our episodes as more or less perceptually similar, and which must therefore antedate all learning and be innate (in the sense of being nonacquired). In other words, if learning is to take place by means of conditioning, as Quine thinks it does, then the learning subject must be initially endowed with the ability to group his episodes along various dimensions, and this ability itself cannot be the product of learning, for, if it were, it too would presuppose some previous ability, and so on, ad infinitum.

Such innate standards of perceptual similarity are subjective, of course, since the relation of perceptual similarity is always confined to a single subject. The episodes that are rated as perceptually similar are episodes of that subject's life. They are more or less similar *for him.* Yet the innate sense of perceptual similarity has, for all its subjectivity, a degree of objective validity as well. Man's inductive expectations are arrived at by extrapolating along lines of perceptual similarity. Experiences that have similar beginnings are expected to turn out similarly. In short "our innate standards of perceptual similarity show a gratifying tendency to run with the grain of nature" (RR, 19). Quine thinks that this concurrence is a product of natural selection: "Since good prediction has survival value, natural selection will have fostered perceptual similarity standards in us and in other animals that tend accordingly. Natural selection will have favored green and blue, as avenues of inductive generalization, and never grue" (RR, 19; *note omitted*).[1]

The detection of a subject's innate standards of perceptual similarity, however, has its problems. To detect perceptual similarity behaviorally, a subject must first be conditioned to respond in a particular way to all episodes in the receptual neighborhood of episode *b* and to withhold that response to all episodes in the receptual neighborhood of episode *c*, and then tested for the response in the face of an episode in the receptual neighborhood of episode *a*. If this *a*-type episode elicits the same type of response that was associated with the *b*-type episodes, then this *a*-type episode is alleged to be more similar to *b*-type episodes than to *c*-type episodes (for this subject). The problem with this criterion is that some internal state of the subject might inhibit or elicit the response in question in the *a* case regardless of present stimulation.

The kinds of internal states Quine has in mind here are the subject's current purposes, his passing memories, and so forth. Quine's problem is that he wants perceptual similarity to be reflected in *behavioral similarity* (i.e., the relation of episodes in terms of overt behavior), but in just so much of the behavioral output as is a function of the current input. However, there does not seem to be any behavioral way to determine just what part, if any, of the subject's behavior on a particular occasion is elicited by the current input while the rest of his behavior on that occasion is brought about by other internal conditions. In other words, the behavioral criterion of perceptual similarity that Quine has been developing is not sufficient for detecting even innate standards of perceptual similarity—because these dispositions, like all dispositions, are susceptible to interference, and the interference, on isolated occasions, is not behaviorally detectable.

Quine's solution to this difficulty lies in his naturalism:

There must be, we saw, an innate standard of perceptual similarity. It underlies our primitive inductions, and is accountable to natural selection by virtue of its survival value. So we may be confident that what we are looking for under the head of

1. The allusion here is to Goodman's paradox concerning grue emeralds. See Nelson Goodman, *Fact, Fiction, and Forecast* (New York: Bobbs-Merrill, 1955), pp. 74–75.

perceptual similarity must persist rather stably, and manifest itself in the subject's behavior a good part of the time, despite
sporadic interferences from his ongoing internal states. If it
were not thus dominant and persistent, it would not have been
so important for survival; it would not have helped our ances-
tors so much in recognizing the wholesome and the toxic, the
predator and the prey. Moreover, such being the nature of this
hypothetical physiological state or mechanism, we may expect
it to change only slowly under the influence of experience.
(RR, 22)

Quine thinks that these reflections show a way of weeding out the episodes in which the behavior of the subject is due largely to internal
interferences, thereby isolating the episodes that are perceptually relevant: "If an episode is perceptually relevant, then *most* episodes that
are not very remote in time from that one, and are receptually similar
to it, should be behaviorally similar to it" (RR, 22–23). These perceptually relevant episodes are the ones the psychologist must use to
gauge a subject's standards of perceptual similarity. "It is a matter of
detecting regular trends beneath the perturbations" (RR, 23).

Further, Quine is of the opinion that these same reflections on innateness and natural selection suggest another, and somewhat better,
index of what behavior is relevant to detecting perceptual similarities,
namely, social uniformity:

We may expect our innate similarity standards to be much
alike, since they are hereditary in the race; and even as these
standards gradually change with experience we may expect
them to stay significantly alike, what with our shared environment, shared culture, shared language, and mutual influence.
So, if we find that one subject's episodes a and b tend to be
perceptually more or less similar according as another subject's
episodes a' and b' are perceptually more or less similar, whenever a is receptually *very* similar to a' and b to b', we may be
encouraged to believe that our plotting of perceptual similarities for the two subjects is proceeding nicely. (RR, 23; *my
emphasis*)

The "catch" to this approach toward gaining behavioral access to standards of perceptual similarity, and one which Quine explicitly acknowledges, comes where he talks about the episodes of one subject

being *very similar* to those of the other. 'Very similar' in this context cannot mean receptually similar. Receptual similarity is a relation among episodes of the same subject. Hence, when Quine talks about the *very similar* episodes among subjects, he is speaking in an uncritical vein. Apparently there is no theoretical way to specify this kind of similarity since even members of the same species have nerve networks which are very different from one another in structure.

In practice this difficulty is overcome by an implicit homology assumption. In the case, for example, of a parent teaching a child, say, a color word ostensively, the parent implicitly assumes that the child's surface impingements are similar to his own (despite their different perspectives), once the parent has satisfied himself that the child's view of the colored surface is not obstructed by some intervening object. For the psychologist mapping the perceptual similarity standards of a segment of the population, the case is similar. He assumes similarity of reception among his subjects once the physical setting has been scouted sufficiently.

A brief summary of what we have seen thus far of Quine's views on perception and learning might be helpful in providing some continuity with what remains to be said with respect to *traces, salience,* and *pleasure*. For Quine, learning is a matter of acquiring habits through conditioning. Such habits are dispositions. In order for learning to take place we must assume that the learning subject has an innate (i.e., not-learned) ability to regard some of his episodes as being more or less similar to other of his episodes. This innate ability is what Quine calls innate standards of perceptual similarity. These innate standards (as well as acquired ones) are second-order dispositions, i.e., dispositions to acquire other habits (or dispositions). They have a tendency to change with experience, but we can expect the innate ones to change slowly since they have proved so successful in the struggle for survival. The fact that standards of perceptual similarity do change with experience has presented some difficulty to the project of establishing a behavioral criterion for perceptual similarity. Quine's solution to this problem has been to point out that in practice the psychologist can get by if he is careful to map similarity standards for a subject over a sufficiently long period, and can then correlate his findings for that subject with those for other members of the community that he has tested under similar stimulatory conditions. Quine's conjecture here, which is based upon considerations of innateness, evolution, heredity, and social uniformity, is that standards of perceptual similarity are more or less uniform throughout society and are slow to change. The theoretical problem with his solution is that it depends upon a notion of similarity of stimulation among subjects and that such a notion does not appear to be amenable to any straightforward nonintuitive specification.

We have thus seen that learning is, for Quine, essentially a matter of establishing habits based on innate standards of perceptual similarity. One episode of a subject is regarded by that subject to be more or less similar to others of his episodes. But how is it, by what mechanism is it possible, that a subject accomplishes this? Quine's answer to this question is given in terms of traces, salience, and pleasure. These terms, 'traces', 'salience', and 'pleasure', have their mentalistic overtones. And while it would be intolerable to deprive ourselves of these useful idioms, "let us remember that this is all meant to be, in the end, a matter of physiological mechanisms, manifested in behavior" (RR, 26).

To begin with, episodes leave traces. "Such *traces*, whatever their physiological nature, are essential to all learning. The trace of an episode must preserve, in some form, enough information to show perceptual similarity between that episode and later ones" (RR, 25). On the other hand, the traces do not preserve everything of an episode. Episodes are global affairs, times in the life of a subject. Perceptual similarity hinges, rather, upon noticing *salient* features of episodes:

> Noticing is a matter of degree, and perceptual similarity is sensitive to this variation. Thus suppose a cat is visible at times *a, b,* and *c*; suppose that the broad visual setting of the cat is much the same at times *a* and *c* but quite different at *b*; but suppose the cat is salient at times *a* and *b*, because of motion or spotlighting or focal position, and not at *c*. Then the subject may find *a* perceptually more similar to *b* than to *c*, despite the sameness of landscape at *a* and *c*. Perhaps *a* is receptually much more similar to *c* than to *b*; still, salience has the power to swing perceptual similarity the other way. (RR, 25)

The physiological conditions of a subject that are necessary for the recognition of salience are of two general types: those that are innate, and those that are acquired. The innate ones account for the ability of such things as focal position, motion, brightness, boundary contrast, and gaudy color to induce salience. It is as though, together with our acquired traces, we had a fund of innate traces that were inducing the salience of the bright colors and shape boundaries and the rest. The acquired traces come, of course, along with the episodes of a subject.

Between the traces of past episodes and present ones there is a certain reciprocal enlivening effect (relative to the recency of the past traces, and the like). A past trace can enhance the salience of a present episode, and the similarities of a present episode to a past one can enliven a past trace. This reciprocity, in general, accounts for the common phenomena of being reminded of past episodes by present ones and of the power of recollected episodes to influence, in turn, how and what we perceive in a present one.

Episodes are pleasant or unpleasant in varying degrees. It has already been pointed out that the strength of a trace varies with recency and also that the trace preserves information needed for perceptual similarity. It must now be added that the strength of the trace varies also with the pleasure or discomfort of the episode and that the trace preserves an index of this pleasure or discomfort.

The encoding of pleasure and discomfort into traces provides the subject's motivation to learn. Thus, where the trace involved is of a pleasant episode, the subject is caused to exert himself in ways designed to increase the similarity of later episodes to the pleasant one; and this drive will vary in strength with the vividness of the trace. Correspondingly, where the trace is that of an unpleasant episode, the subject is encouraged to exert himself in ways designed to decrease the similarity or hinder its increase.

> Learning, thus viewed, is a matter of learning to warp the trend of episodes, by intervention of one's own muscles, in such a way as to simulate a pleasant earlier episode. To learn is to learn to have fun. Behaviorally, the shoe is on the other foot: an episode counts as pleasant if, through whatever unidentified mechanism of nerves and hormones, it implants a drive to reproduce it. The pleasure is measured by the strength of this drive. And all this applies also in reverse, to the avoiding of the unpleasant. (RR, 28–29)

In Chapter 2 we shall see that this general theory of learning is the basis of Quine's theory of language learning, but presently we must survey Quine's grammatical analysis of English.

§1.3   *Grammatical analysis*

Quine's grammatical analysis of the terms, auxiliary particles, and constructions of English, given, for the most part, in chapter three of his *Word and Object*, presupposes an already existing theory of grammatical categories whose origin remains obscure. Nevertheless, it is clear that this theory includes the grammatical categories of *adjective, substantive, intransitive verb, transitive verb, article, preposition,* and *clause,* among others.

In what follows I shall not try to lay out every detail of Quine's grammatical analysis of English, but I shall provide enough detail to prepare the way for the relevant discussions in Chapters 2 and 3. As a standard procedure, I shall point out, where it is helpful in understanding Quine's grammatical analysis, the defining syntactical features of terms and constructions as well as their truth conditions and other important semantical features. As a general format, then, I shall introduce a term or construction, give its defining syntactical features, give its truth conditions or other relevant semantical features, and offer some discussion of the term or construction, when appropriate.

Now, to the laying out itself. A term for Quine "marks out" a category of objects. ('Marks out' should not be taken as 'names'.) Hence some linguistic expressions are terms and some are not: 'wine' is, but 'sake' is not. What are not terms are usually referred to by Quine as particles. Thus terms have *categorematic* usages (i.e., they are used to mark out categories of objects) while particles have *syncategorematic* usages (i.e., particles are never used to mark out categories of objects but are only used *with* terms). Although all full-fledged terms mark out objects, not all terms belong to the same category. In other words, we can distinguish among the categories of terms.

The first distinction to be made among terms, and a central one according to Quine, is the distinction between general terms and singular terms. The distinction between these two categories of terms can be made in at least three ways: syntactically, semantically, and by their roles in predication. The three criteria taken together are, according to Quine, sufficient for making the distinction.

Syntactically, a term is a *general term* if it "admits the definite and indefinite article and the plural ending" (WO, 90). Similarly, a term is a singular term if it "admits only the singular grammatical form and no article" (WO, 90). Semantically, a term is a general term if it "is true of each, severally, of any number of objects" (WO, 90–91). Correspondingly, "a singular term names or purports to name just one object, though as complex or diffuse an object as you please" (WO, 90).

As noted previously, a third way of distinguishing between general and singular terms is by their distinctive grammatical roles in predication. This is the means for differentiating the two which Quine emphasizes: "It is by grammatical role that general and singular terms are properly to be distinguished" (WO, 96). And, further, Quine says that "the basic combination in which general and singular terms find their contrasting roles is that of *predication*" (WO, 96).

However, before examining the construction of predication itself, one should be cautioned not to take Quine's remarks just quoted to be his last words on this matter of distinguishing general and singular terms, for "the fact is that general and singular terms, abstract or concrete, are not to be known only by their role in predication. There is also the use of singular terms as antecedents of 'it', and the use of general terms after articles and under pluralization" (WO, 119). This is a point we shall return to when discussing abstract terms. But now we can turn our attention to an examination of the construction of predication in order to understand the distinction between general and singular terms relative to their respective grammatical roles.

Generally, *predication* is a grammatical construction which "joins a general term and a singular term to form a sentence that is true or false according as the general term is true or false of the object, if any, to which the singular term refers" (WO, 96). This general statement about the nature of predication reveals two aspects of a predication: the syntactical and the semantical. The syntactical aspect of predication is the one of interest to us at the moment, for it is this aspect which reveals the grammatical roles of the general and singular terms. This aspect of predication is vaguely expressed by saying that predication joins a general term and a singular term to form a sentence. More exactly, one can say that predication is the joining of a singular term in subject position with a general term in predicative position.

The adoption of the logical schematism '*Fa*' to represent predication will facilitate the remaining discussion. The general term, represented by '*F*', is what is predicated, or occupies what grammarians call predicative position, and the singular term, represented by '*a*', is the subject of the predication, or occupies what grammarians call the subject position. The predicate, although it is always a general term, can be either (a) an intransitive verb: thus 'Mama *sings*'; (b) an adjective: thus 'Mama is *big*'; or (c) a substantive: thus 'Mama is a *woman*'. Thus, the schematism '*Fa*' is an abbreviation for '*aF*s' (read "*a effs*"), '*a* is *F*', and '*a* is an *F*'. The copula of predication, 'is' or 'is a(n)', is best seen, according to Quine, as a prefix converting general terms from adjectival and substantival forms to verbal form for purposes of predication. Hence, the general term in verbal form can be seen as the

fundamental form of a general term for predication, since no copula-
prefix is necessary for the term to enter the construction of predication.
Conversely, the suffixes '-ing' and '-er' can be used to convert general
terms from verbal form to adjectival or substantival forms to suit purposes other than predication. And, the suffixes '-thing' and '-ish' can
be used to convert adjectives into substantives, and vice versa.

Another type of term to be noted, apart from singular and general
terms, is the mass term. *Mass terms* are best identified by their characteristic lack of divided reference, but like general terms and singular
terms, syntactical as well as semantical properties of mass terms can
be listed. Syntactically, mass terms (like singular terms) resist pluralization and articles. Semantically, mass terms refer cumulatively; that
is, mass terms (like singular terms) do not divide their reference (or, at
least, not much). Take, for example, the mass term 'water'; any sum of
parts that are water is itself water. But mass terms (unlike singular
terms) do not obviously purport to name a unique object. Yet this last
point is mitigated somewhat by the fact that mass terms sometimes occur in predications *before* the copula and sometimes *after* the copula.
With regard to this ambivalence, Quine recommends that "the simplest
plan seems to be to treat . . . [a mass term] as a general term in its
occurrences after 'is', and as a singular term in its occurrences before
'is'" (WO, 97). For example, 'water' in 'That puddle is water' functions as a general term "true of each part of the world's water . . .
down to single molecules but not to atoms" (WO, 98). In general
Quine thinks that mass terms occurring in predicative position should
be construed as general terms which are true of each "bit" or "batch"
of stuff in question. On the other hand, mass terms occurring in subject
position should be construed as singular terms designating scattered
objects. For example, 'water' in 'Water is a fluid' is a singular term
describing all the world's water, scattered though it be. Consequently,
mass terms can function both as general terms and as singular terms,
thanks to their accessibility to predication, scattered objects, and "bits"
and "batches."

We have been assuming that there is but one variety of each kind of
term, but this is not the case. We have only dealt with what Quine calls
absolute general terms and *absolute mass terms*. There are in addition,
however, *relative general terms* (which we shall examine shortly). In
The Roots of Reference Quine introduces the notion of a *relative mass
term*, e.g., 'darker than' and 'same dog as'. Whereas the *absolute* mass
terms occurring in the predicate position of a predication, as 'water'

does in 'That puddle is water', are construed as being true of each part of the world's water down to single molecules of water, *relative* mass terms are true of objects pairwise, as with 'Here is darker than here' and 'Here is the same dog as here'. There is a slight difference to be noted, however, between the relative mass terms of these two examples. The one term, 'darker than', is transitive and asymmetrical, while the other term, 'same dog as', is transitive and symmetrical.

Thus far in our discussion of Quine's grammatical analysis of English we have not mentioned methods of forming compound terms. The nearest we have come to such constructions was our talk of prefixes and suffixes (and a few remarks on relative terms). We shall now turn our attention to three general methods that Quine describes for forming composite terms: (a) demonstrative singular terms, (b) attributives, and (c) conjunctive particles.

A *demonstrative singular term* is formed by prefixing a demonstrative particle such as 'this' or 'that' to a general term and accompanying this construction with an appropriate gesture, namely, pointing. Thus (in conjunction with the appropriate gesture) 'this river' or 'that woman' are considered to be demonstrative singular terms. It sometimes happens that the demonstrative particle 'this' is used as a full-fledged term. This usage can happen in circumstances where the object indicated contrasts with its surroundings sufficiently for the particle and the gesture to effect communication without the general term.

Before going on to the second method of forming composite terms, there is one more construction we should note in connection with demonstrative singular terms. Often the general term following the 'this' or 'that' of a demonstrative singular term will suffice, along with the circumstances of the utterance, to direct attention to the intended object without benefit of a gesture. Accordingly, 'this' and 'that' sometimes tend to become weakened to 'the': thus 'the river' and 'the woman'. Quine calls this kind of degenerate demonstrative singular terms *singular descriptions*.

> Often the object is so patently intended that even the general term can be omitted. Then, since 'the' (unlike 'this' and 'that') is never substantival, a *pro forma* substantive is supplied: thus 'the man', 'the woman', 'the thing'. These minimum descriptions are abbreviated as 'he', 'she', 'it'. Such a pronoun may be seen thus as a short singular description, while its grammatical antecedent is another singular term referring to

the same object (if any) at a time when more particulars are needed for its identification. (WO, 102–3)

The second method which Quine cites for forming composite terms involves "the joining of adjective to substantive in what grammarians call *attributive position*" (WO, 103). An adjective is in attributive position when it is prefixed or suffixed to a substantive: thus 'red' in 'red house' and 'at Macy's' in 'man at Macy's' are adjectives in attributive position. However, not all adjectives used with substantives are used in a genuinely attributive way, e.g., 'mere' in 'mere child'. Of this use of adjectives Quine remarks: "Such an adjective invites the old philosophical word *syncategorematic*. For such an adjective is not a term (in my sense) marking out a category of objects in its own right; it makes sense only with *(syn)* such a term, e.g. 'mother', as part of a further such term, e.g. 'expectant mother'" (WO, 103). In short, not all adjectives are terms. (Sometimes substantives also occur in attributive position, e.g., 'lady cop', 'iron bar', and so forth, but such occurrences are infrequent.)

Returning now to the categorematic use of adjectives in attributive position, we see that the substantive of the attribution may be either a general term or an absolute mass term, e.g., 'white woman' and 'white wine', respectively. A composite general term formed attributively is true of just the things of which the components are both true. Thus in the case of an adjective in attributive use next to a general term ('white woman'), the adjective must be taken as a general term, "for it is only thus that we can reckon the compound a general term true of the things of which the two components are jointly true" (WO, 104). However, in the case of an adjective in attributive use next to an absolute mass term ('white wine'), the adjective must be treated as a mass term. The two mass terms unite to form a compound absolute mass term. Recalling now that an absolute mass term can occur in a predication either as a singular term designating a scattered object, or as a general term true of each "bit" or "batch" of stuff (this follows from the fact that absolute mass terms can occur in subject position or in predicate position of predications), there arise two separate truth conditions for a composite absolute mass term formed by prefixing (or suffixing) an adjective in attributive position to an absolute mass term. If the composite absolute mass term is thought of as a singular term naming two scattered portions of the world, then "the compound becomes a singular term naming that smaller scattered portion of the world which is just the com-

mon part of the two" (WO, 104). On the other hand, if the composite
absolute mass term is thought of as a general term, and its parts likewise function as general terms, then "the compound is true of each of
the things of which the two components are jointly true" (WO, 104).

The third method which Quine gives for forming composite terms
is what might be called "conjunction," and it is a method closely related to the attributive joining of terms. *Conjunction* is accomplished
by joining either two substantives or two adjectives by the use of the
conjunctive particles 'or' and 'and'.

> Used as in '*a* is *F* and *G*', the 'and' compound has the force of
> the compound formed in the attributive way; viz., it is true of
> just the objects that both components are true of. When plu-
> ralized, however, as in '*F*s and *G*s are *H*', the 'and' compound
> commonly functions rather as a term true of all objects that one
> or both components are true of. This force is reserved rather to
> the 'or' compound when the plural is not used. (WO, 105)

As though all of this were not already complex enough, we are
now ready to introduce *relative general terms* such as 'part of', 'bigger than', 'brother of', 'exceeds', and the like. The general terms dealt
with earlier were *absolute* general terms. And, just as absolute general
terms could take the forms of intransitive verbs, adjectives, and substantives, *relative* general terms take the forms of transitive verbs,
adjectives plus preposition or conjunction, and substantives plus preposition. Paralleling the logical schematism of predication '*Fa*' for absolute general terms is the one for relative terms '*Fab*': '*a* is *F* to *b*', or
'*a f s b*'.

The principal semantical difference between the two types of general terms (i.e., the absolute and the relative) lies in their different
truth conditions: "Whereas an absolute general term is simply true of
an object *x*, and of an object *y*, and so on, a relative term is true rather
of *x* with respect to some object *z* (same or different), and of *y* with
respect to *w*, and so on" (WO, 105). Thus, relative general terms are
true of objects pairwise. There are also relative general terms in an
extended sense—triadic ones that are true of objects in sequences of
three; also tetradic ones, and higher. Predication of such terms may be
represented as '*Fab*', '*Fabc*', '*Fabcd*', and so forth.

Quine also describes several ways of combining relative general
terms. One way of combining them is to "pair relative terms off as
mutual *converses:* the one is true of anything *x* with respect to any-

thing *y* if and only if the other is true of *y* with respect to *x*. Thus 'bigger than' and 'less than'" (WO, 106). Sometimes "the key word of a relative term is used also *derelativized*, as an absolute term to this effect: it is true of anything *x* if and only if the relative term is true of *x* with respect to at least one thing. Thus anyone is a brother if and only if there is someone of whom he is a brother" (WO, 106).

However, a more important move made with relative general terms is combining them with singular terms by *application* yielding absolute general terms of a composite kind. "Thus the relative [general] term 'brother of' gives not only the absolute general term 'brother' but also the absolute general term 'brother of Abel'" (WO, 106).

So, according to Quine's grammatical analysis, there are two basic methods for forming composite general terms. One is the joining of one general term *attributively* to another (i.e., adjective plus absolute general term, either a substantive or a mass term in predicative position). The other method is *application*: joining a relative general term to a singular term. These two operations, attributive joining and application, can even be combined to yield more complex general terms. A quotation from Quine reveals the power of these techniques:

> thus 'wicked brother of Abel', formed by joining 'wicked' attributively to 'brother of Abel', or again 'man at Macy's', formed by joining the composite adjectival general term 'at Macy's' attributively to 'man'. Compound general terms obtained by either or both devices can be useful in turn under 'this', 'that', and 'the' in the forming of further singular terms. To composite singular terms, conversely, we can apply relative terms to get further general terms; and so round and round. (WO, 107)

Analogous to the application of relative general terms to singular terms as in 'brother of Abel' is the application of relative general terms to absolute general terms. "In this combination the subsidiary general term is given the plural form, thus 'benefactor of refugees', and the result is again a general term" (WO, 108).

Next we shall introduce another type of general term: the *relative clause*. Contrary to its name, the relative clause is an absolute term (adjectival in status). "It has the form of a sentence except that a relative pronoun stands in it where a singular term would be needed to make a sentence, and often the word order is switched; thus 'which I bought'" (WO, 110). On the semantical side, "a general term of this sort is true of just those things which, if named in the place of the relative pronoun, would yield a true sentence; thus 'which I bought' is true of just those things x such that x I bought, or, better, such that I bought x" (WO, 110).

The real contribution of the relative clause is that it creates from a sentence ' . . . x . . . ' a complex adjective summing up what the sentence says about x. Relative clauses, as general terms in adjectival form, are available for attributive position, just as other adjectives are.

Some relative clauses can function only as general terms, but some can function as either general or singular terms (this is true of other adjectives as well):

> In 'Coffee from which extract is made is grown in the lowlands', the substantive 'coffee' and the adjective 'from which extract is made' are mass terms which stand as singular terms, each the name of a scattered portion of the world; and the compound formed of them, 'coffee from which extract is made', is a singular term naming the smaller scattered portion of the world which is the common part of the two. (WO, 111)

We have already discussed singular descriptions as instances of degenerate demonstrative singular terms, but now we see that general terms in the form of relative clauses provide a further basis for forming singular descriptions, thus: 'the car [which] I bought from you'. We can build this example of a singular description from its elements, to demonstrate the point:

> We have a triadic relative term 'bought from', which, applied predicatively to the singular terms 'I', 'x' (say), and 'you', gives a sentence form 'I bought x from you'. Putting a relative pronoun for the 'x' here and permuting, we get the relative clause 'which I bought from you'. This clause is a general term, adjectival in status. Combining it attributively with the general term 'car', we get the general term 'car which I bought from you'; and then 'the' yields the singular term [i.e., the singular description 'the car which I bought from you']. (WO, 111)

The relative clause (e.g., 'which I bought from you') must be combined attributively with a substantive (e.g., 'car') before the particle 'the' is applied, since 'the' applies to substantives and not to adjectives which, of course, is what the relative clause is. However, if there is no interest in the substantive beyond the grammatical role just described, then 'thing', 'object', or 'person' can be used in place of the substantive; thus 'thing which I bought from you'. The reason for permuting word order is to bring the relative pronoun to the beginning, or near the beginning, of the clause. As this can sometimes be a demanding exercise in complex cases, the relative pronoun can be replaced by the alternative 'such that' construction.

> This construction demands none of the tricks of word order demanded by 'which', because it divides the two responsibilities of 'which': the responsibility of standing in a singular-term position within the clause is delegated to 'it', and the responsibility of signaling the beginning of the clause is discharged by 'such that'. Thus 'which I bought' becomes 'such that I bought it'; 'for whom the bell tolls' becomes 'such that the bell tolls for him'. (WO, 112)

In summary, then, the relative clause, although it looks like a sentence, can be identified by the occurrence of a relative pronoun, 'which', 'who', 'whom', 'that', 'what', standing where a singular term would be needed to make the construction a sentence. The relative clause is a general term, adjectival in status, and it is a term true of just those things which might be named in place of the relative pronoun which occurs in it. When combined attributively (some relative clauses cannot be combined attributively), the relative clause may occur in predications as a singular term or as a general term. Also, the relative clause is a source for constructing singular descriptions. In these constructions the word order is permuted to place the relative pronoun at or near the beginning of the clause. In difficult cases, the relative pronoun can be replaced by the 'such that' construction.

The next category of terms to be examined is the category of *indefinite singular terms*. These terms are formed typically with the help of the indefinite articles, 'a' and 'an'; hence 'a lion', as in 'I saw a lion'. Whereas 'the lion' in 'I saw the lion' is presumed to refer to some specific lion, 'a lion' in 'I saw a lion' is not. It is just a *dummy singular term*. 'I saw a lion' is regarded as true if at least one lion, any one, was seen by me on the occasion in question. It is these indefinite singular terms which serve as pure affirmations of existence:

> 'I saw a lion' is true if there is at least one object satisfying the conditions of being a lion and being seen by one on the occasion in question; otherwise false. Sentences like 'Mama sings'

and 'I saw the lion', which contain definite singular terms, may indeed be said to depend for their truth on the existence of objects named by those terms, but the difference is that they do not clearly become false (and their negations true) failing such objects. Failing objects of reference for their definite singular terms, such sentences are likely to be looked upon as neither true nor false but simply uncalled for. (WO, 112–13; *note omitted*)

Here we see, in rudimentary form, a formulation of Quine's famous dictum 'To be is to be the value of a bound variable'.

Another *particle* besides 'a' and 'an' which can be used to form indefinite singular terms is 'every'. 'Every lion', just like 'a lion', produces a dummy singular term; however, the truth conditions of 'every lion' differ, obviously, from the truth conditions of 'a lion'. These particles, 'an' and 'every', have their variants too: "notably 'some', 'each', and 'any'. The interchangeabilities here are curiously erratic, as one sees by putting 'every', 'some', and 'any' for 'a' in the sentences 'John can outrun a member of the team' and 'John cannot outrun a member of the team' and comparing" (WO, 114).

Another type of term is the *relative general term of identity* "expressed in English by those uses of 'is' that one is prepared to expand into 'is the same object as'. The sign '=' may conveniently be thought of as annexed to English in this sense, enabling us as it does to be brief about the matter without ambiguity" (WO, 114–15). The sign '=' is a relative general term which has the form of a transitive verb. Like any such term, the '=' joins singular terms to make a sentence; thus 'Mama *is* the new treasurer'. Sentences thus formed are true if and only if their component singular terms designate the same object. When such identity statements are true, they can be truly informative and not merely idle on the condition that they are comprised of *unlike* singular terms.

There remain for consideration two more categories of terms: abstract terms, both singular and general. *Abstract singular terms* can be formed by suffixing general terms with '-ness', '-icity', etc.; thus 'carness', 'roundness', 'sphericity'. Consequently, each absolute general term delivers an abstract singular. And, whereas 'car', 'round', and 'sphere' are suited to play the role of '*F*' in '*Fa*', 'carness', 'roundness', and 'sphericity' are suited rather to the role of '*a*' or '*b*' in '*Fa*', '*Fab*', etc.

Now in order for this latter role to exist for abstract singular terms [i.e., the role of '*a*' in '*Fa*', etc.], there have to be some abstract general terms for the supporting role of '*F*': some general terms predicable of abstract objects. Two such abstract general terms are 'virtue' and 'rare'; thus '*Fa*' can be 'Humility is a virtue', or 'Humility is rare'. Again a relative term that is abstract at one end is 'has', as in '*a* has humility'; or '*a* has roundness', which have the form '*Fab*'. The move that ushers in abstract singular terms has to be one that simultaneously ushers in abstract general ones. (WO, 119)

However, if the parsing of certain words as abstract terms, general and singular, depended merely upon "parsing their combinations as predications in certain ways, and vice versa, then decisions on either point would be pretty empty" (WO, 119, *note omitted*). But as we noted earlier in talking of the general-term–singular-term dichotomy, general terms and singular terms (concrete or abstract) are not to be known *only* by their distinctive grammatical roles in predication; there is also the use of singular terms as antecedents of 'it' and the use of general terms occurring after articles in pluralized form. As Quine sees it,

predication is but part of a pattern of interlocking uses wherein the status of a word as general or singular term consists. By the time we encounter abstract general terms in such contexts as 'He has a rare virtue', for instance, we are left with no very evident alternative to recognizing them as abstract general terms and recognizing the sentence even as affirming, outright, the existence of an abstract object. (WO, 119)

§1.4 *Summary and conclusions*

In the three preceding sections I have presented some of the considerations and concepts that are foundational in my exposition of Quine's philosophy. In §1.1, I attempted to indicate Quine's place in the development of modern empiricism by contrasting his notion of enlightened empiricism with Carnap's notion of rational reconstruction and the older empiricism. As noted there, the fundamental aim of enlightened empiricism is to provide a factual, scientific account of the link between observation and theory. Thus, the central question of epistemology is: 'How, given only the stimulation of our senses, do we acquire our theory of the world?' As I see it, Quine's philosophical concerns are dominated by his attempt to provide a systematic and comprehensive answer to this question; this conviction, as I noted in the Introduction, is the guiding principle of this book.

In §1.2, I presented most, if not all, of the key concepts of Quine's general behavioristic theory of perception and learning. These included episode, receptual similarity, perceptual similarity, behavioral similarity, neighborhood, salience, trace, pleasure, and pain. This general theory of learning provides the conceptual foundation for understanding Quine's theory of language learning presented in Chapter 2. Furthermore, Quine's theory of language learning is not merely some piece of theory isolated from his other philosophical concerns, since he reformulates, as we shall see in §2.1, the central question of epistemology as the question of how we acquire our *talk* about the world.

In §1.3, I surveyed Quine's grammatical analysis of English into terms, auxiliaries or particles, and constructions. Familiarity with these grammatical distinctions will facilitate the discussion in Chapter 3 of his program for the regimentation of ordinary language.

Chapter 2: The framework

§2.1 *Enlightened empiricism:*
a genetic approach

We noted in §1.1 that the primary goal of epistemology, according to Quine, is to provide a factual account of how our theory of the world can arise from observation. Since, Quine believes, conceptualization to any significant extent is inseparable from language, the various theories comprising our overall theory of the world could be taken as systems of sentences. The central problem of epistemology, then, is one of giving an account of the relation between observation and our theoretical *talk.*

But how are we to construe observations? Being sensory, they are subjective; yet in using observations in the contexts of language learning and assessing evidence, they must be socially shared. On the other hand, nothing is gained if we construe observations not as sensations but as shared environmental circumstances; for we cannot presume intersubjective agreement about the environing situation either, inasmuch as two people will assess it differently, partly as a result of noticing different features and partly because of holding different theories. Quine suggests a solution to this difficulty over the notion of observation:

> It consists in talking neither of sensation nor of environing situation, but of language: talking of language at the observational end no less than at the theoretical end. I do not suggest that observations themselves are something verbal, but I propose that we drop the talk of observation and talk instead of

observation sentences, the sentences that are said to report observations: sentences like 'This is red', 'This is a rabbit'. No matter that sensations are private, and no matter that men may take radically different views of the environing situation; the observation *sentence* serves nicely to pick out what witnesses can agree on. (RR, 39)

The central problem of epistemology, now, becomes one of giving an account of the relation between our theoretical *talk* and our observational *talk*. This relation has two aspects, one epistemological (evidential), the other semantical (meaning). Besides being the relation through which sentences affirmed in a theory gain support, it is the relation through which they gain their meaning, for we learn our language by relating its terms to the observations that elicit them.

Correlatively, the central problem of accounting for the link between theory and observation has two aspects, expressed by the following questions: (a) how does one sentence serve as evidence for another? and (b) how do sentences acquire meaning? The answers to these questions begin with the roles that observation sentences play in providing both evidential support and meaning for the other kinds of sentences in theories. Observation sentences play an *evidential role* in theories because they are the kinds of sentences that enjoy virtually unanimous acceptance among the members of the speech community. Two theorists may disagree about the truth of some theoretical sentence, but at the level of observation sentences they will find a common ground for assessing relevant evidence. (*Whatever evidence there is for science is sensory evidence.*) Observation sentences also play a *semantical role* in theories, for although most of language consists of interverbal associations, somewhere there have to be nonverbal reference points, nonverbal circumstances which can be intersubjectively appreciated and associated with appropriate utterances. (*All inculcation of meanings of words rests ultimately on sensory evidence.*) Observation sentences are, therefore, the gateway to language and to science; and language is the gateway to enlightened empiricism:

We see, then, a strategy for investigating the relation of evidential support, between observation and scientific theory. We can adopt a *genetic approach*, studying how theoretical language is learned. For the evidential relation is virtually enacted, it would seem, in the learning. This genetic strategy is attractive because the learning of language goes on in the world and is open to scientific study. It is a strategy for the scientific study of scientific method and evidence. *We have here a good reason to regard the theory of language as vital to the theory of knowledge.* (NNK, 74–75; *my emphasis*)

Thus insofar as Quine's philosophy is viewed as an attempt to answer the central question of epistemology, *his* theory of language is vital to *his* theory of knowledge. It is of paramount importance, therefore, to gain an understanding of Quine's conception of language, the "framework" within which he constructs his answer to the central question of epistemology.

§2.2   *The naturalistic-behavioristic conception of language*

Quine's remark that "language is a social art which we all acquire on the evidence solely of other people's overt behavior under publicly recognizable circumstances" (OR, 26) is as concise a statement of the naturalistic-behavioristic thesis of language learning and linguistic meaning (hereinafter sometimes referred to as the NB conception or thesis of language, or the NB thesis) as one is likely to encounter in Quine's writings. The first part of this thesis, that *language is a social art*, suggests that Quine views language primarily as a kind of social activity (namely, people behaving verbally). By emphasizing this social-art aspect of language Quine is rejecting an older mentalistic view of language according to which language is allegedly open to study, ultimately, only through the medium of introspection. On the other hand, when conceived of in Quine's externalized way, language becomes an object open to study by the intersubjective techniques of inquiry characteristic of natural science generally. The second part of the NB thesis, that *we acquire our language on the evidence solely of other people's overt behavior under publicly recognizable circumstances*, suggests that Quine's view of language involves (1) a behavioral theory of linguistic meaning, and (2) a behavioral theory of language learning. Sections 2.2.1 and 2.2.2 examine these topics in turn.

§2.2.1   *Linguistic meaning (semantics)*

The major thrust of Quine's naturalistic-behavioristic approach in semantics is directed against mentalistic semantics (the "idea idea," as he sometimes calls it) and against referential theories of meaning generally. Thus, for Quine, the meaning of an expression is not the object to which the expression refers, whether one assumes that object to be an idea, a proposition, a physical body, or a Platonic form. On the contrary, Quine's claim is that if we must look for meanings at all, then we should look to the public conditions of use—that is, to the overt behavior of people using language. For the NB thesis insists that the learner of a first language has no data to work with when learning a language (which includes learning meanings) other than the overt behavior of other speakers amid publicly recognizable circumstances. Consequently, Quine's theory of meaning, if we call it that, is an attempt to characterize the meanings of expressions in behavioral terms. Whatever meanings are, they are learned by behavioral criteria and, so, must be explicable, if at all, by behavioral descriptions. The "meanings" that are not thus characterizable are just not meanings at all for Quine.

Quine recognizes three levels of explanation of human behavior generally. The first level, which Quine regards as being the least satisfactory, is mentalism. In semantics, mentalism takes the form of explaining the meaning of an expression by reference to the idea, or to some other mentalistic entity, that is said to correspond to the expression. For example, the meaning of 'red' is said to be the idea red, or the mental image of red, and so forth.

The next level of explanation is behaviorism. Quine regards this level to be an improvement over mentalism. In semantics, behaviorism takes the form of explaining the meaning of an expression by reference to certain behavioral dispositions of members of the speech community. As we shall see, Quine's central semantical concept, stimulus meaning, is based upon a speaker's dispositions to assent to and dissent from sentences when they are queried. For Quine, the distinctive and vital role of behaviorism in semantics is in the *partial* explication of semantical concepts, not in their causal explanation nor even, usually, in any full definition. Similarly, when speculating on the rules governing the acquisition and use of language, and on the innate psychological mechanisms of language learning, the theorist should refrain from positing any irreducibly mentalistic mechanisms, and he should try to limit himself to positing only mechanisms for which he can specify some behavioral evidence.

The third level of explanation—the only *real* explanation according to Quine—is the neurophysiological (or, more generally, the physical). But this level of explanation has only a limited application in semantics, as can be seen by reflecting on the way language is learned: we do not as a rule learn the meanings of expressions by correlating them (the expressions) with neurophysiological states, ours or anybody else's. This is not to say, however, that neurophysiology has no significance or relevance to language theory generally. On the contrary, when it comes to explaining behavioral dispositions themselves, or to explaining the underlying mechanisms of language acquisition, surely neurophysiological explanations, when they are available, are very significant and relevant.

Insofar as Quine's semantic theory is concerned with meaning at all it is so only in connection with sentences and not with words. The reason for this is that Quine thinks words derive what meanings they have from the sentences in which they occur. Sentences, not words, are for Quine the primary semantical units of language. I even hesitate to say that Quine regards sentences as the primary semantical units of language since, as we shall see shortly, only a small class of sentences (namely, observation sentences) can be said to have individual meanings. It would be more accurate to say of Quine's view that he regards theories, or significant parts of theories, as the primary semantical units of language.

A further point worth making is that the kind of meaning that Quine is interested in is *cognitive meaning*. Cognitive meaning is characteristic of a certain class of sentences, namely sentences that are used for making assertions. The defining property of such sentences is that, when used, they are either true or false, but not both simultaneously. Cognitive meaning fastens on truth: to know the cognitive meaning of a sentence is to know the conditions under which the sentence is true or false. Thus, cognitive meaning ignores all of the nuances of our merely intuitive notions of meaning, nuances that might be associated with assertions. Quine's motivation for focusing on cognitive meaning is simply his desire to make as much sense of the notion of meaning as is possible in terms of truth and falsity.

Since Quine thinks that meanings are first and foremost meanings of (some) sentences, we begin our inquiry into the details of his semantic theory by examining his classification of sentences. For Quine, "a sentence is not an event of utterance, but a universal: a repeatable sound pattern, or repeatedly approximable norm" (WO, 191).

As one might have expected, Quine's classification of sentences proceeds along behavioral lines. Basically, he thinks there are two kinds of sentences: occasion sentences and standing sentences. An *occasion sentence* is a sentence that would elicit assent or dissent when queried *only* *if* some prompting (usually nonverbal) stimulus were present. For example, 'This man is John's brother' is an occasion sentence, since *each time* it is queried and assented to there must be present some prompting stimulus (e.g. some man). Other typical examples of occasion sentences are: 'His face is dirty' and 'The cat is licking her young'. A *standing sentence* is a sentence that would elicit assent or dissent each time it is queried without being prompted anew by some (usually nonverbal) stimulus. For example, 'John's brother is tall' is a standing sentence since it would be assented to or denied on countless occasions when it is queried despite the absence of John's brother from the present scene. Other typical examples of standing sentences are: 'Copper conducts electricity' and 'Today is Monday'. Standing sentences grade off into occasion sentences: 'The mail has arrived' is a standing sentence for about twenty-four hours, and 'John just sneezed' is a standing sentence for a few minutes.

Within the categories of standing sentence and occasion sentence there are, respectively, the subcategories of eternal sentence and observation sentence. *Eternal sentences* are standing sentences whose truth values are permanently fixed: "An eternal sentence may be general in import, or it may report a specific local event. In the latter case it will gain its specificity through explicit use of names, dates, or addresses. The eternal sentences most characteristic of scientific theory are of course general" (RR, 63). *Observation sentences* are occasion sentences whose occasions are intersubjectively observable and, moreover, are generally adequate to prompt assent from any observer conversant with the language. For example, just about everyone in the speech community would assent to the sentence 'This paper is white' if queried and simultaneously prompted by the sight of white paper.

All observation sentences are occasion sentences, but not all occasion sentences are observation sentences. For example, 'This man is John's brother' is an occasion sentence, since *each time* it is queried and assented to there must be present some prompting stimulus (e.g. some man). But this occasion sentence is not also an observation sentence in Quine's sense, for *not all* present witnesses conversant with the language would assent to it—ideally, only those privy to the identity of John's brother would do so.

The central concept of Quine's semantics is that of stimulus meaning. *Stimulus meaning* is the meaning of a sentence for a given speaker at a particular time. The stimulus meaning of a sentence for a speaker at a time is definable, behaviorally, in terms of the ordered pair of what Quine calls the affirmative stimulus meaning and negative stimulus meaning of a sentence. A stimulation *a* is said to belong to the *affirma-*

tive stimulus meaning of a sentence S for a given speaker if and only if there is a stimulation a' such that if the speaker were given a' and were asked S, then were given a and were asked S again, he would dissent the first time and assent the second. *Negative stimulus meaning* can be defined similarly by interchanging 'assent' and 'dissent'. Stimulus meaning is the ordered pair of the affirmative and negative meanings.[1]

The notion of stimulus meaning can be applied as a general concept of meaning to any of the categories of sentences discussed above. Take, for example, the class of nonobservation occasion sentences. In the case of a single speaker of a single language we can assess his stimulus meanings for sentences like 'He is a bachelor' by querying such sentences of him in various contexts and cataloging his responses. Affirmative and negative responses of the subject will depend in the case of 'He is a bachelor' upon the subject's knowledge of the marital status of the individuals he is confronted with when queried—Quine calls this kind of background information *collateral information*. And, since it would be highly unlikely that any two subjects would know all and only the same men together with the same relevant marital information, it would also be highly unlikely that any two subjects would have equivalent stimulus meanings for the sentence 'He is a bachelor.'

Remaining, for the moment, with the case of a single, monolingual speaker it is possible using stimulus meaning to define cognitive equivalence of occasion sentences. Two occasion sentences are said to be *cognitively equivalent* for a speaker if they have the same stimulus meaning for that speaker. For example, 'He is a bachelor' and 'He is an unmarried man' would ordinarily be cognitively equivalent for a speaker. Furthermore, the concept of cognitive equivalence of occasion sentences can be *socialized* by polling all (or sufficiently many) members of the speech community and generalizing the results.

There is also a way of stretching the notion of socially cognitively equivalent occasion sentences across languages.

> If a bilingual is available, we can treat the two languages as his single tandem language; and then we can indeed define cognitive equivalence of occasion sentences generally, for him, even between the languages. But this is still cognitive equivalence only for him and not for a linguistic community, or pair of com-

1. This handy formulation of the definition of 'stimulus meaning' is borrowed from Paul Ziff's "A Response to Stimulus Meaning," *The Philosophical Review* 79 (January 1970).

munities. Only if we have a whole subcommunity of bilinguals can we summate over the individuals, as we did in the monoglot case, and derive a bilingual relation of cognitive equivalence of occasion sentences at the social level. (UPM, 8)

Now that cognitive equivalence for occasion sentences is available, it is an easy matter to specify, behaviorally, other useful semantical concepts. One such concept is the *cognitive synonymy* of words and phrases: "a word is *cognitively* synonymous to a word or phrase if substitution of the one for the other always yields cognitively equivalent sentences" (UPM, 5). Furthermore, Quine thinks that if a given word is interchangeable with a given word or phrase in all occasion sentences, invariably yielding a cognitively equivalent sentence, then the interchangeability can be depended upon to hold good in all standing sentences as well.

If this be granted, then a conceptual foundation for cognitive synonymy is pretty firmly laid. The courses, as stonemasons call them, are as follows. First there is the relation of sameness of overall stimulation of an individual at different times [viz. the receptual similarity of episodes]. This is defined, theoretically, by sameness of triggered receptors. Next there is the relation of cognitive equivalence of occasion sentences for the individual [viz. sameness of stimulus meaning]. This is defined by his disposition to give matching verdicts when the two sentences are queried under identical overall stimulations. Next there is the relation of cognitive equivalence of occasion sentences for the whole linguistic community [viz. social cognitive equivalence]. This is defined as cognitive equivalence for each individual. Finally there is the relation of cognitive synonymy of a word to a word or phrase. This is defined as interchangeability in occasion sentences *salva equivalentia*. We could take the nominal further step, if we liked, and define the cognitive meaning of a word as the set of its cognitive synonyms. (UPM, 6)

As we have noted, to say that two occasion sentences are cognitively equivalent for a subject is to say that the two sentences in question have the same stimulus meaning for that subject: he would assent to and dissent from the one in just those situations where he would do likewise for the other. The question naturally arises, then, how does a speaker decide on some occasion which of two cognitively equivalent sentences to use?

To seek an answer to this kind of question within the framework of Quine's semantic theory, however, would be to misunderstand its nature and purpose. Quine's semantic theory is based upon the concept of stimulus meaning, which in turn is based upon the behavioral technique of offering sentences under intersubjectively observable conditions for assent and dissent. Stimulus meaning, the cornerstone of Quine's semantic theory, is therefore an index of a subject's dispositions to affirm and to deny various queried sentences and not an index of a subject's dispositions *to use* or *not to use* those sentences. Such a theory aims at discovering truth conditions of sentences, not at providing a causal explanation of speech.

If, outside of his semantic theory, Quine were pressed for an answer to the question posed, I fancy he would respond, ultimately, in neurophysiological and anatomical terms. Each of the two occasion sentences in question has its underlying disposition to be uttered. Such dispositions are neurophysiological states; the one offering less resistance to the activation of the speech muscles at the time would dominate. On such a view, the question of "deciding" to use one rather than the other of a pair of cognitively equivalent occasion sentences is largely metaphorical (*see* UPM, 2–3).

What Quine wants to emphasize about his semantic theory is that *just because* it is based upon the query–assent-dissent technique it is freed from the burden of accounting for the causal factors of speech. He takes this to be one of the cardinal virtues of his theory.

As a general concept of meaning, stimulus meaning is less successful in generating other useful semantical concepts when it is applied to the category of standing sentences than when it is applied to the category of occasion sentences. The reason for this is that standing sentences, unlike occasion sentences, have few times at which prompting stimulations are relevant or needed. In other words, standing sentences are not linked closely to the present nonverbal stimulations that give substance to the concept of stimulus meaning and, consequently, to the concept of cognitive equivalence. Take, for example, the pair of standing sentences 'Snow is white' and 'The sea is salty'. A subject would reasonably be expected to assent to one of these whenever he would assent to the other, but little of semantical value is gained if, as a result of this circumstance, we announce the two to be cognitively equivalent.

Nevertheless, the concept of cognitive equivalence can be extended beyond occasion sentences to standing sentences, with some success. Standing sentences, it will be recalled, grade off into occasion sentences in proportion to the diminution of the times during which each queried sentence continues to elicit assent or dissent without the eliciting query being accompanied anew with a prompting nonverbal stimulation. The limiting case is the occasion sentence itself, which requires a new, prompting, nonverbal stimulation accompanying each query for an affirmation or a denial to be elicited. Thus the more a standing sentence resembles an occasion sentence, the more applicable the criterion of cognitive equivalence: like verdicts under like stimulation (sameness of stimulus meaning). As Quine points out, that criterion can be extended to apply to *all* standing sentences provided that it is regarded merely as a necessary condition of cognitive equivalence and not as a sufficient one. (For occasion sentences the criterion is both necessary and sufficient.) Thus we could say that any two standing sentences are cognitively equivalent *only if* they both have the same stimulus meaning for that speaker.

On the other hand, Quine also shows that it is possible to state a criterion for the cognitive equivalence of standing sentences that is sufficient but not necessary. One standing sentence is cognitively equivalent to another *if* it can be transformed into the other by a sequence of replacements of words or phrases by cognitive synonyms, or by other sorts of paraphrase, that have already been found to preserve cognitive equivalence among occasion sentences. "These conditions do not quite add up to a definition of cognitive equivalence for standing sentences. If a pair of standing sentences meets the necessary condition and not the proposed sufficient one, the question of their cognitive equivalence has no answer. But in their incomplete way the conditions do make the notion widely applicable to standing sentences" (UPM, 8).

The application of stimulus meaning to standing sentences also yields a notion (or, perhaps, notions) of analyticity. A standing sentence is *stimulus analytic* for a subject if he would assent to it after every stimulation. Similarly, a standing sentence is *stimulus contradictory* for a subject if he would dissent from it after every stimulation. Both of these concepts, stimulus-analytic standing sentence and stimulus-contradictory standing sentence, can be generalized to the *social* level for those standing sentences that are stimulus analytic or stimulus contradictory for just about everyone in the speech community. The former notion applies to sentences like '2 + 2 = 4', 'No bachelor is married', and 'There have been black dogs'; the latter notion applies to sentences like '2 + 2 = 5', 'Some bachelor is married', and 'There have never been any black dogs'.

In *The Roots of Reference* Quine recognizes a subclass of socially stimulus-analytic standing sentences that he leaves unnamed but which we may dub *socially psychogenetically stimulus-analytic* standing sentences. A standing sentence is socially psychogentically stimulus analytic "if *everybody* learns that it is true by learning its words" (RR, 79). For example, if everyone in the speech community learns the word 'bachelor' by discovering that those speakers from whom they are learning their language are disposed to assent to it in just those circumstances where they will assent to 'unmarried man', then, in virtue of this discovery, everyone in the speech community has learned the truth of the standing sentence 'A bachelor is an unmarried man'. Such sentences qualify as socially psychogenetically stimulus analytic.

> Even so, we have here no such radical cleavage between analytic and synthetic sentences as was called for by Carnap and other epistemologists. In learning our language each of us learns to count certain sentences, outright, as true; there are sentences whose truth is learned in that way by many of us, and there are sentences whose truth is learned in that way by few or none of us. The former sentences are more *nearly* analytic than the latter. The *analytic* sentences are the ones whose truth is learned in that way by all of us; and these extreme cases do not differ notably from their neighbors, nor can we always say which ones they are. (RR, 80)

The most significant application of the concept of stimulus meaning, however, is to that subclass of occasion sentences called observation sentences. Indeed, the very idea of an observation sentence (in Quine's sense) is crucial to the success of Quine's semantic theory, to his language acquisition theory, and to his whole epistemological enterprise in general, i.e., to his genetic approach toward answering the question of how we acquire our theory of the world.

An *observation sentence*, it will be recalled, is an occasion sentence that just about everyone in the speech community, if queried, would assent to or dissent from (for example, 'This paper is white' queried in the conspicuous presence of white paper).

It should be kept in mind that observation sentences are a subclass of occasion sentences. Without this stipulation the definition of 'observation sentence' would allow sentences like 'There have been black dogs' to count as observation sentences, since just about every member of the speech community would assent to them. Such sentences are, rather, to be classified as socially stimulus-analytic *standing* sentences. The difference between the two is that as occasion sentences observation sentences require a new prompting (usually nonverbal) stimulation accompanying each query, whereas standing sentences do not.

Another feature of observation sentences is that they can be learned ostensively. When this occurs, the learning takes place under conditions where the teacher and his pupil have *virtually* identical episodes. The teacher and the pupil must, for example, see the red ostended surface when the child learns 'red', and at least one of the two must also notice that the other is seeing red at the time. In such situations what the teacher is teaching is the *similarity basis* of the sentence in question, that is, "the distinctive trait shared by the episodes appropriate to that observation sentence; the shared trait in which their perceptual similarity consists" (RR, 43). Of course, such learning requires, also, that the teacher and the pupil possess similar standards of perceptual similarity.

In the realm of observation sentences, then, meaning and evidence merge. The *meaning of* and *evidence for* (the truth of) any observation sentence are identical and public. Their meanings are public because their evidence is intersubjectively observable and agreed upon. Observation sentences, says Quine, "wear their meanings on their sleeves" (WO, 42).

Two further points about observation sentences deserve mention. First, because of their public dimension, observation sentences are usually about bodies and not about sense data. Second, universal assent to an observation sentence may sometimes be mistaken. Every member of the speech community might assent to the query of 'This is paper' when simultaneously confronted with a presentation of, say, a deceptive piece of cloth. In both of these respects Quine's notion of an observation sentence differs from the older notion of a protocol sentence, which was championed by some of the logical positivists.

§2.2.2 *Language learning*

Quine claims that language is a social art and that all one has to go on in learning it are intersubjective cues as to what to say and when to say it. Exposed to a linguistic environment, and endowed with a set of innate standards of perceptual similarity (among other presumed but unknown innate endowments) needed for detecting and systematizing salient features of his environment, assisted and motivated by traces of episodes encoded with pleasure and pain, and endowed with an instinct for babbling and mimicry, a child undertakes the learning of his first language.

The initial method of his learning is *ostension*. He learns, by observing the overt behavior of his elders, under publicly recognizable circumstances, to associate sentences as unstructured wholes with appropriate nonverbal stimulations. In short, he learns, inductively, the range of stimulus conditions governing the correct use of a particular expression. This method of learning sentences approximates the psychological schematism of direct conditioning. The conditioning involved is not quite the simplest kind: we do not say 'red' or the like whenever we see something red. We do then, however, assent to the query 'Red?' when asked. Sentences learned by ostension are thus learned as unstructured wholes conditioned to nonverbal stimulation. "But this method is notoriously incapable of carrying us far in language [learning]" (LP, 57). Most of the sentences of our language are not tied, even derivatively, to any fixed ranges of nonverbal stimulation.

A second general method of language learning, which accounts for the learning of the higher reaches and greater portion of language, is what Quine calls *analogic synthesis*. Sentences learned by this method are built up from learned parts by analogy with the way in which those parts have previously been noticed to occur in other sentences that, themselves, may or may not have been learned as unstructured wholes. Unlike the method of ostension, however, virtually nothing is known about the underlying psychological mechanisms responsible for such learning.

The structure resulting from these two general methods of language learning, the language acquired, consists of a socially conditioned, continuously evolving network of dispositions to respond verbally in various types of stimulus situations. In the next two sections we shall examine some of the details of Quine's speculations concerning the learning of English by these two methods.

§2.2.2.1 *Ostensive learning*

Ostensive learning is basic to language acquisition. The first sentences a child learns, he learns ostensively. Such learning requires observationality. For example, in learning (or in teaching) ostensively the (one-word) sentence 'Red', both the teacher and the pupil must see the present, red, ostended surface, and at least one of them must also see that the other sees the red surface at the time. Hence, the first sentences learned are observation sentences.

The following passage from *The Roots of Reference* provides an example of such learning, and it also reveals how the general learning theory of §1.2 plugs into the language learning setting.

> Suppose the child happens to utter the word ['red'] in the course of the random babbling that is standard procedure in small children, and suppose a red ball happens to be conspicuously present at the time. The parent rewards the child, perhaps only by somehow manifesting approval. Thus in a certain brief minute in the history of overall impingements on the child's sensory surfaces there were these features among others: there were light rays in the red frequencies, there were sound waves in the air and in the child's headbones caused by the child's own utterance of the word 'red', there were the impacts on the proprioceptors of the child's tongue and larynx occasioned by the utterance, and there were the impacts, whatever they were, that made the episode pleasant. On a later occasion a red shawl is conspicuously present. Its color makes for a degree of perceptual similarity between the pleasant earlier episode and the present, thus enlivening the trace of that episode. The child contorts his speech muscles so as to add what more he can to the similarity: he again says 'red', and we may hope that the similarity is yet further enhanced by a recurrence of the reward. (RR, 29)

In the following brief summary of some of Quine's speculations concerning the parts of English that can be learned ostensively, we shall be concerned with the learning of observation sentences and of what Quine calls observation terms. Both observation sentences and observation terms (even when the latter are composed of strings of words) are to be regarded in the context of this discussion as unstructured wholes that are learned by associating them directly with their various intersubjectively appreciable stimulus conditions. But, while both observation sentences and observation terms can be *fully* acquired ostensively, terms in the full-blooded sense of the term 'term' can only be *partially* acquired ostensively. Observation terms represent just so much of a full-blooded term's empirical meaning as can be acquired ostensively. In other words, one can learn to *respond* with an observation term to appropriate stimulus conditions, but responding is not *referring*. Observation terms may eventually become terms in the full-blooded sense (they may "mark out" categories of objects) but only when they are systematically, yet multifariously, connected with the higher reaches of language, which are themselves not learnable by ostension but require for their learning the devices of analogic synthesis. For now it will be convenient to regard them as terms (in the lesser sense) rather than as mere sentences, since doing so will spare us the burden of inventing a classificatory scheme to differentiate among observation sentences; we may, instead, simply borrow the classificatory scheme used to differentiate terms that was detailed in §1.3. Thus, 'Water' and 'Dog' are both, indiscriminately, one-word observation *sentences*, while both 'water' and 'dog' are, as observation *terms*, discriminable: the former is an absolute mass (observation) term, and the latter is an absolute general (observation) term.

In discussing Quine's speculations concerning ostensive language learning I shall focus systematically on six factors:

(1) *Grammatical item*. The grammatical items of concern will be either sentences, terms, particles, or modes of composition.

(2) *Example*. I shall provide an example (or examples) of each of the kinds of grammatical items in question.

(3) *Psychological mechanism*. Since all of the grammatical items under consideration are learnable ostensively, they all involve the psychological schematism of conditioning that includes perceptual similarity, the pleasure principle (i.e., learning is learning to have fun), and induction as key elements. In addition, references to convergence of images, transfer of conditioning, generalization, and abstraction will occur. In those instances where reference to a psychological mechanism occurs in parentheses, it should be understood as applying to the instance of the grammatical item which occurs in parentheses following '*Example:*'.

(4) *Gestures*. Ostensive learning usually requires the assistance of gestures such as static pointing and dynamic or sweeping gestures. Reference to the gesture involved in the learning of a grammatical item will be made, when relevant.

(5) *Similarity basis*. The similarity basis of one of the examples given for each grammatical item will be described. In general, the similarity basis is that distinctive trait shared by the episodes appropriate to the grammatical item being learned; it is the shared trait in which the perceptual similarity of the episodes consists. In those instances where

reference to a similarity basis occurs in parentheses, it should be understood as applying to the instance of the grammatical item which occurs in parentheses following 'Example:'.

(6) *Discussion.* A short discussion will be given for each grammatical item. Since some of this discussion makes use of Quine's notion of *quasi-quotation*, I shall now pause to explain that notion.

Logicians have developed a technique to signal that an expression is being talked about or *mentioned* (rather than being *used*). The technique consists in merely placing the expression within single quotation marks, e.g., 'Boston'. Throughout the remainder of this book, I shall signal the mention of an expression additionally by setting it off from the body of the text and prefacing it with a numeral in parentheses. For example, by this technique I may now *mention* the word of my previous example thus:

(1) Boston.

Now consider the expressions:

(2) Boston is a city,
(3) 'Boston' is composed of six letters of the alphabet,
(4) Boston is composed of six letters of the alphabet.

In (2) 'Boston' is being *used* to refer to the city of Boston; in (3) 'Boston' is being *mentioned*—it asserts that the expression 'Boston' has six letters; in (4) 'Boston' is being *used*, but the result is nonsensical (or, perhaps, false), for it asserts that Boston, the city, is composed of six letters of the alphabet.

This technique of signaling the mention of an expression has its limitations, however. For example, logicians sometimes need to speak of specific contexts of unspecified objects, as when they say such things as:

(5)   The result of writing the dyadic logical connective '$\equiv$' between *any two* well-formed formulas is itself a well-formed formula.

But (5) is inconveniently long. Isn't there a shorter way to express (5)? Suppose we adopt the Greek letters 'ϕ' and 'ψ' to serve as metalogical variables whose range of values is well-formed formulas; we could then (so it seems) express (5) more briefly as

(6)   If 'ϕ' and 'ψ' are well-formed formulas, then '$\phi\equiv\psi$' is a well-formed formula.

However, (6) won't do, for '$\phi \equiv \psi$' is *not* a well-formed formula; it is a hybrid of two meta-logical variables (belonging to the meta-language) and a dyadic logical connective (belonging to the object language). Moreover, the Greek letters occurring in (6) designate only the Greek letters themselves, not the unspecified expressions as desired. In short, quotation is insufficient to accomplish the task at hand. To remedy this kind of situation, Quine recommends rewriting (6) as

(7)　If $\ulcorner \phi \urcorner$ and $\ulcorner \psi \urcorner$ are well-formed formulas, then $\ulcorner \phi \equiv \psi \urcorner$ is a well-formed formula.

The notation enclosing the Greek letters in (7) Quine calls *corners*, the technique of doing so he calls *quasi-quotation*. Quasi-quotation amounts to quoting the constant contextual background, ' $\equiv$ ', and imagining the unspecified expressions written in the blanks.

We can facilitate our discussion of Quine's theory of language acquisition by utilizing this technique of quasi-quotation. The Greek letters of the quasi-quotation with which we shall be concerned should be construed as variables that range over both sentences and terms. Sometimes our discussion of Quine's theory of language acquisition will focus on sentences. In those contexts the Greek letters represent unspecified mentioned sentences. For example:

(8)　$\ulcorner \alpha \ ? \ \urcorner$ - 'Yes'

should be construed in the manner of

(9)　'Is the cat licking her paw?' - 'Yes'.

Sometimes our discussion will focus on terms. In those contexts the Greek letters represent unspecified mentioned terms. For example:

(10)　$\ulcorner \alpha \ \beta \ \urcorner$

should be construed in the manner of

(11)　'red wine'.

We may now profitably begin our inquiry into Quine's speculations concerning ostensive language learning.

Grammatical item: Observation sentences.
Example: 'Red', 'This is red', etc.
Psychological mechanism: Induction.
Gesture: Static pointing.

Similarity basis: The red episodes that a subject has associated with an accomplished speaker's assenting to the query 'Red?', or with an accomplished speaker's utterance of 'Red', or with the accomplished speaker's approval of the subject's utterance of 'Red'.

Discussion: The child's discovery of the similarity basis of an observation sentence like 'Red' takes time; it is a matter of his making the correct extrapolations. For example:

> In learning 'red' he has to learn that it is a question of sight, not some other sense. He has to find the proper direction in the scene, and how much to count: how big a patch. He has to learn what aspect of the patch to count; he might think that what mattered in his first red patch was the shape and not the color. Also there is the question of chromatic latitude: how orange can red get? Having been rewarded for saying 'red' on one exposure, he can only conjecture what similarity might warrant saying it again. We may expect him to have to make a number of trials and eliminate a number of errors before he is shunted onto the right track for good. (RR, 43)

Thankfully, this whole process of extrapolation can be expedited if the red in the various episodes is naturally salient or is rendered so with pointing gestures from the child's teacher.

Grammatical item: Expression of assent; (general technique of assent).
Example: 'Yes'; ($\ulcorner$ α ?$\urcorner$-'Yes').
Psychological mechanism: Induction; (generalization).
Gesture: None.
Similarity basis: A language-dependent similarity: the shared feature in which the similarity lies is perhaps an introspective sense of willingness to repeat a queried sentence; a sense of freedom from inhibition.
Discussion: It is possible that in a *particular case* a child might babble 'red' when a red object is present, and pleasure is present, followed by the sound of a parent's utterance 'yes'. In a subsequent episode there may be present a red object and the sound of the parent's query 'Red?'. Based on this partial similarity with the former episode, the child attempts to increase the similarity by uttering the sound 'yes', hoping again to receive pleasure in the form of reward from the parent. In such a way the child could learn to assent to the specific observation sentence 'Red'.

In time the child will learn the *general trick* of assenting when an observation sentence he has previously learned is queried for the first time. He learns this by generalizing from several particular cases he has learned separately in ways similar to the one suggested above. Hence, this feat is clearly a case of the language-dependent learning of language. The successful child learns the equivalence: assent to a sentence entails the same rewards or penalties as a repetition of the sentence would entail.

Grammatical item: General technique of dissent.
Example: ⌐ α ? ¬ - 'No'.
Psychological mechanism: Induction.
Gesture: None.
Similarity basis: A language-dependent similarity: the shared feature in which the similarity lies is perhaps an introspective sense of unwillingness to repeat a queried sentence; a sense of inhibition.
Discussion: After having acquired the general trick of assent, the child could move directly to the general trick of dissent, ⌐ α ? ¬ - 'No', without first learning to dissent to particular sentences, by simply coming to appreciate that dissent is rewarded where assent is penalized and vice versa.

Quine has noted three reasons why the learning of the idioms of assent and dissent are indispensable in the child's progress in the art of learning to use, query, and respond to sentences. First, the child must learn how and when to assent to his parents' queries rather than to persist in his childish blurting out of sentences like 'Red' in the presence of red in hopes of being rewarded for the utterance: "If the child were to persist in volunteering the names of passing colors and other observables, he would soon bore his purveyor of rewards beyond the point of diminishing returns" (RR, 45). Second, in order to improve and perfect his own usage, the child must learn to query sentences for others' assent, since the utterances volunteered by others are too sporadic to meet his needs. Third, there are observation sentences whose proper occasions of use cannot be discovered by watchful waiting but only by query and assent. Such are observation sentences with overlapping ranges of stimuli: "By just passively noting the episodes of impingement in which one's elders volunteered 'rabbit' or 'animal', one would have no way of making sure that all the things cited as rabbits would count also as animals, or whether any of the things cited as animals might count also as rabbits. By query and assent, on the other hand, it is the work of a moment" (RR, 46).

Grammatical item: Absolute mass terms.
Example: 'red', 'water', 'sugar', etc.
Psychological mechanism: Induction.
Gesture: Static pointing.
Similarity basis: The same as that given previously for the observation sentence 'Red'.
Discussion: To have learned an observation term is, in general, to have learned when to assent to or dissent from it in conformity with the way in which the relevant segment of the speech community assents to or dissents from it as an occasion sentence. So the similarity basis of the observation term 'red' will be identical with the similarity basis of the observation sentence 'Red' for a speaker who is a member of the relevant segment of the speech community. Regarding 'red' as an observation *term* rather than as an observation *sentence* is merely a way of acknowledging that 'red' can, as the resources of a person's language grow, find its way into longer sentences as a word describing or naming objects: describing bodies or surfaces or naming a color.

A significant feature of absolute mass terms is that they are closed with respect to aggregation. "Two squares do not together constitute a square, nor two apples an apple; but when you add sugar to sugar the total is still sugar. On this score, color words like 'red' behave like mass terms" (RR, 52). The respective similarity bases of 'red', 'sugar', and 'water', as for all absolute mass terms, have nothing to do with shape. It is also noteworthy that red, like sugar and water, can be present in simultaneous portions.

Grammatical item: Singular terms: proper names.
Example: 'Mama', 'Fido', 'Jumbo', etc.
Psychological mechanism: Induction.
Gesture: Sweeping gesture.
Similarity basis: Presentation of Mama exhibiting continuity of displacement, continuity of visual distortion or deformity, and continuity of discoloration.
Discussion: As an observation term, 'Mama' can be learned ostensively just as absolute mass terms like 'red' and 'sugar' can, namely, by learning inductively the appropriate similarity basis. One big difference between the learning of 'Mama' and the learning of the other terms is, however, that Mama, when she is present, is visibly continuous and, unlike the masses red and sugar, she is not present in simultaneous portions. At worst, Mama is sometimes partially eclipsed by some intervening object, but "these casual eclipses offer little threat to

Mama's integrity as a single Gestalt; for they are fleeting and they are independent of Mama's movements, responding rather with parallax to the movements of the observer" (RR, 53).

As we have already noted, the similarity bases of absolute mass terms do not include shape; the fact that red and water are presented in multifariously shaped patches and pools, respectively, is irrelevant to the ostensive learning of 'red' and 'water'. But with 'Mama' the case is different, for shape is very much the point when it comes to the similarity that links the various presentations of Mama:

> Her visual shapes are many in the course of her various orientations and contortions, but they are joined by observed continuity of deformation. We do not keep Mama under observation, but we do watch her often enough as she changes visual shape in our field. The similarity that links the many presentations of Mama for us under the one name is not just static visual similarity, but a similarity that depends also on continuity of deformation and displacement [and discoloration]. We may next recognize Mama because our new glimpse is visually similar to some earlier view that observably evolved from attested views by continuous deformation. Chains of such links are what hold Mama together. (RR, 53)

The kind of similarity that links presentations of Mama together is the kind of similarity that links the presentations of any *body* together. According to Quine, man has an innate predisposition (instinct) for recognizing this kind of similarity: "Man is a body-minded animal, among body-minded animals. Man and other animals are body-minded by natural selection; for body-mindedness has evident survival value in town and jungle" (RR, 54).

Grammatical item: Absolute general terms.
Example: 'dog'; ('animal'), etc.
Psychological mechanism: Induction; (generalization, abstraction).
Gesture: Sweeping gesture.
Similarity basis: Presentations of dogs each exhibiting continuity of displacement, continuity of visual distortion or deformity, and continuity of discoloration; (a second-order similarity between the similarity bases of various dogs).
Discussion: The same body-unifying kind of similarity that played a role in the learning of 'Mama' figures also in the learning of 'dog' since Mama and dogs are bodies. However, in learning 'dog', unlike

the case of learning 'Mama', one has to learn more than when the object is present. One also has to learn that 'dog' divides its reference; for unlike Mama more than one dog can be present at the same time. Thus, in learning 'dog' one must learn what to count as one dog and what to count as another. Consequently, "the similarity basis of such a term is rather sophisticated: a second-order similarity, as it were, of similarities" (RR, 56). This second-order similarity is a similarity between the similarity bases of particular dogs. The child has to recognize that in a mixed population of dogs and cats, say, that any two dogs are perceptually more similar to each other than is any dog to any cat. The learning of 'animal' is an analogous matter. Here the child has to recognize, for example, that each member of a pair of cats, or a pair of dogs, or a paired cat and dog is perceptually more similar to the other member of that pair than is any single cat or dog to any inanimate object.

Grammatical item: Relative mass terms.
Example: 'darker than', 'same dog as', etc.
Psychological mechanism: Induction.
Gesture: Pairwise pointing.
Similarity basis: Presentations of pairs of points or unbounded regions in which one's being darker than the other is or can be made salient by the appropriate gesture.
Discussion: The learning of relative mass terms does not differ much from the learning of absolute mass terms like 'red'. Both can be taught by punctual ostension. The relative case differs from the absolute case only in taking points or unbounded regions two by two: 'Here is darker than here'. As noted in §1.3, relative mass terms like 'darker than' or 'Here is darker than here' are asymmetrical and transitive, while others like 'same dog as' or 'Here is the same dog as here' are symmetrical and transitive.

Grammatical item: Relative general terms.
Example: 'smaller than', etc.
Psychological mechanism: Induction.
Gesture: Pairwise sweeping gesture or pairwise pointing.
Similarity basis: Presentations of pairs of bounded regions or objects in which the trait of one being smaller than the other is salient or can be made salient by the appropriate gesture.
Discussion: The learning of 'smaller than', and the like, requires pairs of sweeping ostensions accompanying such pleonastic expres-

sions as 'This is smaller than this' sufficient to indicate the bounds of the regions or objects concerned. Sometimes it will be possible to get by with pairs of merely static gestures if the bounded regions or objects are already salient.

Grammatical item: Mode of composition: attributive composition.
Example: 'yellow paper'; ($\ulcorner \alpha \, \beta \, \urcorner$).
Psychological mechanism: Induction, or convergence of images; (generalization).
Gesture: Usually none required.
Similarity basis: Presentations of yellow superimposed on paper; (language-dependent similarity).
Discussion: Once 'yellow' and 'paper' have been learned ostensively as observation terms, their utterance by the teacher enlivens traces of episodes in the learner's memory in which yellow was salient and episodes in which paper was salient. These enlivened memory traces—heuristically regarded by Quine as images—enhance the salience of any yellow paper present at the time. "Salience of yellow paper is thus enhanced doubly. All our mentor has to do to perfect our training in the compound 'yellow paper' is discourage assent in those less striking cases where the yellow and the paper are separate" (RR, 60).

After a time the child can catch on to the *general trick* of forming on his own attributive compounds like $\ulcorner \alpha \, \beta \, \urcorner$. He can learn this general trick by noticing a language-dependent similarity, namely, that occasions for assenting to attributive compounds are similar to one another in that the two component terms always serve to heighten the salience of some one part of the present scene. "This account not only depends on our present reasonable doctrine that a learned word has power to enhance the salience of an appropriate part of a current episode; it also assumes that the overlapping of two such verbal heightenings would itself be noticed and used as a point of similarity" (RR, 60).

Grammatical item: Mode of composition: 'in' compound.
Example: 'Mama in the garden'; ($\ulcorner \alpha \text{ in } \beta \, \urcorner$).
Psychological mechanism: Induction, convergence of images; (generalization).
Gesture: Usually none required.
Similarity basis: Presentations of Mama embedded in the garden; i.e., Mama and the garden partially overlapping; (language-dependent similarity).
Discussion: Once having learned 'Mama' and 'the garden' as ob-

servation terms, the child can learn 'Mama in the garden' (or the pleonastic 'Mama is in the garden') in the same fashion in which he learned 'yellow paper' after he had acquired 'yellow' and 'paper'. The difference between the two is that Mama and the garden overlap only *partially* whereas the yellow and the paper of our previous example overlapped *totally*. The acquisition of the *general trick* of forming 'in' compounds, $\ulcorner \alpha$ in $\beta \urcorner$, is also similar to the learning of the comparable feat for attributive compounds. From the various particular cases of 'in' composition already acquired, the child generalizes $\ulcorner \alpha$ in $\beta \urcorner$ by means of a language-dependent similarity; he comes to see that all utterances of 'in' compounds share the trait of heightening the salience of portions of the scene that are embedded one within the other.

Grammatical item: Particle: '-like'.
Example: 'dog-like'; ($\ulcorner \alpha$ -like $\urcorner$).
Psychological mechanism: Induction; (generalization).
Gesture: None.
Similarity basis: Presentations of dog-like objects; (language-dependent similarity).
Discussion: Terms such as 'dog-like' could be learned as simple, uncompounded, observation terms like 'dog' itself. The *general trick* of forming such observation terms, $\ulcorner \alpha$ -like $\urcorner$, is, again, a matter of generalizing from instances along the lines of a language-dependent similarity: "What the proper occasions for assenting to $\ulcorner \alpha$ -like $\urcorner$ have in common is a perceptible but insufficient impulse to assent to α itself" (RR, 62).

Grammatical item: Eternal sentence; (eternal predication construction).
Example 1: 'Snow is white' (joining of two mass terms); ($\ulcorner \alpha$ is $\beta \urcorner$).
Example 2: 'Fido is a dog' (joining of a singular term—a proper name—with an absolute general term); ($\ulcorner \alpha$ is $\beta \urcorner$).
Example 3: 'Fido is smaller than Jumbo' (joining of two singular terms—proper names—and a relative general term); ($\ulcorner \alpha \gamma \beta \urcorner$).
Example 4: 'A dog is an animal' (joining of two absolute general terms); ($\ulcorner$ Every α is $\beta \urcorner$).
Psychological mechanism: Transfer of conditioning; (generalization).
Gesture: The eternal predications containing terms denoting bod-

ies may require sweeping gestures for their teaching—gestures indicating the spatial extent of the intended bodies.

Discussion: The ostensive learning of any occasion sentence as an unstructured whole conditioned to ranges of recurring presentations of prompting stimuli is clearly a matter of the pupil's coming to appreciate the various kinds of conditions under which the utterance of that sentence is regarded as true or as false. On the other hand, the ostensive learning of standing sentences, while ultimately still a matter of the pupil coming to appreciate the truth conditions of sentences, takes place in a manner slightly different from the ostensive learning of occasion sentences.

The simplest kind of standing sentences that may be learned ostensively are those formed by joining predicatively two mass terms, as in the first example above: 'Snow is white'. Quine's account of the ostensive learning of such sentences involves a *transfer of conditioning*. (Incidentally, this is a different psychological mechanism than the convergence of images that figured in Quine's account of the ostensive learning of the attributive joining of two mass terms, e.g., 'white snow'.) Suppose, for example, that a child has learned the mass terms 'snow' and 'white' ostensively. Suppose further that when the child's parent queries 'Snow is white?' the sound of the word 'snow' enlivens a memory trace of the child in which snow was salient. Since the child in virtue of already having learned 'white' ostensively is disposed to assent to the query 'White?' in the presence of snow, he will, upon hearing the word 'white' following closely upon the heels of 'snow' in 'Snow is white?', voice his assent as though snow itself were present. In this case the child *transfers* his verbal response of assent from the snow stimulus to the associated verbal stimulus, 'snow'. In short, the *snow image*, the enlivened memory trace in which snow is salient, activated by the sound of 'snow', is sufficiently similar to presentations of snow itself so as to trigger the affirmation response to 'White?' even though no snow is present.

The other kinds of eternal sentences, typified by our *Examples 2, 3,* and *4,* can all be learned in ways similar to the way just conjectured for 'Snow is white'. The only difference of note is that these others may require the use of sweeping gestures for their learning, since they contain terms denoting bodies, while 'Snow is white' does not.

But, of course, the child does not merely learn specific, singular, eternal sentences like 'Snow is white' and 'Fido is a dog', nor merely specific universal categoricals like 'A dog is an animal'; he also learns, by generalizing from these individual cases, the singular and general modes of composition that they represent: ⌐ α is β ¬ and ⌐ Every α is β¬. The child begins to sense a similarity among the ways of coming to appreciate that snow is white, that Fido is a dog, and that a dog is an animal. What the child senses as being common to each pair of terms—the similarity basis of the mode of composition—is a tendency in the sound of the first term of each pair to dispose him to assent to the second term of each pair. So, in effect, when the child learns these modes of composition, he is, as with the learning of occasion sentences, learning truth conditions. In the case of occasion sentences, he learns in which circumstances a particular sentence is true and in what circumstances it is false. In learning the eternal predication construction, he learns how to judge whether a given pair of terms produces a true predication, true for good, or a false one, false for good. "First and last, in learning language, we are learning how to distribute truth values" (RR, 65).

In *Word and Object* Quine claimed that truth functional modes of forming compound sentences could be learned ostensively. But in *The Roots of Reference* he acknowledges that this is not quite so. *Negation* offers no problems in this quarter, but conjunction and alternation do.

In learning the truth function of *conjunction* ostensively the child must learn to assent to conjunctions when and only when he would assent to each of the component sentences of the conjunction; and he must learn to dissent to conjunctions when he would dissent to any of the component sentences of the conjunction. But what rule must he follow when each of the component sentences of a conjunction would, if queried separately, elicit not assent or dissent but abstention? Under such conditions the queried conjunction is indeterminate; the indeterminacy is between dissent and abstention. For example, suppose the sentences 'It is a mouse' and 'It is a chipmunk' are both queried of a subject, and he abstains on both counts as a consequence of having received only fleeting presentations of the critter in question. Still, if he were then queried with the conjunction 'It is a mouse *and* it is a chipmunk', he would *dissent* since he knows that whatever it is, it cannot be both a mouse and a chipmunk, either simultaneously or concurrently. But now consider the pair of sentences 'It is a mouse' and 'It is in the kitchen', queried under the same conditions. If each of these were queried separately and resulted in abstention, then, more than likely, the result would likewise be *abstention* when their conjunction were queried.

A similar discrepancy occurs in the ostensive learning of truth functional *alternation*. Here the indeterminacy is between assent and abstention. Supposing again that the separate queries of 'It is a mouse' and 'It is a chipmunk' each resulted in abstention, still the query of their alternation might elicit *assent* or *abstention*.

At the level of ostensive learning, therefore, a distinction emerges between truth functions and what Quine calls *verdict functions*. While standard truth functional logic is a two-valued logic, verdict logic is a three-valued logic whose values are assent (A), dissent (D), and abstention (Ab). Table 2.1 gives the verdict table definitions of verdict-conjunction and verdict-alternation, respectively.

Table 2.1.   Verdict conjunction and verdict alternation

α	β	⌐ α and β ⌐	α	β	⌐ α or β ⌐
A	A	A	A	A	A
A	D	D	A	D	A
A	Ab	Ab	A	Ab	A
D	A	D	D	A	A
D	D	D	D	D	D
D	Ab	D	D	Ab	Ab
Ab	A	Ab	Ab	A	A
Ab	D	D	Ab	D	Ab
Ab	Ab	? (D or Ab)	Ab	Ab	? (A or Ab)

Verdict functions approximating to conjunction and alternation could be forged by specifying abstention at the . . . [bottom] of the tables. These are more primitive than the genuine truth-functional conjunction and alternation, in that they can be learned by induction from observation of verdict behavior. They are independent of our parochial two-valued logic, and independent of other truth-value logics. Truth values represent a more advanced, more theory-laden level of linguistic development; and it is in terms of theory, different theories for different subject matters, that we eventually learn (if at all) what verdict to give to the cases of conjunction and alternation that are indeterminate at the . . . [bottom] of the verdict tables. Two-valued logic is a theoretical development that is learned, like other theory, in indirect ways upon which we can only speculate. Some theorists, notably the intuitionists, favor

another logic, and there is nothing in the observable circumstances of our utterances that need persuade them to assign
meaning to our two-valued scheme. (RR, 78)

I shall omit from my account several additional terms, particles,
and modes of composition learnable ostensively that Quine discusses
in *The Roots of Reference*. (The additional items are these: values
'good (-tasting)' or 'good (-feeling)', 'good (-looking)', and 'good
(-behaving)'; color idiom 'color', 'sameness of color', '-colored', 'is a
color', 'is the same color as', ⌐ α-colored ¬, ⌐ α is a color¬, 'This
color is the same as this', ⌐ α is a tint¬; shape idiom 'shape', ⌐ α-
shaped¬, ⌐ α is a shape¬, ⌐ α is a shape word¬.) Enough has been
said already to grasp the drift of Quine's theory of ostensive language
learning. We may now turn our attention to his speculations pertaining
to that part of language acquired by means of analogic synthesis.

§2.2.2.2   *Analogic synthesis*

Quine believes that ostensive learning will not take one very far in language learning. In particular, one cannot learn by ostensive means the
language for referring to objects. At best the child can learn to associate certain verbal responses with various sensory presentations. But
this kind of recognition and discrimination of sensory presentations,
together with verbal accompaniments, does not constitute referring. A
child may learn, ostensively, to respond with 'Red' under all the appropriate stimulatory occasions, but it would be premature to conclude
from this that he was referring to an object.

In order to account for the learning of language that lies beyond the
range of ostensive learning, Quine introduces the concept of analogic
synthesis. The general idea of analogic synthesis is that most sentences
a person learns are built up from parts of other sentences that the person has already acquired and are based on analogies with the ways
those parts have previously been noticed to occur in those other sentences. In the whole of *Word and Object* Quine provides but one concrete example or instance of such learning: "It is evident how new sentences may be built from old materials and volunteered on appropriate
occasions simply by virtue of the analogies. Having been directly conditioned to the appropriate use of 'Foot' (or 'This is my foot') as a sentence, and 'Hand' likewise, and 'My foot hurts' as a whole, the child
might conceivably utter 'My hand hurts' on an appropriate occasion,
though unaided by previous experience with that actual sentence"
(WO, 9).

This sole example of analogic synthesis does not tell the whole story of how the portion of language that lies beyond the range of ostensive learning is acquired. What Quine has to say on the matter additionally, which is considerable, is conditioned by his epistemological interest: how can we acquire our theory of the world? A theory of the world is largely a theory of what there is in the world, and what a theory says there is in the world is a matter of reference. So Quine's speculations regarding the acquisition of the higher reaches of language are "limited to one important aspect: the referential aspect, the acquisition of an apparatus for speaking of objects" (RR, 81).

According to Quine, learning the referential apparatus of English is a contextual process that utilizes analogic synthesis. To learn how to refer, a child needs to learn how to use "a cluster of interrelated grammatical particles and constructions: plural endings, pronouns, numerals, the 'is' of identity, and its adaptations 'same' and 'other'" (OR, 32). In *Word and Object* Quine says that "the contextual learning of these various particles goes on simultaneously, we may suppose, so that they are gradually adjusted to one another and a coherent pattern of usage is evolved matching that of society. The child scrambles up an intellectual chimney, supporting himself against each side by pressure against the others" (WO, 93).

It was Quine's dissatisfaction with "so brief and metaphorical an account of the matter" (RR, ix–x) that prompted him to write *The Roots of Reference*. In the third part of that work, "Referring to Objects," Quine offers a speculative account of how a child could acquire the referential apparatus of English by a series of grammatical transformations and *irreducible leaps of analogy*. Actually, Quine's account is an idealization of this process. He understands quantification to be an encapsulation of this referential apparatus, and his attention is, as a matter of convenience, directed toward speculations regarding how a child could acquire the idiom of quantification. "By considering what steps could lead the small child or primitive man to quantification, rather than to the less tidy referential apparatus of actual English, we arrive at a psychogenetic reconstruction in skeletal outline. We approximate to the essentials of the real psychogenesis of reference while avoiding inessential complications" (RR, 100).

Before proceeding to examine some of Quine's speculations concerning language learned by analogic synthesis, I should like to alleviate a certain tension that may be building in the reader's mind. In §1.1 we drew a contrast between Carnap's program of rational reconstruction and Quine's program of enlightened empiricism in these terms:

Carnap was contented to come up with *any* adequate reconstruction of our theory of the world (viz. science), whereas Quine, disdainful of "all this make-believe," opted instead for a "factual account" of the matter. But it now would appear, in light of the revelation that Quine intends to settle for an idealized account of how a child might acquire the idiom of quantification, that Quine's commitment to the goal of providing a factual account of how our theory of the world, i.e., of how (theoretical) language is acquired, seems to be waning. This is an important matter, for to relinquish the goal of a factual account is virtually a relinquishing of enlightened empiricism itself.

This apparent conflict in Quine's thought between a factual account and an idealized account is only a mirage. Recall that Quine has been quoted as saying that the new empiricism, enlightened empiricism, may include something like the old rational reconstruction, for imaginative constructions can afford hints of actual psychological processes. And while it is true that the conspicuous difference between the old and new epistemology is that the epistemologist of enlightened empiricism is free to make use of empirical psychology, he or she may nevertheless pursue the inquiry at one or more removes from the laboratory, at one or another level of speculativity:

> Such speculations would gain, certainly, from experimental investigation of the child's actual learning of language. Experimental findings already available in the literature could perhaps be used to sustain or correct these conjectures at points, and further empirical investigations could be devised. But a speculative approach of the present sort seems required to begin with, in order to isolate just the factual questions that bear on our purposes. For our objective here is still philosophical— a better understanding of the relations between evidence and scientific theory. Moreover, the way to this objective requires consideration of linguistics and logic along with psychology. This is why the speculative phase has to precede, for the most part, the formation of relevant questions to be posed to the experimental psychologist.
>
> In any event the present speculations, however inaccurate, are presumably true to the general nature of language acquisition. (NNK, 78)

The reader's anxiety that Quine is abandoning enlightened empiricism thus dispelled, we may proceed to an examination of Quine's speculations concerning how a child could learn the idiom of quantification.

We have already seen how individual predications (the joining of a singular term and a general term as in 'Fido is a dog') could be learned inductively by transfer of conditioning. The predicative construction, $\ulcorner \alpha$ is $\beta \urcorner$, is, perhaps, acquired inductively by generalizing upon a language-dependent similarity shared by all individual predications, that is, the sound of the first term of a predication disposes one to assent to the second term of the predication.

We have also seen how individual universal categoricals (the joining of two general terms as in 'Every dog is an animal') could be learned inductively by transfer of conditioning. The universal categorical construction, $\ulcorner$ Every α is $\beta \urcorner$, is acquired much as $\ulcorner \alpha$ is $\beta \urcorner$ is acquired. The child whose language learning has progressed to this point has made a significant advance beyond the learning of observation sentences as unstructured wholes. The child's acquisition of such observation sentences indicates merely that he has learned to *respond* verbally to the stimuli he recognizes and discriminates, but with the advent of the universal categoricals he is well on his way toward acquiring theoretical language with which he will be able to actually *refer* to objects. In fact, Quine has suggested that universal categoricals represent the earliest phase of what could properly be called reference. However, another step toward acquiring theoretical language, equally important for the child, is his mastery of the relative clause.

Relative clauses, it will be recalled from §1.3, are usually absolute terms, e.g., 'something that chases its tail'. These relative clauses can find their way into predications; for example, 'Dinah is something that chases her tail'. But notice that this predication is only a long-winded version of the shorter predication 'Dinah chases her tail', which a child could produce simply by substituting the proper name 'Dinah' for the pronoun 'something that' of the relative clause. Quine's suggestion is that the child catches on to this trick of substitution (a substitutional transformation rule) by observing that adults are prepared to assent to a predication of a relative clause in just those circumstances where they are prepared to assent to the simpler sentences obtained by substitution. In effect, the child has learned that the pronouns of relative clauses perform the work of substitutional variables whose values are the range of terms serving as substituends; we see here the beginnings of the idiom of substitutional quantification.

But, having learned this much, the child is struck by a further analogy between relative clauses and the more ordinary general terms like 'dog': relative clauses can be put into other positions where general terms have been observed to occur. One such notable position is that of the α in the universal categorical construction ⌐Every α is β⌐, producing, for example, 'Everything that chases its tail is an animal'.

Once the relative clause finds its way into the place of α in ⌐Every α is β⌐, it cannot be eliminated from that position, for it arrived there by dint of an irreducible leap of analogy (and not by means of a two-way substitutional transformation). "The further point to notice now about this leap is that along with forsaking eliminability it forsakes the substitutional status of the [pronoun-] variables themselves" (RR, 99–100). The pronouns of relative clauses are no longer forerunners to substitutional variables only; they have now become forerunners to objectual variables as well. For such categoricals to be true, they must be true of everything satisfying their predicates. Their substituends are now specifically *singular* terms, but the objects that are the values of these new pronoun-variables may very well be more plentiful than are the singular terms available for naming them. Consequently, such categoricals usher in a new phase of reference, namely, a way of referring to unnameable objects.

The idioms of quantification, namely, 'everything x is such that' and 'something x is such that', encapsulate in pristine form all that is worth preserving of (substantival) relative clauses for the purpose of objective reference.

> Seeing the referential apparatus as epitomised in quantification, we see it as consisting essentially of two sorts of device: there are the quantitative particles 'every' and 'some', as applied to general terms in the categorical constructions, and there are the variables or pronouns as used in abstracting new general terms in the form of relative clauses. *The relative clause and the categorical thus stand forth as the roots of reference*. The objectual variable is an outgrowth of these two roots, not of one alone; for the variable of the relative clause begins as substitutional. (RR, 101; *my emphasis*)

This is by no means a complete survey of Quine's speculations concerning the psychogenesis of reference, but it suffices as an indication of how one might begin with ostensive learning, which is ultimately concerned with the observational edge of language, and work one's way into the discursive interior of language where scientific theory can be expressed.

Predication is at hand, and the universal categorical, the relative clause, and the truth functions. Once this stage is reached, it is easy to see that the whole strength of logical quantification is available. . . .

By further conjectures in the same spirit, some of them more convincing and some less, we can outline the learner's further progress, to where he is bandying abstract terms and quantifying over properties, numbers, functions, and hypothetical physical particles and forces. *This progress is not a continuous derivation, which, followed backward, would enable us to reduce scientific theory to sheer observation.* It is a progress rather by short leaps of analogy. (NNK, 77–78; *my emphasis*)

In §1.1 we noted the insight that lies at the bottom of Quine's salvation of empiricism, namely, his denial of the thesis that the *individual* sentences of a theory admit of confirmation and infirmation. Rather, it is, he thinks, theories as wholes which admit of confirmation and infirmation. We now have Quine's *explanation* of why this holistic view is true: scientific (i.e., referential) language is the product of irreducible leaps of analogy; it is, therefore, not reducible to sheer observation. This same theory of how scientific language is acquired is also at the bottom of Quine's claim that our scientific theory of the world is, in principle, underdetermined by all possible observations. If all of language were learnable ostensively, by induction, this would not be the case. Both of these topics, holism and underdetermination, and their connection with Quine's theory of language learning are discussed in detail in Chapter 3.

§2.3   *Summary and conclusions*

In the Introduction I stated that Quine's philosophy is a systematic attempt to answer, from a uniquely empiricistic point of view, what he understands to be the central question of epistemology: 'How, on the basis of observation, could we construct our theory of the world?' I have tried to show in Chapter 2 how and why Quine reconstrues this as a question of how theoretical *talk* is linked to observational *talk*. This question is one of how language is learned; hence Quine's insistence that the theory of language is vital to the theory of knowledge.

Quine's theory of language learning has not been without its critics, the most notable one being the linguist-philosopher Noam Chomsky. Consequently, a question of some importance is whether Quine's theory is defensible. Because in this essay I have assigned such great importance to Quine's theory of language learning, I feel compelled to attempt a response to this question, which is Chapter 4 of the book.

Quine's theory of language (i.e., his theory of linguistic meaning—semantics—and his theory of language learning) is what I have called the "framework" of his philosophy. His semantic theory is centered around his behavioral specification of the various kinds of sentences and his notion of stimulus meaning. His theory of language is grounded on the naturalistic-behavioristic thesis, the thesis that language is a social art which is acquired by social emulation and social feedback, all of which takes place amid publicly observable circumstances. It would be fairly close to the mark, therefore, to conclude that the naturalistic-behavioristic thesis is the central axiom of Quine's philosophy.

When I say this thesis is an "axiom," I do not mean that it is without empirical support, even though Quine never states an argument for the thesis. I think he regards it as something most people would believe to be true on the basis of their own experience. When I say the thesis is "central," I mean, to put the point in a Quinian turn of phrase, that it is the last thesis Quine would be disposed to relinquish.

Chapter 3: The edifice

§3.1 *The naturalistic-behavioristic conception of*
language and the Quinian system

We are now ready to examine Quine's systematic philosophy, which is constituted in large part by his attempt to answer the question of how a person could acquire scientific knowledge about the world. This will involve examining the various doctrines and theses that comprise Quine's philosophy, tracing out some of the important relationships that hold among some of these, and revealing how all of this takes place within the framework of the naturalistic-behavioristic conception of language. My principal method in this chapter will be to show first, through quotations, how Quine himself sees the NB conception of language as fundamental to much of his philosophy and then, by detailed discussion, to show how Quine's major doctrines develop within the framework of the NB conception of language.

The fundamental nature of the role played in Quine's philosophy by the NB conception of language is nowhere better expressed in Quine's writings than in the early pages of his Dewey Lectures, "Ontological Relativity," where he says:

> Philosophically I am bound to Dewey by the naturalism
> that dominated his last three decades. With Dewey I hold that
> knowledge, mind, and meaning are part of the same world that
> they have to do with, and that they are to be studied in the same
> empirical spirit that animates natural science. There is no place
> for a prior philosophy.

63

When a *naturalistic* philosopher addresses himself to the philosophy of mind, he is apt to talk of language. Meanings are, first and foremost, meanings of language. Language is a social art which we all acquire on the evidence solely of other people's overt behavior under publicly recognizable circumstances. Meanings, therefore, those very models of mental entities, end up as grist for the *behaviorist's* mill. Dewey was explicit on the point: 'Meaning . . . is not a psychic existence; it is primarily a property of behavior.' (OR, 26–27; *note omitted; my emphasis*)

Once language is understood in this naturalistic way, as a social art to be studied empirically, it is immediately obvious that there cannot be any useful sense to the claims that language is private or that meaning is private.

Uncritical semantics is the myth of a museum in which the exhibits are meanings and the words are labels. To switch languages is to change the labels. Now the naturalist's primary objection to this view is not an objection to meanings on account of their being mental entities, though that could be objection enough. The primary objection persists even if we take the labeled exhibits not as mental ideas but as Platonic ideas or even as the denoted concrete objects. Semantics is vitiated by a pernicious mentalism *as long as we regard a man's semantics as somehow determinate in his mind beyond what might be implicit in his dispositions to overt behavior*. It is the very facts about meaning, not the entities meant, that must be construed in terms of behavior. . . . (OR, 27; *my emphasis*)

When with Dewey we turn . . . toward a naturalistic view of language and a behavioral view of meaning, what we give up is not just the museum figure of speech. We give up an assurance of determinacy. Seen according to the museum myth, the words and sentences of a language have their determinate meanings. To discover the meanings of the native's words we may have to observe his behavior, but still the meanings of the words are supposed to be determinate in the native's *mind*, his mental museum, even in cases where behavioral criteria are powerless to discover them for us. When on the other hand we recognize with Dewey that 'meaning . . . is primarily a property of behavior', we recognize that there are no meanings, nor likenesses nor distinctions of meaning, beyond what are implicit in people's dispositions to overt behavior. For naturalism the question whether two expressions are alike or unlike in meaning has no determinate answer, known or unknown, except insofar as the answer is settled in principle by people's speech dispositions, known or unknown. If by these standards there are indeterminate cases, so much the worse for the terminology of meaning and likeness of meaning. (OR, 28–29)

It is important to note explicitly what Quine says *results* when, with Dewey, we turn toward a naturalistic view of language and a behavioral view of meaning: (1) we give up the museum figure of speech, (2) we give up assurance of determinacy, and (3) we recognize that there are no meanings or likenesses or distinctions of meaning beyond those that are implicit in people's speech dispositions.

I shall argue in the remainder of this chapter that, fully expanded, (1)–(3) amount to the following Quinian doctrines and theses: (a) indeterminacy of translation, (b) inscrutability of reference, (c) ontological relativity, (d) underdetermination of theory, (e) revisibility or holism thesis, (f) rejection of intensional objects, including meanings, propositions, attributes, and relations, (g) rejection of synonymy, (h) rejection of analytic-synthetic distinction, (i) rejection of radical epistemological reductionism, (j) rejection of modal logic, (k) pragmatic philosophy of science.

§3.2 *Radical translation, indeterminacy, inscrutability, and relativity*

The essence of Quine's almost infamous doctrine of the *indeterminacy of translation* can be stated as the claim that "manuals for translating one language into another can be set up in divergent ways, all compatible with the totality of speech dispositions, yet incompatible with one another" (WO, 27). In order to understand how this can happen we need only examine an extreme case of such translation, which Quine calls *radical translation*, where the language being translated into (say) English is completely without preexisting aids to translation—as a Martian language would presumably be.[1]

---

1. A "Martian" language is used not merely for dramatic effect, since a true case of terrestrial radical translation would be rare. However, there is a danger involved in

Without getting bogged down in the intricate details of the activity of radical translation, perhaps we can show by the following general account of a fictitious linguist's activities how Quine thinks indeterminacy arises. The linguist begins, we may suppose, by observing the Martians speaking—all one has to go on in learning a language is the overt behavior of others, and so forth. No doubt one of the linguist's first tasks will be phonemic analysis; but we, like Quine, can omit that part of translation since the philosophical point Quine is intent to make is unaffected by the linguist's concern with Martian phonemes. The most elementary steps in translating the Martian language (as in learning any language) consist in translating the Martian utterances keyed to present events that are conspicuous to the linguist *and* to his subject: "A rabbit scurries by, the . . . [Martian] says 'Gavagai', and the linguist notes down the sentence 'Rabbit' (or 'Lo, a rabbit') as tentative translation, subject to testing in further cases" (WO, 29).

One of the next tasks for the linguist is to settle on Martian expressions for assent and dissent. This is a necessary step for two reasons. First, what the linguist is interested in is not the language-in-use of any particular Martian subject but, rather, his language-in-disposition. There may be many situations where a subject *could* say something keyed to present stimulation, but where he *does not*. The linguist's solution to this difficulty is to put himself in position to query the Martian with Martian sentences, to see if the Martian *would* assent to, or dissent from, these sentences under various stimulatory conditions. Second, and more important, the linguist must be able to discriminate among Martian terms that overlap in their reference, and he can do this only if he has settled on Martian expressions for assent and dissent. (The analogue to this in the normal language learning context of the child was discussed in §2.2.2.1.)

---

talking of translating Martian talk (which Quine never does, although he sometimes talks of Martians translating human talk), which is that we could be charged with leaving out of account part of the nonverbal behavioral data that could be relied upon by the linguist who endeavors to translate human languages. In other words, humans translating human talk can rely on supposed commonly shared features of human interests and behavior to facilitate translation and to eliminate indeterminacies, but no such data would (presumably) be available in translating the "talk" of "green" people. Similar remarks pertain to assumptions about shared innate standards of perceptual similarity. Quine's point about indeterminacy of translation, however, is unaffected by considerations about how much or how little the linguist and his subjects have in common. Consequently, perhaps we can agree to overlook the "greenness" of our Martians now that we have noted it.

The method by which the linguist arrives at his identifications of the Martian expressions for assent and dissent is not foolproof. In general, he relies upon what appears to be assent behavior and dissent behavior. A Martian sign for assent might be recognizable by this partial criterion: a speaker will assent to a sentence, if queried, under circumstances producing similar episodes in the receptual neighborhood of the episodes near to which he volunteers the same sentence. A partial criterion for dissent is that a speaker will dissent under no circumstances producing episodes in the receptual neighborhood of the episodes near to which he volunteers the sentence. But the linguist could run into difficulties, especially if the sentences he is working with happen not to be observation sentences. It is also possible that Martianese has no unique expressions for assent and dissent. Still, the linguist makes the best guess he can. If extraordinary difficulties attend all his subsequent steps of translation, he may discard his first hypothesis and guess again.

Once the expressions of assent and dissent are in hand, the next task for the linguist will be to equate the observation sentences of English and Martianese. This is done by learning to utter Martian sounds sufficient to the task of querying a Martian speaker for assent or dissent under various public stimulus conditions. Working inductively, the linguist is able to make approximate identifications of stimulus meanings. Of course the linguist cannot compare his own stimulus meaning for some sentence of English with his subject's stimulus meaning for some sentence of Martianese: stimulus meanings are subjective. But the linguist can learn that the Martian is prepared to assent to or dissent from the query 'Gavagai?' under just those same public conditions where the linguist would be prepared to assent to or dissent from the query 'Rabbit?'. Hence, the linguist concludes that the two stimulus meanings—his for 'Rabbit' and the Martian's for 'Gavagai'—are approximately the same.

But even this early step of translating is taken on the grounds of some (probably unconscious) subtle hypothesizing on the part of the linguist, for he has to suggest to himself "reasonable" English translations for various Martian observation sentences. For example, in the case of equating the Martian's 'Gavagai' with 'Rabbit' or 'Lo, a rabbit' the linguist is assuming, reasonably enough, that the Martians have a fairly short expression for responding to rabbit stimulations. At any rate, the linguist can go on entering new Martian observation sentences into his manual for translating Martianese into English now that he has settled on some Martian expressions for assent and dissent. (It will be recalled from §2.2.1 that once the linguist goes bilingual, he can then translate *all* of the Martian occasion sentences, not just the observation sentences, by equating his own stimulus meanings introspectively.)

What is extremely important to notice about this level of translation is that the linguist can get things wrong—he can make mistakes (for example, incorrect inductive generalizations). He may find, for example, that on some future occasion his stimulus meaning for 'Rabbit' and the Martian's stimulus meaning for 'Gavagai' diverge. Thus, stimulus situations offer an objective criterion for adjudicating between the proposed equating of a single expression of Martianese with one or the other of two nonequivalent English expressions. This is an important feature of translation, for if it were not absent from some later stages of radical translation, indeterminacy of (radical) translation would not occur—at least not to the same philosophically interesting extent. At the level of stimulus meaning more than just Martian observation sentences can be objectively translated. Whatever parts of language the Martian child could learn ostensively, the linguist could, in principle, translate at this level. Truth functions could be partially translated (into verdict functions, for example), and cognitively equivalent occasion sentences could at least be recognized.

Steps of translating beyond the ones already indicated necessarily involve the explicit utilization of *analytical hypotheses*. The linguist segments Martian utterances into conveniently short recurrent parts and thus compiles a list of Martian "words." Various of these he hypothetically equates to English words and phrases. Such are his analytical hypotheses. But, analytical hypotheses are not, as one might at first think, merely or even generally equations of Martian and English words like: 'gavagai' means 'rabbit'. In fact, Quine explicitly says that analytical hypotheses are not in general held to equational form:

> There is no need to insist that the . . . [Martian] word be equated outright to any one English word or phrase. Certain contexts may be specified in which the word is to be translated one way and others in which the word is to be translated in another way. The equational form may be overlaid with supplementary semantical instructions *ad libitum*. Since there is no general positional correspondence between the words and phrases of one language and their translations in another, some analytical hypotheses will be needed also to explain syntactical constructions. These are usually described with help of aux-

iliary terms for various classes of . . . [Martian] words and phrases. Taken together, the analytical hypotheses and auxiliary definitions constitute the linguist's . . . [Martian-to-English] dictionary and grammar. (WO, 69–70)

If the linguist is to get much beyond Martian observation sentences, he must therefore make explicit use of analytical hypotheses. But how, it may be asked, does the linguist arrive at (in the sense of 'discover' not 'justify') his analytical hypotheses? Typically, Quine suggests, "the linguist apprehends a parallelism in function between some component fragment of a translated whole . . . [Martian] sentence and some component word of the translation of the sentence" (WO, 70). (As one might apprehend a parallel function of 'ne . . . pas' in 'Il ne parle pas française' and 'not' in 'He does not speak French'.) In so doing, the linguist is guided in formulating his analytical hypotheses by a projection of prior linguistic habits. Thus, his method of utilizing analytical hypotheses is a way of catapulting himself into the foreign language by the momentum of his own home language. In this subtle way, the linguist superimposes his home language and conceptual scheme upon the Martians' language in almost every act of translation.

It is at just this stage in translating that indeterminacy of a philosophically interesting kind occurs. The indeterminacy of translation is, one might say, of two varieties. One variety is *indeterminacy of intension* or "meaning" (taken in some intuitive sense) and can affect any Martian expression deemed significant enough to "have meaning"; the other variety is *indeterminacy of extension*, or *indeterminacy of reference*, and affects Martian terms. (Quine calls this latter variety *inscrutability of reference*, or *inscrutability of terms*.) The former variety of indeterminacy amounts to the claim:

(A) Consistent with all possible dispositions to behavior on the parts of all concerned, different systems of analytical hypotheses can be formulated which render different English translations of the same use of a Martian expression which, on intuitive grounds, differ in "meaning"; *and* there is no sense to the question of any one translation being the uniquely correct one.

Similarly, the latter variety of indeterminacy amounts to the claim:

(B) Consistent with all possible dispositions to behavior on the parts of all concerned, different systems of analytical hypotheses can be formulated which render the same use of a Martian expression as either a nonterm or a term, and if a term, then either as a singular term or as a general term, and if either, then either as an abstract singular or general term or as a concrete singular or general term; and, further, if the Martian expression is translated as a term of divided reference, then there will be further alternative systems of analytical hypotheses which will settle the reference of this term differently, thereby imparting different ontologies to the Martian speakers; *and* neither in the matter of termhood, nor in the matter of reference, is there any sense to the question of there being a uniquely correct translation.

What (A) and (B) assert, essentially, is that "meaning" *and* reference are indeterminate on behavioral grounds and that to inquire beyond the (possible) behavioral evidence for a unique "meaning" or a unique referent of a Martian expression is folly. These are major consequences of the naturalistic turn: (1) we give up hope of determinacy (of "meaning" and reference), and (2) we recognize that there is no fact of the matter regarding unique translation (i.e., there is no unique "meaning" or unique referent of Martian expressions beyond what can be established on behavioral evidence).

Take, for instance, Quine's 'gavagai' example of the inscrutability of reference. Suppose that our linguist concludes from his inductively well-established correlation of the observation *sentences* 'Gavagai' and 'Rabbit' that 'gavagai' is a concrete general *term* and is uniquely translated as 'rabbit'. In other words, the linguist is convinced that 'gavagai' and 'rabbit' refer to just the same objects.

Yet, if Quine's indeterminacy thesis is true, then the linguist is, while acting reasonably enough in equating 'gavagai' with 'rabbit', nevertheless mistaken if he thinks the correlation of the observation sentences 'Gavagai' and 'Rabbit' fixes the reference of the term 'gavagai' uniquely; it is quite possible (i.e., consistent with all possible behavioral evidence) that 'gavagai', if a term at all, might be an abstract singular term referring to rabbithood, or a concrete general term true not of rabbits but, say, of undetached rabbit parts, or of rabbit stages. At the level of ostensive learning (or translation) reference is behaviorally inscrutable (as are "meanings" of terms taken in some intuitive sense, i.e., the sense in which 'rabbit' and 'rabbit stage' are said to differ in "meaning"; of course, stimulus meanings are scrutable behaviorally). The problem of inscrutability arises because the only difference between rabbits, undetached rabbit parts, and rabbit stages is in their individuation. The scattered portion of the world that is made up of rabbits, and that which is made up of undetached rabbit parts, and that which is made up of rabbit stages are all three just the same scattered portions of the world. "The only difference is in how you slice it. And how to slice it is what ostension or simple conditioning, however persistently repeated, cannot teach" (OR, 32).

In trying to decide whether to equate 'gavagai' with 'undetached rabbit part', or with 'rabbit', the linguist might query the Martian with 'gavagai' while at the same time pointing to an undetached rabbit part. But this technique is ineffective as a means for deciding the issue; the trouble is that in pointing to a part of the rabbit, the linguist is also pointing to the rabbit. On the other hand, if the linguist queries the Martian with 'gavagai' while indicating the whole rabbit with a sweeping gesture, he will still fall short of the desired result, since the sweeping gesture indicates as well a multitude of undetached rabbit parts. "It seems clear that no even tentative decision between 'rabbit' and 'undetached rabbit part' is to be sought at this level [i.e., at the level of ostension]" (OR, 32).

The only way for the linguist to settle such instances of the inscrutability of reference is by fixing upon the Martian equivalents of English "plural endings, pronouns, numerals, the 'is' of identity, and its adaptations 'same' and 'other'" (OR, 32). These, it will be recalled from §2.2.2.2, constitute the cluster of interrelated grammatical particles and constructions with which the individuating of terms of divided reference in English is connected. Once the linguist has fixed these equivalents, he can begin to ask the Martian questions like 'Is this gavagai the same as that one?', 'Is this one gavagai or two?', and so forth. And, once the linguist is able to ask the Martian such questions as these, he will be well on his way to determining whether to equate 'gavagai' with 'undetached rabbit part' or with 'rabbit'. However, *before* the linguist is able to formulate such questions, he will have to formulate a system of analytical hypotheses in connection with other Martian expressions, notably the important and helpful expressions just mentioned that comprise the cluster of interrelated grammatical particles and constructions governing reference.

But, while this method of translation is, in principle, the best that one could hope for given Quine's naturalistic-behavioristic characterization of the translation (and language learning) situation(s), it is not sufficient, after all, for settling *absolutely* the indeterminacy between translating 'gavagai' as 'rabbit', or as 'undetached rabbit part', or as

'rabbit stage', and the like. For if one workable overall system of analytic hypotheses provides for translating a given Martian expression
into 'is the same as', perhaps another workable but systematically different system would translate the same Martian expression, instead,
into something like 'belongs with'. Thus, when the linguist attempts to
ask 'Is this gavagai the same as that?', he could as well unwittingly be
asking 'Does this gavagai belong with that?'. Therefore, the Martian's
assent cannot be used to settle the reference of 'gavagai' absolutely.

It is at this stage in translating, where analytical hypotheses come
clearly to the surface, that the indeterminacy of translation is most manifest, for according to that thesis it is possible to formulate alternative
systems of analytical hypotheses all of which are consistent with the totality of speech dispositions of all concerned and which nevertheless
produce translations that are inconsistent with one another. It is significant, too, that what is indeterminate is not just "meaning" but also
reference. Not only is the absolute "meaning" (beyond the stimulus
meaning) of 'gavagai' indeterminate as between 'rabbit', 'rabbit stage',
and so forth, but also the reference of 'gavagai' is indeterminate.

Thus it is not possible on behavioral grounds (and Quine's naturalistic-behavioristic thesis asserts that there are no other grounds)
to settle *absolutely* the "meaning" or reference of Martian terms. Ostensive learning can settle the stimulus meanings of observation sentences like 'Gavagai' and 'Rabbit', but ostension will never be able to
teach that the terms 'gavagai' and 'rabbit' are terms and, if they are
terms, that they have the same "meaning," or even that they are coextensive. Further, resorting to analytical hypotheses only settles the
"meaning" and reference of 'gavagai' in a *relative* way. For it is quite
possible that another linguist working independently might arrive at
another system of analytical hypotheses having the effect of equating
'gavagai' with 'undetached rabbit part'. Presumably, both linguists
could account for all the Martian's speech dispositions. But, by making different adjustments in their respective systems of analytical hypotheses utilized in translating the grammatical particles and constructions that bear on reference, the two linguists could produce manuals
for Martian-to-English translation that differ in the ontologies they attribute to the Martians. Quine finds this "plausible because of the
broadly structural and contextual character of any considerations that
could guide us to . . . [Martian] translations of the English cluster of
interrelated devices of individuation. There seem bound to be systematically very different choices, all of which do justice to all dispositions to verbal behavior on the part of all concerned" (OR, 34).

Hence, *relative to* some set of analytical hypotheses, our linguist could (we suppose) equate 'gavagai' with 'rabbit'. However, and this is the point of the indeterminacy thesis, there are no grounds for declaring this particular system of analytical hypotheses sacrosanct; and, since this is the case, there can be no useful sense to the question about what the Martian's 'gavagai' *really* means or *really* refers to. 'Really' thus queried is idle talk. As Quine insists, there is no fact of the matter. To think that there is some fact of the matter (a mental one, presumably) is to revert to the myth of the museum. Hence, Quine's claim that when with Dewey we turn toward a naturalistic view of language and a behavioral view of meaning what we give up is not just the museum figure of speech; we also give up the assurance of *determinacy*.

One might suspect that the problem of indeterminacy is peculiar to the context of radical translation and is, therefore, insignificant. But this would be a mistake, for it overlooks the analogous behavioral parameters of radical translation and ordinary language learning (and with ordinary translation for that matter). Both the linguist and the child learning a first language must begin with observation sentences, both must master the assent/dissent language game, and both must utilize, consciously or unconsciously, analytical hypotheses to eke out the language. True, the situations are not completely analogous, since the linguist already has prior linguistic habits to facilitate his acquisition of Martianese while the Martian child does not, but this difference is insufficient to prohibit indeterminacy from infecting the domestic scene.

Consider, for example, the case of an English speaker among fellow English speakers. Must he always construe their strings of phonemes as identical with his own? Certainly imitating the sounds of others in one's linguistic environment (i.e., homophonic translation) is basic to language learning, but the question is: Do we ever systematically deviate from such imitation (i.e., engage in heterophonic translation)? Sometimes we do, for we find it to be in the interests of communication to recognize that our neighbor's use of some word, such as 'groovy' or 'square', differs from our own, and so we translate that word of his into a different string of phonemes in our idiolect.

In a similar fashion we could systematically reconstrue our neighbor's apparent reference to rabbits as references to rabbit stages, and we could "reconcile all this with our neighbor's verbal behavior, by cunningly readjusting our translations of his various connecting predicates so as to compensate for the switch of ontology. In short, we can reproduce the inscrutability of reference at home" (OR, 47).

Quine maintains that "the problem at home differs none from radical translation ordinarily so called except in the willfulness of this suspension of homophonic translation" (OR, 47). In other words, the inscrutability of reference is engendered in the intralinguistic context through a person's willfully suspending homophonic translation of one of his neighbor's terms, while, at the same time, anchoring his own terms, through homophonic translation, to their conventional usages, which are manifest in the verbal behavior of the other members of the speech community.

> But if there is really no fact of the matter, then the inscrutability of reference can be brought even closer to home than the neighbor's case; we can apply it to ourselves. If it is to make sense to say even of oneself that one is referring to rabbits . . . and not to rabbit stages . . . then it should make sense equally to say it of someone else. After all, as Dewey stressed, there is no private language. (OR, 47)

Although Quine does not say so explicitly, we may plausibly interpret him as saying implicitly that inscrutability is engendered in the egocentric context by an analogue to the willful suspension of homophonic translation applied this time to our own talk where we *willfully* "contemplate alternative denotations for our familiar terms. We begin to appreciate that a grand and ingenious permutation of these denotations, along with compensatory adjustments in the interpretations of the auxiliary particles, might still accommodate all existing speech dispositions" (OR, 48).

But this development presents something of a conundrum, for:

> We seem to be maneuvering ourselves into the absurd position that there is no difference on any terms, interlinguistic or intralinguistic, objective or subjective, between referring to rabbits and referring to rabbit parts or stages. . . . Surely this is absurd, for it would imply that there is no difference between the rabbit and each of its parts or stages. . . . Reference would seem now to become nonsense not just in radical translation but at home. (OR, 47–48)

Quine's resolution of this absurd consequence of the naturalistic-behavioristic conception of language is his doctrine of *ontological relativity*. The absurdity we are concerned with arose from the following considerations:

All we have to go on in learning a language is the overt behavior of others (so holds the NB thesis). However, behavior is not sufficient for settling the reference of the terms we learn. We cannot settle the reference of Martian expressions in the context of radical translation except by using some nonunique system of analytical hypotheses. Similarly, in our own home language we cannot settle the reference of our neighbor's terms, nor the reference of our own terms, except relative to the predicates and auxiliary devices of our language. In the case of radical translation we came to realize that the various systems of analytical hypotheses used for translating Martian expressions in different ways were behaviorally indeterminate, that is, that (all possible) behavioral evidence was insufficient grounds for preferring one system of analytical hypotheses over another. In the case of the home language we came to realize that with a little ingenuity and a lot of perversity we could permute the denotations of our neighbor's terms, or our own terms, and together with compensatory adjustments in the interpretations of the auxiliary particles that bear on the matter of reference we could still accommodate all of our neighbor's, or our own, speech dispositions. "This was the inscrutability of reference, applied to ourselves; and it made nonsense of reference. Fair enough; reference *is* nonsense except relative to a coordinate system" (OR, 48).

It is meaningless, therefore, Quine insists, to ask whether, in general, our terms 'rabbit', 'rabbit part', etc., *really* refer, respectively, to rabbits, rabbit parts, etc., rather than to some ingeniously permuted denotations.

> It is meaningless to ask this *absolutely*; we can meaningfully ask it only *relative to* some background language. When we ask, 'Does "rabbit" really refer to rabbits?' someone can counter with the question: 'Refer to rabbits in what sense of "rabbits"?' thus launching a regress; and we need the background language to regress into. The background language gives the query sense, if only relative sense; sense relative in turn to it, this background language. Querying reference in any more absolute way would be like asking absolute position, or absolute velocity, rather than position or velocity relative to a given frame of reference. Also it is very much like asking whether our neighbor may not systematically see everything upside down, or in complementary color, forever undetectably. (OR, 48–49; *my emphasis*)

Consequently, Quine does not see the absurd consequence of the NB conception of language as a *reductio ad absurdum* of that view; rather, he sees it as a sober reminder to us all to refrain from loose talk of reference. Reference is a perfectly respectable semantical notion despite its being behaviorally inscrutable, but it is respectable only relative to some background language, some system of predicates and auxiliary devices bearing on reference.

But what of reference in the background language itself? If it is meaningful to question the reference of a term only relative to some background language, then to question meaningfully the reference of a term of the background language itself would seem to require some further background language. Are we involved, then, in an infinite regress? Quine's *first* answer to this is: "in practice we end the regress of background languages, in discussions of reference, by acquiescing in our mother tongue and taking its words at face value" (OR, 49). Taking the words of our mother tongue at face value is to revert to homophonic translation except when communication seems to demand an occasional departure. (This solution to the regress makes sense when it is recalled that what differentiated the inscrutability in the home language from that in the context of radical translation was the *willfulness* of the suspension of homophonic translation in the former.)

Apart from what we do in practice, however, how are we to handle the regress? Quine's reply is given in terms of a relational theory of what the objects of theories are: "What makes sense is to say not what the objects of a theory are, absolutely speaking, but how one theory of objects is interpretable or reinterpretable in another" (OR, 50). This quotation expresses the essence of Quine's doctrine of *ontological relativity*, which rests, of course, upon the NB conception of language: for the doctrine of relativity is really nothing more than a generalization of the doctrine of the inscrutability of reference, which itself is a consequence of the NB conception of language. If the NB thesis is true, then reference is inscrutable; and reference will become scrutable only relative to some nonunique translation. But the reference of the terms of a language or a theory is nothing but the ontology of the language or theory. Thus, if reference is relative, so is ontology.

In all there are, according to Quine, three aspects or levels to the ontological (or referential) relativity of theories. The first of these is expressed by the claim that it makes no sense to say what the objects of a theory are beyond saying how to interpret or reinterpret that theory in another. There is no sense to specifying the objects of a theory *absolutely*. Consider the answer to the question 'What is an *F*?': 'An *F* is a *G*'; 'What is a gavagai?': 'A gavagai is a rabbit'. "The answer makes only *relative* sense: sense relative to the uncritical acceptance of '*G*' [and of 'rabbit']" (OR, 53; *my emphasis*).

The second aspect or level of ontological relativity has to do with the choices among competing manuals for translating talk of *F*s into talk of *G*s—translating the talk of the object theory into talk of the background theory. In Quine's radical translation context, for example, the field linguist has a choice among rival sets of analytical hypotheses, which would translate 'gavagai' as either, say, 'rabbit' or as 'undetached rabbit part'. It is only relative to some such set of analytical hypotheses that object theory talk can be translated into background theory talk. "Commonly of course the background theory will simply be a containing theory, and in this case no question of a manual of translation arises. But this is after all just a degenerate case of translation still—the case where the rule of translation is the homophonic one" (OR, 55).

The third aspect of the doctrine of ontological relativity emerges when we attempt to distinguish between substitutional and referential (or objectual) quantification in the object theory relative to a background theory and some manual for translating. Sometimes it is possible to show within a theory having an infinite number of names and having the means for treating of the theory's notations and proofs within the terms of the theory that the quantifications of the theory are referential (or objectual) rather than substitutional. If it could be shown, for example, that every time a name is substituted for the variable in a certain open sentence the resulting sentence is true, but at the same time we prove that the universal quantification of the open sentence is false, then we have thereby shown that the universe of the theory contains some nameless objects. "This is a case where an absolute decision can be reached in favor of referential quantification and against substitutional quantification, without ever retreating to a background theory" (OR, 64).

On the other hand, however, it is possible that in such a theory as outlined above there is no such open sentence: whenever an open sentence is such that each result of substituting a name in it can be proved, its universal quantification can be proved in the theory as well. Under these circumstances one would be likely to construe the universe of the theory as devoid of nameless objects, but he need not. He could still maintain that the theory's universe contains nameless objects. "It could just happen that the nameless ones are *inseparable* from the named ones, in this sense: it could happen that all properties of nameless objects that we can express in the notation of the theory are shared by named objects" (OR, 65).

Quine cites as an example of this kind of thing a theory containing all real numbers. Since the real numbers are indenumerable, and yet their names are denumerable, some of the reals are nameless. But it still might be the case that within this theory the nameless reals are inseparable from the named reals. If so, then it would be impossible, within the theory, to prove a distinction between referential and substitutional quantification. Every quantification expressible in the theory that is true when referentially construed remains true when substitutionally construed and vice versa.

> We might still make the distinction from the vantage point of a background theory. In it we might specify some real number that was nameless in the object theory; for there are always ways of strengthening a theory so as to name more real numbers, though never all. Further, in the background theory, we might construe the universe of the object theory as exhausting the real numbers. In the background theory we could, in this way, clinch the quantifications in the object theory as referential. But this clinching is doubly relative: it is relative to the background theory and to the interpretation or translation imposed on the object theory from within the background theory. (OR, 65)

In concluding this section on radical translation, indeterminacy, inscrutability, and relativity, I should like to point out that, for Quine, the fact that inscrutability of terms occurs is a matter beyond dispute: "Over the inscrutability of terms itself there is little room for debate. A clear example from real life was seen in connection with the Japanese classifiers" (RIT, 182; *note omitted*). The example of the Japanese classifiers, Quine claims, shows that a particular three-word construction of Japanese can be translated into English such that the third word of the construction can be construed either as an individuative term or as a mass term if compensatory adjustments are made in the translations of the construction's second word. Quine argues that neither of the two ways can be singled out as *the* correct translation since there simply is no fact of the matter to be right or wrong about. One way of handling the classifier provides for a more efficient translation into English, the other better conveys a feeling for the Japanese idiom; but both fit the verbal behavior of Japanese speakers equally well (*see* OR, 35ff.).

However, the general thesis of indeterminacy has no grand example and so must be argued for. So far as I can detect, Quine offers three lines of argument in favor of the indeterminacy claim: (1) the argument drawn from the holism thesis (sometimes called Duhem's thesis or re-visibility thesis) together with Peirce's thesis, (2) the argument drawn from Quine's naturalism and his attitude of scientific realism together with the underdetermination of physical theory (sometimes called the doctrine of empirical slack), and (3) Quine's conviction that indeterminacy is plausible because any considerations that guide us in translating the individuative apparatus of a language (English, at least) are so broadly structural and contextual in character as to allow divergent translations.

§3.3 Holism, underdetermination, indeterminacy, and the naturalistic-behavioristic conception of language

Each of Quine's three explicit arguments for the indeterminacy thesis listed above is intimately bound up with the NB conception of language. The relations of each argument to the NB conception of language we may investigate by a series of questions:

(a) What is Quine's holism thesis (Quine's doctrine of underdetermination)?

(b) How does the holism thesis (the doctrine of underdetermination) serve to support the indeterminacy thesis?

(c) How is the holism thesis (the doctrine of underdetermination) related to the NB conception of language?

(d) Why does Quine think as we shall come to see that the observational criteria of theoretical terms are so flexible and fragmentary?

(e) How does this claim about the flexibility and fragmentariness of the observational criteria for theoretical terms support the doctrine of underdetermination?

§3.3.1 What is Quine's holism thesis?

Quine's holism thesis has rightly been called the Duhem thesis and sometimes the Duhem-Quine thesis. The thesis claims that scientific statements are not separately vulnerable to adverse observations, because it is only jointly as a theory that such statements imply their observable consequences. Any one of the statements of the theory can be adhered to in the face of adverse observations by revising other statements in the theory. Suppose for example, that some experiment has produced a result contrary to what some currently held theory predicts. The theory is composed of a bundle of conjoint hypotheses or is resoluble into such a bundle. What the experiment reveals is that at least one of those hypotheses is false, but it does not show which: "It is only the theory as a whole, and not any one of the hypotheses, that admits of evidence or counter-evidence in observation and experiment" (PL, 5).

> And how wide is a theory? No part of science is quite isolated from the rest. Parts as disparate as you please may be expected to share laws of logic and arithmetic, anyway, and to share various common-sense generalities about bodies in motion. Legalistically, one could claim that evidence counts always for or against the total system, however loose-knit, of science. Evidence against the system is not evidence against any one sentence rather than another, but can be acted on rather by any of various adjustments. (PL, 5)

Quine believes that observation sentences are usually exceptions to this rule since their evidence is pretty well exhausted by the observations they report. But, even so, in the case of an observation contrary to some time-honored theory, it is possible to go with the theory and not the conflicting observation, by dismissing the observation as an illusion or the like: "The tail thus comes, in an extremity, to wag the dog" (WO, 19).

§3.3.2 *How does the holism thesis serve to support the indeterminacy thesis?*

"If we recognize with Peirce that the meaning of a sentence turns purely on what would count as evidence for its truth, and if we recognize with Duhem that theoretical sentences have their evidence not as single sentences but only as larger blocks of theory, then the indeterminacy of translation of theoretical sentences is the natural conclusion" (EN, 80–81).

Let us call Quine's version of Peirce's thesis (P):

(P) The meaning of a sentence turns purely on what would count as evidence for its truth.

(P) is a form of verificationism. It is a thesis that equates the concepts of meaning and evidence. Consider in this vein the stimulus *meaning* of an observation sentence; it is, roughly, that class of stimulations which would count as *evidence* for the truth of the sentence.

Let us call Quine's version of Duhem's thesis (D):

(D) Single theoretical sentences do not always or usually have a separable fund of *evidence* to call their own; they have their funds of evidence only when connected to larger blocks of theory.

Now, if (P) is regarded as a statement of the equivalence of the concepts of meaning and evidence, then (D) could as well be read as:

(D') Single theoretical sentences do not always or usually have a (separable) *meaning* to call their own; they have their meanings only when connected to larger blocks of theory.

The point of (D) is that evidence may be allocated in theories in various ways to the individual sentences; (D') makes the analogous point in connection with meaning. In a word, (D')—the semantic corollary of (D)—*is* the indeterminacy of translation thesis, in abbreviated form! We are coming to appreciate a point made in §2.1: For Quine, the semantical relationships and the evidential relationships among the sentences of a theory are isomorphic.

§3.3.3   *How is the holism thesis related to the naturalistic-behavioristic conception?*

Let us review some of the important aspects of the NB conception of language presented in Chapter 2. First, the view was said to comprise, among other things, certain claims about language acquisition, linguistic meaning, and sensory evidence. Language learning was said to consist largely in two general techniques for learning sentences: ostension (or direct conditioning) and analogic synthesis. The discussion of meaning, as far as it went, centered around the concepts of stimulus meaning and cognitive meaning. "Meaning" in any general intuitive sense was shunned. Evidence was talked of a little, mainly in connection with the discussion of observation sentences. Observation sentences were said to play a dual role in theories: they play an *evidential* role in theories because their public dimension of general acceptance (a feature they owe to their potential for being learned ostensively) provides scientists with a means for reconciling their differences of opinion about the truth of theoretical sentences; they play a *semantical* role in theories because even though most of language consists in the association of sentences and their parts with other sentences and their parts, still, somewhere, there must be nonverbal reference points, nonverbal circumstances that can be intersubjectively appreciated and associated with appropriate utterances, *if* language is to be learned at all (along the lines in which Quine thinks it is learned). It is here, in Quine's theory of meaning and evidence and in his theory of how language is learned, that the holism thesis finds its deepest roots.

Suppose with Quine that observation sentences are the gateway to language. They are the first sentences learned by child and linguist alike, the first sentences conditioned to present stimulation. Their stimulus meanings are intersubjectively appreciable; they wear their meanings on their sleeves. But only a small portion of language is (or could be) acquired in this way. The rest of language learning takes place by analogic synthesis and is much more contextual. Language grows as a fabric of sentences. Somehow the child learns to carry his observation terms over into theoretical contexts, variously embedded. In doing so, he is connecting his observation sentences with standing sentences in multifarious ways. It is only by such means, however ill understood, that anyone masters the nonobservational part of language. The child learns the observational part of his language in well understood ways, and then he must build out somehow, imitating what he hears and linking it tenuously and conjecturally to what he knows, until by means of social correction he achieves fluent dialogue with his community.

> This discourse depends, for whatever empirical content it has, on its devious and tenuous connections with the observation sentences; and those are the same connections, nearly enough, through which one has achieved one's fluent part in that discourse. The channels by which, having learned observation sentences, we acquire theoretical language, are the very channels by which observation lends evidence to scientific theory. It all stands to reason; for language is man-made and the locutions of scientific theory have no meaning but what they acquired by our learning to use them. (NNK, 74)

Hence, by virtue of (P), observation sentences are the gateway not only to language but also to science as well: "To learn a language is to learn the meaning of its sentences, and hence to learn what observations to count as evidence for and against them. The evidence relation and the semantical relation of observation to theory are coextensive" (RR, 38). Not only are they coextensive, they are as well co-devious and co-tenuous, since a person's progress in learning his or her language "is not a continuous derivation, which, followed backward, would enable us to reduce scientific theory to sheer observation. It is a progress rather by short leaps of analogy" (NNK, 77–78). No wonder any one of the statements in a theory can be adhered to, come what may, by revising the truth values of other statements in the theory. Empirical evidence simply cannot be allocated to the individual sentences of a theory in any unique way—and this is just what (D) claims. On the other hand, as Quine once put the point in a conversation, if we stayed close to the ground, say, by limiting our theories to observation sentences, then there would be no problem here. Each sentence, by virtue of being an observation sentence, would have its unique stimulus conditions. The holism thesis, then, would be without point! Or, if languages were learned in a way radically different from that which the NB conception depicts—where, say, each sentence of the theory had a unique meaning—then Duhem's thesis would again be pointless.

In summation we could say that Quine's holism or Duhem's thesis is the claim that scientific statements are not separately vulnerable to adverse observations because only jointly as a theory do they imply their observable consequences. Further, in virtue of the verificationism of Peirce's thesis the semantic corollary of the holism thesis *is* the thesis of indeterminacy: if the holism thesis is true, and if Peirce's thesis is true, then, Quine concludes, the indeterminacy thesis is true. And, as we have seen, the holism thesis itself depends, ultimately, upon the NB conception of language. Also, Peirce's thesis is intimately related to the NB conception: the behavioral theory of meaning of the NB conception is largely an elaboration of Peirce's thesis itself. Quine makes all this abundantly clear when he says:

> Should the unwelcomeness of the conclusion [(D'), the indeterminacy of translation, which was inferred from (D) and (P)] persuade us to abandon the verification theory of meaning [(P)]? Certainly not. The sort of meaning that is basic to translation, and to the learning of one's own language, is necessarily empirical meaning and nothing more. A child learns his first words and sentences by hearing and using them in the presence of appropriate stimuli. These must be external stimuli, for they must act both on the child and on the speaker from whom he is learning. Language is socially inculcated and controlled; the inculcation and control turn strictly on the keying of sentences to shared stimulation. Internal factors may vary *ad libitum* without prejudice to communication as long as the keying of language to external stimuli is undisturbed. Surely one has no choice but to be an empiricist so far as one's theory of linguistic meaning is concerned (EN, 81; *note omitted*).

Let us now turn to the set of questions regarding Quine's doctrine of the underdetermination of physical theory.

§3.3.4   *What is the doctrine of underdetermination?*

Essentially, the doctrine is that physical theory (i.e., our theory about the world) transcends our observations of the world, and that different, competing, physical theories can, therefore, be developed from the same set of observations. In a word, physical theory is *underdetermined* by the observations that support it, thereby engendering a fair amount of empirical slack in our beliefs about the world:

> Naturally it [physical theory or our theory about the world] is underdetermined by past evidence; a future observation can conflict with it. Naturally it is underdetermined by past and future evidence combined, since some observable event that conflicts with it can happen to go unobserved. Moreover, many people will agree, far beyond all this, that physical theory is underdetermined even by all *possible* observations. Not to make a mystery of this mode of possibility, what I mean is the following. Consider all the observation sentences of the language: all the occasion sentences that are suited for use in reporting observable events in the external world. Apply dates and positions to them in all combinations, without regard to whether observers were at the place and time. Some of these place-timed sentences will be true and others false, by virtue simply of the observable though unobserved past and future events in the world. Now my point about physical theory is that physical theory is underdetermined even by all these truths. Theory can still vary though all possible observations be fixed. Physical theories can be at odds with each other and yet compatible with all possible data even in the broadest sense. In a word, they can be logically incompatible and empirically equivalent. This is a point on which I expect wide agreement, if only *because the observational criteria of theoretical terms are commonly so flexible and fragmentary* [*my emphasis*—RG]. People who agree on this general point need not agree as to how much of physical theory is empirically unfixed in this strong sense; some will acknowledge such slack only in the highest and most speculative reaches of physical theory, while others see it extending even to common-sense traits of macroscopic bodies. (RIT, 178–79; *note omitted*)

Why Quine believes that the doctrine of underdetermination is true I will consider in §3.3.6.2. Here my concern is to explain further the doctrine of underdetermination. Notice that Quine says that a theory is underdetermined by past observations because a future observation could conflict with the theory; that a theory is underdetermined by past *and* future observations because some conflicting observation may go unnoticed; and that theories can still be underdetermined by all possible observations because the observational criteria of theoretical terms are so flexible and fragmentary. The logical basis of this third characterization of underdetermination is obviously very different from that of the first and second. In the first two cases Quine tells us that physical theory may *in fact* be underdetermined; in the third case he tells us that physical theory is *in principle* underdetermined.

Recently Quine has raised some doubts about the intelligibility of the underdetermination thesis. He has concluded that in its full generality the thesis of underdetermination is untenable, and that a more modest version of the underdetermination thesis is tenable but vague. Thus a complete answer to the question of what the doctrine of underdetermination is can be had only by recounting Quine's latest thoughts on the matter, complex though they be.

Recall that the thesis up for clarification concerns the relation between observation and theory: "If all observable events can be accounted for in one comprehensive scientific theory . . . then we may expect that they can all be accounted for equally in another, conflicting system of the world" (EES, 313). This relation is asymmetrical: the theory implies the observations and not vice versa. But even this asymmetrical relation, as it stands, is vague. We need a clarification of 'theory', 'implies', and 'observation'. In clarifying these terms, Quine limits his discussion to theories stated (or statable) in standard logical language: truth functions, quantification, and a finite lexicon. This does much to clarify 'implication', 'equivalent', and 'incompatibility', since these can be strictly defined in such a language.

The notion of observation gains some clarity if, instead of talking about observations as an observer's private sensations, we talk about observation sentences. As is evidenced by the fact that they are learnable ostensively, observation sentences possess an intersubjective aspect that private sensations lack. In short, observation sentences pick out what different observers, speaking the same language, can agree about. However, observation sentences are not the kinds of sentences that are implied by scientific theories since they are occasion sentences, which are true or false relative to the conditions prevailing at the time of their utterance or query. The sentences implied by scientific theories, on the contrary, are standing sentences.

The solution to this difficulty lies with a method for converting observation sentences into standing sentences. We can adopt some arbitrary numerical system of spatio-temporal coordinates and assign each observation sentence expressible in the language to each combination of spatio-temporal coordinates. The resulting sentences are *standing* sentences, which Quine, confusingly enough, calls *pegged observation sentences*. Some of these newly acquired standing sentences will be true and others false. "The true ones do not depend for their truth on anyone's having made the observations; it matters only that the observable state or event in question occur, in fact, at the specified place-time" (EES, 317).

This leaves 'theory', still, for clarification. Here Quine introduces the notion of a *theory formulation*. A theory formulation "is simply a sentence—typically a conjunctive sentence comprising the so-called axioms of the theory" (EES, 318). However, the theory formulation does not typically imply any particular pegged observation sentences. "Typically a theory will descend to particulars only conditionally upon other particulars, assumed as *boundary conditions*" (EES, 317; *my emphasis*). The set of pegged observation sentences stating the boundary conditions would have been, presumably, already verified. The theory formulation, then, would imply *observation conditionals* whose antecedents would be statements of boundary conditions (a conjunction of verified pegged observation sentences) and whose consequents would be some particular pegged observation sentence. The class of observation conditionals implied by a theory formulation is said to comprise the *empirical content* of the theory. Such is, in general, the asymmetrical logical relation between theory (formulation) and observation (conditionals).

How are we to tell, though, whether two theory formulations are formulations of the same theory? Suppose two theory formulations to be identical except that one uses the predicates 'electron' and 'molecule' in just those places where the other uses 'molecule' and 'electron'. Suppose, also, that neither 'electron' nor 'molecule' figures essentially in any observation conditional implied by either of the two theory formulations. Thus the two theory formulations would be logically incompatible but empirically equivalent, for each of the two would assert claims about electrons and molecules that the other would deny, yet their empirical consequences would be identical. But would two such theory formulations be, therefore, *different* theory formulations? Quine thinks not. For by simply reconstruing the predicates of one of the theory formulations, the apparent logical inconsistency dissolves. By a *reconstrual* of the predicates Quine has in mind "any mapping of our lexicon of predicates into our open sentences (*n*-place predicates to *n*-variable sentences)" (EES, 320). Thus, for Quine, two theory formulations are identical if they are empirically equivalent (i.e., both imply the same set of observation conditionals) *and* there is a reconstrual of predicates that transforms the one theory formulation into a logical equivalent of the other.

> We have now settled the individuation of theories, within our parochial confines [i.e., within the confines of a standard logical language and an arbitrary numerical system of spatio-temporal coordinates]. We have said when to count two formulations as expressing the same theory. Given this equivalence relation, it is a routine matter to say what a *theory* is. The method is artificial but familiar: theories are the equivalence classes of that equivalence relation. The theory expressed by a given formulation is the class of all the formulations that are empirically equivalent to that formulation and can be transformed into logical equivalents of it or vice versa by reconstrual of predicates. (EES, 321; *my emphasis*)

Given our newly clarified concepts of theory, implication, and observation, together with our new vocabulary, we can now state the *general* thesis of underdetermination as follows:

> (U) For *any* one theory formulation there is another that is empirically equivalent to it but logically incompatible with it, and cannot be rendered logically equivalent to it by a reconstrual of predicates.

Consequently, the foregoing example of the two theory formulations using the predicates 'molecule' and 'electron' in duality *fails to exemplify underdetermination* since a reconstrual of predicates *is* possible. What is needed for an illustration of the underdetermination thesis are theory formulations that are empirically equivalent, logically incompatible, and irreconcilable by a reconstrual of predicates. Even so, these conditions—stated in (U)—are insufficient for ruling out instances of underdetermination of a frivolous sort. Suppose, for example, that we possessed an adequate theory of nature, and then we added to it some gratuitous further sentences that have no effect on the theory's empirical content. By adding different gratuitous sentences to the theory we can construct theories that are logically compatible with the original theory and irreconcilably incompatible with one another.

This possibility is easily schematized: Suppose *A* is our original theory and that nowhere in *A* does the sentence '*p*' occur. Hence, we could produce the two theories ⌐*A* ∧ *p*⌐ and ⌐*A* ∧ ~*p*⌐ by adding '*p*' and '~*p*', respectively, to *A*; the resulting theories are both logically compatible with *A*, yet incompatible with each other. Nevertheless, we would not want to admit that these newly constructed theories, ⌐*A* ∧ *p*⌐ and ⌐*A* ∧ ~*p*⌐, exemplify undetermination in any philosophically interesting sense. (U), therefore, appears to be too weak.

There are other problems for (U) as well. Take, for instance, a theory formulation whose implied observation conditionals are finite in number. The conjunction of this finite set of sentences would be its own theory formulation. It would be implied by every empirically equivalent theory formulation and inconsistent with none. Such a theory would be a counterexample to (U). Much the same sort of difficulty arises where a theory irreducibly implies infinitely many observation conditionals, for it may happen that all these can be encompassed by a single universally quantified conditional or by finitely many. No theory formulation that implies just those observation conditionals can conflict with it. To put the point bluntly: "In its full generality, the thesis of under-determination thus interpreted is surely untenable" (EES, 323). This conclusion prompts Quine to reconsider the thesis of underdetermination:

> The only hope for a thesis of under-determination, evidently, is in application to theories that imply observation conditionals infinite in number and too ill-assorted to be exactly encompassed by any finite formulation; tightly encompassed, that is, without theoretical foreign matter. The thesis needs to be read as a thesis about the world. It needs to be read as saying, for one thing, that the observation conditionals that are in fact true in the world are thus ill-assorted. And it needs to be read as saying, further, that we can encompass more of these true observation conditionals in a loose formulation than in any tight one. And it needs to be read as saying, finally, that for any such loose formulation there will be others, empirically equivalent but logically incompatible with it and incapable of being rendered logically equivalent to it by any reconstrual of predicates.
>
> Here, evidently, is the nature of under-determination. There is some infinite lot of observation conditionals that we want to capture in a finite formulation. Because of the complexity of the assortment, we cannot produce a finite formulation that would

be equivalent merely to their infinite conjunction. Any finite formulation that will imply them is going to have to imply also some trumped-up matter, or stuffing, whose only service is to round out the formulation. There is some freedom of choice of stuffing, and such is the under-determination. (EES, 324)

As I understand Quine here, a *tight formulation* is a theory formulation that, though finite, is equivalent to an infinite conjunction of the observation conditionals it specifies. A *loose formulation* is a theory formulation that, besides specifying an infinite number of observation conditionals, also specifies some theoretical sentences. Underdetermination lurks where there are two irreconcilable formulations each of which specifies exactly the desired set of observation conditionals plus extraneous theoretical matter, and where no formulation affords a tighter fit.

Stated in these terms, the underdetermination thesis seems to be a product of our insistence upon finite theory formulations. Why not just settle for all the desired observation conditionals as they stand, in all their infinite variety? The problem with this approach lies in the matter of how to specify the desired class of observation conditionals without a finite theory formulation. Quine describes work of William Craig, which shows how one could, *in principle*, produce a specification of the desired class of observation conditionals, without a finite formulation (*see* LK, 63–64). However, "this result does not belie underdetermination, since the Craig class is not a finite formulation, but an infinite class of sentences. But it does challenge the interest of underdetermination by suggesting that the finite formulation is dispensible; and indeed the Craig class, for all its infinitude, is an exact fit, being a class of visible equivalents of the desired class" (EES, 325).

Nevertheless, there is no place for Craig's technique *in practice* because of the astronomical amount of time and space required in applying it. Also, the results of the technique, i.e., the specification of the Craig sentences, must be checked against their corresponding finite formulation sentences anyway. The upshot of this result of Craig's is, then, that the underdetermination thesis is less of a *theoretical* thesis than one might at first suppose. However, the thesis retains significance in terms of what is *practically* feasible. A tempered version of the thesis, the most favorable version available, might run as follows:

(U′) We, humanly, are capable of encompassing more true observation conditionals in a loose theory formulation than in any tight system that we might discover and formulate independently of any such loose formulation; and that for each such formulation there will be others empirically equivalent to it but logically incompatible with it and incapable of being rendered logically equivalent to it by any reconstrual of predicates.

Whether there are, in fact, such systems is, for Quine, an open question. He thinks that it stands to reason that any adequate system of the world we can come up with will be a loose one. And, he thinks there will always be possible other formulations empirically equivalent to it and logically incompatible with it. The open question concerns the impossibility of reconciling such formulations by a reconstrual of predicates. A last-ditch version of the thesis of underdetermination runs as follows:

(U″) Our system of the world is bound to have empirically equivalent alternatives which, if we were to discover them, we would *see no way* of reconciling by reconstrual of predicates.

Of this final formulation of the underdetermination thesis, Quine confesses: "This vague and modest thesis I do believe" (EES, 327).

§3.3.5   *How does the doctrine of underdetermination serve to support the indeterminacy thesis?*

Suppose, with Quine, that we were to engage in the radical translation of a foreign physicist's theory of the world:

As always in radical translation, the starting point is the equating of observation sentences of the two languages by an inductive equating of stimulus meanings. In order afterward to construe the foreigner's theoretical sentences we have to project analytical hypotheses, whose ultimate justification is substantially just that the implied observation sentences match up. But now the same old empirical slack, the old indeterminacy between physical theories [or, better, underdetermination], recurs in second intension. *Insofar as the truth of a physical theory is underdetermined by observables, the translation is underdetermined by translation of* [the foreign physicist's] . . . observation sentences. If our physical theory can vary though all possible observations be fixed, then our translation of his physical theory can vary though our translations of all possible observation reports on his part be fixed. Our translation of his observa-

tion sentences no more fixes our translation of his physical theory than our own possible observations fix our own physical
theory. (RIT, 179–80; *my emphasis*)

It should be kept in mind that we are not looking to Quine at this
point for a justification of the doctrine of underdetermination. Quine's
argument for indeterminacy on the basis of underdetermination is directed to those who already agree to the truth of the underdetermination thesis. The most we can cite (thus far) as evidence for the truth of
the doctrine of underdetermination is Quine's remark, quoted earlier,
to the effect that he expects wide agreement on the matter, if only because the observational criteria of theoretical terms are commonly so
flexible and fragmentary.

Quine's argument for indeterminacy on the basis of underdetermination in the passage just quoted seems to be as follows: Observation by itself is insufficient for fixing in any unique way the theoretical
sentences of a theory. In this respect the theory is said to be methodologically underdetermined by observation, or to have empirical
slack. When, in the setting of radical translation, a linguist translates
such a theory, he does so by translating the observation sentences of
the theory by equating stimulus meanings. Beyond this, he must use
analytical hypotheses. By means of these analytical hypotheses the linguist proceeds to take up the empirical slack of the theory. However,
the analytical hypotheses themselves are methodologically underdetermined by the observation sentences (in fact, by all possible observation sentences) of the theory being translated. Consequently, the linguist could have chosen some other system of analytical hypotheses,
thus taking up the empirical slack of the theory in, perhaps, incompatible ways (i.e., in ways that would yield logically incompatible translations of some standing sentences of the theory). It is at this point, then,
that the same old empirical slack recurs in second intension: the translation is methodologically underdetermined talk about talk which, itself, is methodologically underdetermined in the theory! It should be
added that the degree of indeterminacy of translation that one must
recognize will depend upon the amount of empirical slack one is willing to recognize in physics.

On this interpretation of Quine's argument, the underdetermination
thesis is the basis for the indeterminacy thesis: the empirical activity of
translating suffers a methodological underdetermination analogous to
that of physical theory itself. However, this is only half of the story,
and, perhaps, the less important half, for Quine goes on to say:

The indeterminacy of translation is not just an instance of the empirically underdetermined character of physics. The point is not just that linguistics, being a part of behavioral science and hence ultimately of physics, shares the empirically underdetermined character of physics. On the contrary, the indeterminacy of translation is additional. (RIT, 180)

If indeterminacy is *not just* an instance of the empirically underdetermined character of physics, then whatever additional properties it has cannot follow solely from the doctrine of underdetermination. Hence, the thesis of indeterminacy must be based upon something in addition to Quine's underdetermination thesis. That something-in-addition is Quine's naturalism and his attitude of scientific realism.

Notice that what we have witnessed so far in Quine's argument is a certain parallelism between theories and their translations:

In respect of being under-determined by all possible data, translational synonymy and theoretical physics are indeed alike. The totality of possible observations of nature, made and unmade, is compatible with physical theories that are incompatible with one another. Correspondingly the totality of possible observations of verbal behavior, made and unmade, is compatible with systems of analytical hypotheses of translation that are incompatible with one another. Thus far the parallel holds. (RC, 302–3)

What we must seek is a failure of this parallelism that will reveal a relevant difference between physical theory and translation and that will thereby explain how indeterminacy of translation is *additional* to underdetermination. Where, then, does the parallelism fail?

Essentially in this: theory in physics is an ultimate parameter. There is no legitimate first philosophy, higher or firmer than physics, to which to appeal over physicists' heads. Even our appreciation of the partial arbitrariness or under-determination of our overall theory of nature is not a higher-level intuition; it is integral to our under-determined theory of nature itself, and of ourselves as natural objects. So we go on reasoning and affirming as best we can within our ever under-determined and evolving theory of nature, the best one that we can muster at any one time; and it is usually redundant to cite the theory as parameter of our assertions, since no higher standard

offers. It ceases to be redundant only when we are contrasting alternative theories at a deep level, e.g. with a view to a
change.

Though linguistics is of course part of the theory of nature,
the indeterminacy of translation is not just inherited as a special
case of the under-determination of our theory of nature. It is
parallel but additional. Thus, adopt for now my fully realistic attitude toward electrons and muons and curved space-time, thus
falling in with the current theory of the world despite knowing
that it is in principle methodologically under-determined. Consider, from this realistic point of view, the totality of truths of
nature, known and unknown, observable and unobservable,
past and future. The point about indeterminacy of translation is
that it withstands even all this truth, the whole truth about nature. This is what I mean by saying that, where indeterminacy of
translation applies, there is no real question of right choice;
there is no fact of the matter even to *within* the acknowledged
under-determination of a theory of nature. (RC, 303)

The illuminating disanalogy between physical theory and translation is, then, in short, that physical theory is an ultimate parameter and
translation is not. Despite the underdetermined character of physics,
the currently accepted physical theory serves as the last word regarding the truths of nature, there being no legitimate first philosophy. But
matters are otherwise with linguistics. No manual of translation enjoys
the status of an ultimate parameter. For example, the only justification
that could be given for the claim that 'gavagai' refers to rabbits rather
than to something else is an appeal to one of several possible, partially
arbitrary manuals of translation, which, far from being an ultimate parameter, has merely conventional acceptance on its side. So, while we
can expect to settle our questions like 'Are there really electrons?' in
science, we cannot hope to settle our questions like 'What did the Martian's "gavagai" really refer to?' in semantics (i.e., in linguistics). The
former kind of question has a (physical) fact of the matter, by dint of
physics being the court of last appeal; the latter kind of question has no
(physical) fact of the matter because when all the (physical) facts are
in, the question (i.e., the indeterminacy) remains unanswered. Translation, therefore, is indeterminate, for there is no fact of the matter for
the translation to be right or wrong about. On the other hand, if we
adopt Quine's posture of naturalism and his attitude of scientific real-

ism, it does not follow that physics, despite its being methodologically underdetermined, is therefore indeterminate: for physics to be indeterminate, there would have to be some other form of knowledge about the world beyond science, and it is just this that Quine's naturalism denies.

§3.3.6　*How is the doctrine of underdetermination related to the naturalistic-behavioristic conception?*

Recall that Quine was quoted as saying that he expected general acceptance of the doctrine of underdetermination (or the doctrine of empirical slack) if only because of the widely acknowledged fact that the observational criteria of theoretical terms are commonly so flexible and fragmentary. The task of explaining the link between the underdetermination thesis and the naturalistic-behavioristic conception of language, then, boils down to answering two further questions: (1) Why does Quine think that the observational criteria of theoretical terms are so flexible and fragmentary? and (2) How does this claim about the flexibility and fragmentariness of observational criteria for theoretical terms serve to support the underdetermination thesis?

§3.3.6.1　*Why does Quine think that the observational criteria of theoretical terms are so flexible and fragmentary?*

The short answer to this question is: because he is committed to the naturalistic-behavioristic conception of language. A longer and more specific answer must be sought in terms of that portion of the NB conception of language pertaining to the learning of theoretical language. The general outline of this account is the same as that given in §2.2.2.2, "Analogic synthesis." As noted there, Quine's account of how theoretical (or referential) language is learned is idealized and speculative, but, he thinks, true to the essential nature of actual language acquisition. Details aside, the aspect of Quine's account that is presently important rests with his claim that theoretical language is acquired by a series of irreducible, short leaps of analogy, which are taken on only fragmentary evidence. No wonder, then, that he takes the observational criteria of theoretical terms to be flexible and fragmentary: observational evidence does not settle the form that the developing theoretical language must take inasmuch as the same set of observation sentences could support statements of very different theories (which is just what the doctrine of underdetermination amounts to).

§3.3.6.2   *How does this claim about the flexibility and*
fragmentariness of observational criteria for theoretical terms
support the doctrine of underdetermination?

The claim of flexibility and fragmentariness of observational criteria is a claim about the freedom that the form of a theory may enjoy relative to all possible observations. When spelled out in terms of theory formulations this claim simply *is* the doctrine of underdetermination. At the level of observational language the eventual form the theoretical language may take is an open question. At that level there just is no foreseeing that the theoretical language will be recognizable as quantification or as relative clauses and categoricals: "The steps by which the child was seen to progress from observational language to relative clauses and categoricals and quantification had the arbitrary character of historical accident and cultural heritage; there was no hint of inevitability" (NNK, 80).

At the conclusion of the previous section, which dealt with radical translation, indeterminacy, inscrutability, and relativity (§3.2), I remarked that there were three lines of argumentation which Quine draws in support of the thesis of indeterminacy of translation. First, there is the argument drawn from the conjunction of Duhem's and Peirce's theses; second, there was the argument based on the underdetermination of physical theory, Quine's naturalism, and his attitude of scientific realism; third, I noted that Quine was convinced that the indeterminacy thesis is plausible because any considerations that guide us in translating the individuative apparatus of a language are so broadly structural and contextual in character as to allow divergent translations. This third source of support for the indeterminacy thesis is simply the recurrence in second intension of the flexibility and fragmentariness of the observational criteria of the theoretical terms of the language being translated. Consequently, even though this third source of support for indeterminacy may be graphically *illustrated* by Quine's artifice of radical translation, at a deeper level it is *explained* by the fact that in the language being translated, the observational criteria for theoretical terms are flexible and fragmentary, which, in turn, is ultimately explained in terms of how that language is learned. It would seem, then, that the third source of support for the indeterminacy thesis reduces to the second; and it also would seem, then, that Quine's artifice of radical translation is inessential to his central philosophical point about meaning and reference. As Quine himself clearly recognizes, indeterminacy of "meaning" and reference begin at home.

§3.4   *Analyticity, synonymy, and reductionism*

> Modern empiricism has been conditioned in large part by
> two dogmas. One is a belief in some fundamental cleavage
> between truths which are *analytic*, or grounded in meanings
> independently of matters of fact, and truths which are *syn-
> thetic*, or grounded in fact. The other dogma is *reductionism*:
> the belief that each meaningful statement is equivalent to some
> logical construct upon terms which refer to immediate experi-
> ence. Both dogmas, I shall argue, are ill-founded. (TDE, 20)

So begins Quine's famous "Two Dogmas of Empiricism" (hereaf-
ter, TDE). Essentially, his attack on the analytic-synthetic distinction
has two fronts. On the first front Quine argues that the analytic-synthetic
distinction has not been clearly drawn; on the second front he argues
that it is a mistake to think that the distinction needs drawing. His attack on reductionism is intended to show that the program of reductionism is impossible and that it rests upon a mistaken view of how
theories are related to experience. Quine's arguments against the analytic-synthetic distinction and reductionism are all related in one way
or another to the naturalistic-behavioristic conception of language.

Quine begins his assault by pointing out that the analytic-synthetic
distinction predates Kant to some extent in the forms of Leibniz's truths-
of-reason/truths-of-fact dichotomy and Hume's relations-of-ideas/
matters-of-fact dichotomy. Quine does not criticize these earlier dichot-
omies, but he does mention two critical points concerning Kant's: "it
limits itself to statements of subject-predicate form, and it appeals to a
notion of containment which is left at a metaphorical level" (TDE, 21).
Quine also alludes to a more recent version of the distinction couched in
the claim that analytic statements are those whose denials are self-
contradictory. But, for Quine, this latter characterization of analyticity
is no better off than its predecessors, for the notion of self-contradic-
toriness, in the broad sense needed for the definition of analyticity,
stands in exactly the same need of clarification as does the notion of
analyticity itself.

This form of argumentation becomes a familiar salvo on the first
front: E is not an acceptable explanation of analyticity if E itself stands
in need of further clarification. Quine has been criticized for demanding an unreasonably high standard of clarity for any proposed accounts
of analyticity (and synonymy). His reply is that he seeks "no more,
after all, than a rough characterization in terms of dispositions to ver-

bal behavior" (WO, 207). This statement of Quine's (not found in TDE) reveals an *implicit standard of clarity* at work in his thinking in TDE, and it partially accounts for the dissatisfaction with all of the characterizations of analyticity and synonymy suggested on the first front. In this implicit way, Quine's first-front argument, that the analytic-synthetic distinction has never been clearly made, rests on his NB conception of language.

Despite the lack of clarity in previous attempts at characterizing analyticity, Quine extracts from them what he takes to be an intuitive criterion of analyticity: "a statement is analytic when it is true by virtue of meanings and independently of fact" (TDE, 21). Two statements that, so philosophers have thought, meet this criterion are these:

(1) No unmarried man is married,
and
(2) No bachelor is married.

Statements of the general form of (1) are logical truths. "If we suppose a prior inventory of *logical* particles, comprising 'no', 'un-', 'not', 'if', 'then', 'and', etc., then in general a logical truth is a statement which is true and remains true under all reinterpretations of its components other than the logical particles" (TDE, 22–23). The notable characteristic of statements like (2) is that they can be turned into logical truths by putting synonyms for synonyms. For example, in the case of (2) one could substitute 'unmarried man' for 'bachelor'. But if the theory of logical truth is sufficient to explain the analyticity of statements like (1), "we still lack a proper characterization of this second class of analytic statements, and therewith of analyticity generally, inasmuch as we have had in the above description to lean on a notion of 'synonymy' which is no less in need of clarification than analyticity itself" (TDE, 23).

It seems plausible, at first, that this notion of synonymy can be got at through some relevant notion of *definition*. Thus, one might claim that statements like (2) can be transformed into those like (1) by definition, by, for example, defining 'bachelor' as 'unmarried man'. Quine thinks that there are, basically, three different kinds of definition that might be relevant here. Let us call them lexical definitions, explications, and conventional definitions.

If one claimed that 'bachelor' is defined as 'unmarried man', he might have in mind that lexicographers have ordinarily glossed the two as synonyms. But, Quine protests, such *lexical definitions* cannot be

regarded as a clarification of synonymy itself; for, as an empirical scientist, the lexicographer is basing his dictionary synonyms on "his belief that there is a relation of synonymy between those forms, implicit
in general or preferred usage prior to his own work. The notion of synonymy presupposed here has still to be clarified. . . . Certainly, the
'definition' which is the lexicographer's report of an observed synonymy cannot be taken as the ground of the synonymy" (TDE, 24).

In *explication* one defines an expression by giving a definiens that
refines or supplements the meaning of the definiendum. A good example of this is the explication of 'relations-in-extension' as 'classes of
ordered pairs'. In this kind of definition the definiens shares a partial
parallel function with the definiendum. In this spirit of definition we
might accept 'unmarried man' as the definiens of 'bachelor'. But, alas,
this will not do for Quine either, since, in order that a given definition
be suitable for purposes of explication, what is required is just that
each of the favored contexts of the definiendum, taken as a whole in its
antecedent usage, be synonymous with the corresponding contexts of
the definiens.

So it cannot be claimed that 'bachelor' and 'unmarried man' are
synonymous by lexical definition or by explication without presup-
posing some preexisting synonymy, which itself is in need of further
clarification. No solution is to be found in the realm of *conventional
definitions* either, of course. Not that such definitions depend upon preexisting synonymies; they do not. But, by conventional definition we
could as well say that 'bachelor' and 'married man' are synonymous.
Synonymy is clear at last, but only at the cost of becoming vacuous.
Gaining any clarity on the matter of synonymy through definition
seems hopeless.

A more fruitful approach to the problem might be through a notion
of *substitution*. Perhaps we could say that "the synonymy of two linguistic forms consists simply in their interchangeability in all contexts
without change of truth value—interchangeability, in Leibniz's phrase,
salva veritate" (TDE, 27; *note omitted*). The question is, then, whether
interchangeability is a sufficient condition of synonymy. Quite obviously, if the language we are working with is extensional, that is, if it is
a language where the predicates that are true of the same things are
interchangeable *salva veritate*, then interchangeability surely is not a
sufficient condition for synonymy since terms like 'cordate' and 're-
nate' are interchangeable *salva veritate* but not, apparently, synonymous. However, if the language is sufficiently rich in intensional idiom,

it appears as though interchangeability *salva veritate* is a sufficient condition. Consider the statement

(3) Necessarily all and only bachelors are bachelors.

This statement is evidently true when 'necessarily' is construed to be truly applicable only to analytic statements. If 'bachelor' and 'unmarried man' are interchangeable *salva veritate*, then the result

(4) Necessarily all and only bachelors are unmarried men

should, like (3), be true. But if (4) is true, then

(5) All and only bachelors are unmarried men

is analytic, for we said that 'necessarily' applied truly only to analytic statements. Hence, the reduction of the analytic statements like (2) to those like (1) is complete.

The difficulty with this suggested solution to the problem is that the adverb 'necessarily', which is applied truly only to analytic statements, and upon which the solution turns, simply does not make sense to Quine. "To suppose that it does is to suppose that we have already made satisfactory sense of 'analytic'. Then what are we so hard at work on right now?" (TDE, 30). Consequently, Quine thinks the criterion of interchangeability *salva veritate* is not a sufficient condition of synonymy.

Quine's inability to make satisfactory sense of the notion of synonymy either by means of definitions or in terms of substitution *salva veritate* suggests to him that perhaps, instead of trying to clarify synonymy outright (so as to reduce statements like (2) to statements like (1) and thereby to render the concept of analyticity as perspicuous as is the concept of logical truth), he might better try to clarify analyticity outright, and then define 'synonymy' in terms of analyticity. For example, assuming the concept of analyticity has been acceptably clarified, 'bachelor' could then be said to be synonymous with 'unmarried man' if, and only if, (5) is analytic.

Quine finds it difficult to get started at this task in ordinary language because of the very obscurity of analyticity: "I do not know," says Quine, "whether the statement 'Everything green is extended' is analytic. Now does my indecision over this example really betray an incomplete understanding, an incomplete grasp of the 'meanings', of 'green' and 'extended'? I think not. The trouble is not with 'green' or 'extended', but with 'analytic' " (TDE, 32). The proponents of analyticity suggest that the difficulty that Quine is encountering is generally attributable to the vagueness of ordinary language and that the distinction is clear when we have a precise artificial language with explicit semantical rules. This, however, Quine thinks is a mistake. I shall report on only one of Quine's arguments in this regard, for the others are analogous. Suppose that for a given artificial language *L* we are given a set of rules for generating, recursively, all of the analytic statements of the language. The rules would have the form of (6):

(6) A statement *S* in *L* is analytic if. . . .

Of course the problem here is the same as with the earlier 'necessarily' example: both specifications of analyticity presuppose a prior understanding of 'analyticity'. In the case of (6), if no such presumption is made, then the proposed definition is of the vacuous conventional type. Quine proceeds to show analogous flaws in variously formulated instances of semantical rules: "Not all the explanations of analyticity known to Carnap and his readers have been covered explicitly in the above considerations [some of which I have omitted], but the extension to other forms is not hard to see" (TDE, 36). Consequently, Quine sees no hope of illuminating the notion of analyticity from the side of artificial language.

These arguments—the first-front arguments, as I have dubbed them—are designed to show that the analytic-synthetic distinction resists being clearly drawn. Ostensibly, these arguments have little to do with the NB conception of language. However, there is the matter of Quine's standard of clarity implicitly at work in those arguments, and, as we saw from a quoted remark of Quine's, his standard of clarity is wholly behavioristic and, thus, part of the NB conception. In short, Quine's complaint with the concepts of synonymy and analyticity on the first front is that they have not been made *behaviorally* respectable. Let us now turn to the second-front arguments, the arguments designed to show that it is a mistake to think that the analytic-synthetic distinction needs drawing.

Quine makes one more attempt to clarify the concept of synonymy. He suggests that the *verification theory of meaning* might be of some service in developing an acceptable concept of synonymy. This theory is, according to Quine, "that the meaning of a statement is the method of empirically confirming or infirming it" (TDE, 37). Apparently, by making use of this verification theory, one could claim that "statements are synonymous if and only if they are alike in point of method of empirical confirmation or infirmation" (TDE, 37).[2] From this concept of synonymy it is but a short step to the position that a statement is analytic if it is synonymous with a logical truth, thereby effecting the desired reduction of statements of type (2) to those of type (1). "So, if the verification theory can be accepted as an adequate account of statement synonymy, the notion of analyticity is saved after all" (TDE, 38).

Quine's rejection of this verification argument differs from his arguments against previously suggested characterizations of synonymy and analyticity. Earlier, his arguments took the form of the claim that there is no hope of explaining analyticity in terms of synonymy (or synonymy in terms of analyticity) if in explaining synonymy (or analyticity) the explanation either uses some expression standing equally in need of further clarification, or if the explanation presupposes some preexisting synonymy (or analyticity). This line of argument was intended to show the futility of trying to transform statements like (2) into statements like (1) through definition or synonym substitution. It was also intended to show the futility of trying to clarify analyticity outright (e.g., Carnap's semantical rules) in hopes of then being able to say that two expressions are synonymous if the substitution of the one for the other in an analytic statement yields an analytic statement. Quine's intention on the first front was to show that no known characterization of synonymy or of analyticity wholly escaped these difficulties. Further, Quine is confident that similar arguments could be extended to similar characterizations of synonymy and analyticity, if proposed. Quine's arguments thus far considered purport to show only that the analytic-synthetic distinction resists being clearly drawn due to the obscurity of analyticity and synonymy. Quine opens his second front with his reply to the verification argument, to wit, that the thought that the analytic-synthetic distinction need be made rests on a mistaken view of how the sentences of a theory are related to the world.

If, as the verification argument alleges, two statements are synonymous if and only if they are alike in point of empirical confirmation or infirmation, then, Quine thinks, we would do well to look into the notion of empirical confirmation and infirmation as it applies to statements. "What, in other words, is the nature of the relation between a statement and the experiences which contribute to or detract from its confirmation?" (TDE, 38).

2. The account of synonymy, here, would be in terms of statements but once in hand could be used to define synonymy of terms (cf. "Two Dogmas of Empiricism," pp. 37f.).

Quine puts aside any answer to this question given in terms of *radical reductionism*, that is, the view that all of the statements of a theory can be translated into statements about immediate experience. His grounds for doing so are simply that no one has ever succeeded in constructing such a language or even in showing how such a language could be constructed. Further, Quine notes, even the once ardent supporters of such a reductionism have abandoned the idea. However, in a weaker and subtler form of reductionism "the notion lingers that to each statement, or each synthetic statement, there is associated a unique range of possible sensory events such that the occurrence of any of them would add to the likelihood of truth of the statement, and that there is associated also another unique range of possible sensory events whose occurrence would detract from that likelihood" (TDE, 40–41).

Consequently, what we mean when, with the verification theory of meaning, we say that two statements are *synonymous* if and only if they are alike in point of method of confirmation or infirmation is that the two statements in question are associated with the same (or nearly the same) unique range of possible sensory events such that the occurrence of any of them would add to the likelihood of the truth of both statements, or, conversely, would detract from the likelihood of both statements. In other words, whatever sensory events would confirm the one statement would confirm the other, and whatever sensory events would infirm the one statement would infirm the other. And now, with this criterion of the synonymy of statements secured, we can say that a statement is analytic if it is synonymous with some logical truth.

Wherein lies the fallacy? It lies in "the dogma of reductionism [which] survives in the supposition that each statement, taken in isolation from its fellows, can admit of confirmation and infirmation at all" (TDE, 41). In other words, the specification of the meaning of the verificationists' 'alike-in-point-of-method-of-confirmation-and-infirmation' as 'unique-range-of-possible-sensory-events-such-that-etc.' turns on a false doctrine about the relation between the statements of a theory, generally, and experience. Statements simply do not in general, Quine claims, have any such unique confirming and infirming classes of experiences. What makes one think this mistaken view plausible is the obvious truism that the truth of statements does depend upon a linguistic component and upon an extralinguistic component, and this truth leads one, naturally but erroneously, to the dogmatic conclusion "that the truth of a statement is somehow analyzable into a linguistic component and a factual component" (TDE, 41). The factual component, if we are empiricists, is taken to be some range of confirming and infirming experiences associated with the statement, while in the extreme case, where the linguistic component is all that matters to truth, the statement is taken to be analytic. However, Quine thinks "that it is nonsense, and the root of much nonsense, to speak of a linguistic component and a factual component in the truth of any individual statement" (TDE, 42).[3] For when we do, we are led to believe that it is significant in general to speak of the confirmation and infirmation of *individual* statements, the dogma of reductionism, and it seems significant to speak also of a limiting kind of statement which is vacuously confirmed, ipso facto, come what may; such statements being of course the analytic ones, and such statements being of course the very raison d'être of the dogma of the analytic-synthetic distinction.

A close examination of Quine's attack on the verificationist proposal in TDE reveals the following argument:

(P₁) The truth of theories depends upon language and upon extra-linguistic fact.

From the obvious circumstances expressed by (P₁) we are persuaded, illogically (i.e., by committing the fallacy of division), to conclude:

(C₁) The truth of *each statement* of a theory is analyzable into a linguistic component and a factual component.

Further, (C₁), the illicitly drawn conclusion of (P₁), is the *common root* of two dogmas:

(D₁) Each statement of a theory, considered separately, has a unique range of confirming experiences and a unique range of infirming experiences associated with it.

(D₂) Those statements of a theory whose truth depends solely upon the linguistic component (i.e., which are true in the face of all possible experiences) are analytic.

Whether Quine's *genetic account* of (C₁) is accurate is of little logical import, for even if (P₁) were true and (C₁) were not a logical consequence of it, this fact alone would prove nothing about the truth or falsity of (C₁). Consequently, Quine's genetic account of the plausi-

---

3. This seems to be an overstatement of Quine's current position since he would apparently find it acceptable to speak of the factual component and the linguistic component of *some* individual sentences (or statements), namely, observation sentences.

bility of (C_1) is uninteresting as a means for refuting (C_1). More to the point regarding the truth or falsity of (C_1) is what might be called Quine's *pragmatic reductio*. Quine claims that if we hold (C_1) to be true, then, as empiricists, we are led also to hold (D_1) and (D_2) to be true. But, he protests, surely we ought to have been impressed with the difficulties:

> (R_1) The problem of arriving at any explicit theory of empirical confirmation of a synthetic statement.
>
> (R_2) The problem of drawing any straightforward analytic-synthetic distinction.

In other words, if (C_1) were true, then both (D_1) and (D_2) ought to be true; but, as we can see from (R_1) and (R_2), both (D_1) and (D_2) are false; therefore, (C_1) must be false.

However, even if Quine's *pragmatic reductio* is directed more to the issue than is his genetic account of (C_1), it, too, falls short of being an outright refutation of (C_1), for the truth of the conjunction of (R_1) and (R_2) is not inconsistent, even on intuitive grounds, with the truth of (C_1). It might be protested on Quine's behalf that logical inconsistency is too high a standard to require for the refutation of a claim of the nature of (C_1). But, on the other hand, it might be maintained, and with equal plausibility, that merely showing that some view gives rise to various seemingly irresoluble perplexities is not, of itself, sufficient justification for rejecting the view in question.

The conflict here is over the proper canons of rational justification. But when the issue is stated in this general and abstract way, the conflict is more than likely irresoluble—since the concept of sufficient reason, which is at the heart of the matter, varies from situation to situation. Nevertheless, in all fairness to Quine's position, it does seem reasonable to prefer one doctrine over another if the preferred doctrine circumvents the seemingly irresoluble perplexities of its predecessor and *in addition* does not give rise to problems of a more vexatious sort than it alleviates. Under such conditions, the pragmatic reductio form of argument accrues additional persuasive force.

Consequently, it is clear that Quine's attack on the verificationist argument is incomplete without his "countersuggestion . . . that our statements about the external world face the tribunal of sense experience not individually but only as a corporate body" (TDE, 41; *note omitted*). (Here, in a footnote, Quine claimed that "this doctrine was well argued by [Pierre] Duhem" (TDE, 41) in his *La Théorie physique: son objet et sa structure* (Paris, 1960), pp. 303–28, and Quine also cited Armand Lowinger's *The Methodology of Pierre Duhem* (New York: Columbia University Press, 1941), pp. 132–40.) This *countersuggestion* is the additional move needed to make Quine's *pragmatic reductio* convincing. Merely showing that the positivistic (C_1) is the root of much nonsense (i.e., perplexity) is not enough to swing the argument. Quine needs to show, in addition, that there is an acceptable alternative to (C_1) which avoids the problems of (C_1).

Now, if my analysis of Quine's attack on the verification argument is correct, then to properly evaluate the force of his *reductio* we must seek whatever support he presents for the truth of his countersuggestion. In other words, what evidence does Quine offer in support of his contention that our statements about the world face the tribunal of sense experience as a corporate body? In the context in which Quine issues his countersuggestion, he supports it merely by the bald assertion that "Taken collectively, science has its double dependence upon language and experience; but this duality is not significantly traceable into the statements of science taken one by one" (TDE, 42). But of course this is no support at all, for it is merely a restatement, in negative form, of his countersuggestion. The crucial question concerns *why* the duality is not traceable into the individual statements of the theory. Surely the answer to this question must lie with the doctrine of holism that Quine develops in the final section of "Two Dogmas of Empiricism," for he says there that

> *If* this view [i.e., holism] is right, it is misleading to speak of the empirical content of an individual statement—especially if it is a statement at all remote from the experiential periphery of the field. Furthermore it becomes folly to seek a boundary between synthetic statements, which hold contingently on experience, and analytic statements, which hold come what may. Any statement can be held true come what may, if we make drastic enough adjustments elsewhere in the system. (TDE, 43; *my emphasis*)

So, as the antecedent of the first sentence of the above quotation testifies, it is, indeed, Quine's holism doctrine that is the basis for his countersuggestion. Yet the nearest thing to an argument in support of holism to be found in the whole of TDE is an appeal, in a footnote, to relevant arguments of Duhem and Lowinger. It appears, then, that Quine's whole position in TDE is succinctly stated by the conditional just quoted, and that the truth of the antecedent of that conditional is merely assumed and never proved in TDE.

Nevertheless, in §3.3.3, I argued that the holism doctrine (i.e., Duhem's thesis, or the revisibility thesis) is firmly grounded in Quine's theory of language learning and in his theory of meaning (i.e., in the NB conception of language); hence my claim at the beginning of this section that Quine's argument against the dogma of reductionism is bound up with the naturalistic-behavioristic conception of language. Moreover, Quine's second-front argument (namely, that it is a mistake to think that the analytic-synthetic distinction needs to be made) also rests upon the doctrine of holism, and, consequently, it too is intimately bound up with the NB conception. As for Quine's first-front argument (namely, that the distinction resists being clearly drawn), we have taken note of Quine's implicit behavioristic standard of clarity at work there. Consequently, it seems fair to conclude that Quine's rejection of both the dogma of reductionism and the analytic-synthetic dogma is a natural consequence of his allegiance to the NB conception of language. I think this remark is true despite the absence of any explicit appeal to the NB thesis in "Two Dogmas of Empiricism." I think that it is quite clear that if Quine were pressed today to support the antecedent of his conditional (quoted above), beyond merely appealing to Duhem and Lowinger, he would call attention to the way (theoretical) language is learned. Notice, too, a point made at the end of §2.2.2.2, namely, that Quine's theory of language not only supports the claim that holism is true, it also provides a partial explanation of *why* holism occurs.

§3.5   *Unity of science*

Quine and certain other philosophers in the twentieth century who have usually been associated with the philosophical movements of logical positivism, logical empiricism, or scientific empiricism have maintained the thesis of the *unity of science*. This thesis is sometimes conceived as having two parts: the thesis of physicalism and the thesis of extensionality.

Carnap, who was a prominent advocate of the unity of science, held that *physicalism* is the thesis "that every descriptive term in the language of science (in the widest sense, including social science) is connected with terms designating observable properties of things. This connection is of such a kind that a sentence applying the term in question is intersubjectively . . . confirmable by observations."[4] This char-

4. Rudolf Carnap, "Physicalism," in *Dictionary of Philosophy*, ed. Dagobert D. Runes (Totowa, N.J.: Littlefield, Adams and Co., 1977), p. 235.

acterization of physicalism may or may not be consistent with Quine's version of that thesis (which is explained in §3.5.2), depending on how one construes the term 'connection' occurring in Carnap's characterization. (For example, is the connection a holistic one, or is it a reductive one?) Nevertheless, the general idea conveyed by what Carnap says is consistent with Quine's views. This general idea is that the language of physics can be made the universal language of all of science, social science included. Of particular note is the fact that physicalism, applied to psychology, is the logical basis for the method of behaviorism, and, further, behaviorism seeks the elimination of all intentional language from the science of psychology. Thus, behaviorism is an attempt to do psychology without using terms like 'believes', 'desires', 'hopes', 'thinks', 'wants'. This is not to say, of course, that such a universal language of science, replete with vocabulary, is presently in hand. Rather, the thesis of physicalism is a proposal for developing such a language for the future.

The other part of the unity of science thesis, the *thesis of extensionality*, is the further claim that the universal language of science, when completed, will be purely extensional. A purely extensional language of the kind envisioned would be one that contains only those grammatical constructions (or modes of composition) where in general: (a) a singular term can be supplanted by any other co-designative term (i.e., a term referring to the same object) without disturbing the truth value of the containing sentence (for example, by supplanting 'Tully' in 'Tully was a Roman' by 'Cicero'); (b) a general term can be supplanted by any other co-extensive term (i.e., a term true of the same objects) without disturbing the truth value of the containing sentence (for example, supplanting 'is a creature with kidneys' in 'Fido is a creature with kidneys' by 'is a creature with a heart'); (c) a component sentence can be supplanted by any other sentences of the same truth value without disturbing the truth value of the containing sentence (for example, supplanting 'Lincoln was assassinated' in 'Lincoln was assassinated and Kennedy was assassinated' by 'Nixon was president').

The thesis of the unity of science, then, taken as the tandem theses of physicalism and extensionality, implies that neither intentional language nor intensional language would have a place in an ideal, purely scientific account of the world. The problem for Quine, then, as for any advocate of the unity of science, is to show that the intentional idioms of psychology and the intensional idioms of the other sciences can be *eliminated* without detriment to our general theory of the world.

In the next two major sections under §3.5, namely, §3.5.1, ("Toward an extensional language for science") and §3.5.2. ("Physicalism"), we shall examine what contributions Quine has made toward the realization of the ideals of the unity of science movement.

§3.5.1   *Toward an extensional language for science*

Quine notes that when one reflects upon the referential apparatus of everyday English "one encounters various anomalies and conflicts that are implicit in this apparatus" (WO, ix). Yet, for many purposes these anomalies (vagueness, ambiguity, and other failures of reference) present no serious problems, but when it comes to doing science and philosophy they do make for serious problems, for they make it difficult for us to have comprehensive but still simple theories; they limit generalization, complicate deduction, and obscure ontic commitments. Thus, so far as science and philosophy are concerned, these anomalies and conflicts of reference must be removed. The problem is *how* to get rid of them. We cannot burrow under our present language to make an ideal reconstruction of it, nor can we get an entirely new language. So, though repairs to the language must be made, they must be made within the language itself, by means of the resources already present in the language. The essence of the method that Quine advocates for making these repairs involves adopting some of the devices and mechanisms that give precision in language and adapting them and extending them to a wider use. Thus he recommends that we "reflect . . . on the development and structure of our own referential apparatus" (WO, ix) and propose remedies that we are "moved to adopt . . . in the spirit of modern logic" (WO, ix). These remedies may be neither perfect nor final, but Quine thinks they will be useful in helping us toward "understanding the referential work of language and clarifying our conceptual scheme" (WO, 158).[5]

Based upon this idea of adapting and extending the use of precise and simple referential devices and mechanisms already found within everyday language, Quine extrapolates an overall remedy: the regimentation of scientific and philosophical (specifically, ontological) language around the devices and techniques of mathematical logic. "The basic structure of the language of science has been isolated and schematized in a familiar form. It is the predicate calculus: the logic of quantification and truth functions" (FM, 160). The grammar of this strictly regi-

---

5. This passage owes something to Irwin C. Lieb's review of Quine's *Word and Object*, in *International Philosophical Quarterly* (February 1962).

mented language is simple: there are predicates, variables, quantifiers, and truth functions. Such a language is, of course, extensional.

By translating our theory (or theories) of the world into this object-oriented idiom (i.e., the predicate calculus), we gain generality (for the range of values of our variables may be unlimited), we facilitate deduction (for the logical connections among sentences is made perspicuous), and we clarify the ontic commitments of the theory (for to exist is simply to be regarded as a value in the range of values of the bound variables of the regimented theory). Further, it is *only* relative to this regimented language, according to Quine, that it makes sense to inquire into the question of ontology: What is there? A person's "ontology [what his theory says there is] is indeterminate, except relative to some agreed translation of his notation into our regimented one" (FM, 161). A note of caution should be added, however: when we translate everyday language or some theory into the regimented language (the canonical idiom, as Quine calls it), we are not making explicit in the regimented language what was implicit in everyday language or in the theory in question; we are not exposing hidden meanings or hidden references. Rather, our translations are freely created, ontic-oriented analogues of the originals, which can supplant the originals because they share with the originals some partial parallel functions for which the originals were originally wanted. The next four sections delve more deeply into this matter of paraphrase.

§3.5.1.1 *Failures of reference, communication, and simple paraphrase*

In §1.3 we examined Quine's grammatical analysis of English. Familiarity with his analysis facilitated our discussion of his theory of language learning in §2.2.2. But there is a more important and less didactic role for grammatical analysis in Quine's philosophy: *grammatical analysis* is the first phase of a three-phase program of philosophical analysis, which I shall refer to as *Quinian analysis*. The remaining two phases of this method of analysis are *simple paraphrase*, to be dealt with in this section, and *explication*, which will be dealt with in the next section.

I should like to make clear from the start that 'simple paraphrase' is my term and not Quine's. He uses the single term 'paraphrase' to denote both the activities of simple paraphrase and explication, but he does recognize, implicitly, the distinction I shall draw between the two. Further, I shall use 'simple paraphrase' and 'paraphrase' co-extensively and reserve 'explication' for denoting another kind of activity to be explained in §3.5.1.2.

One vitally important function of everyday language is communication; but all too often communication is hampered by various indeterminacies and irregularities, which plague everyday language. Nevertheless, much of the time these indeterminacies and irregularities, when they take the forms of vagueness or ambiguity, can be eliminated by the relatively simple technique of paraphrasing. Quine makes some specific recommendations for eliminating vaguenesses and ambiguities by the technique of simple paraphrase. His paraphrastic program is not, however, a program of language reform. On the contrary, Quine regards the activity of paraphrase as part of common linguistic practice wherein "we are accustomed daily to paraphrase our sentences under the stress or threat of failure of communication" (WO, 125). Quine's paraphrastic program is merely a continuation of this technique, which is routinely found among the everyday linguistic practices of the marketplace and whose primary motivation is to facilitate or ensure communication.

Communication is sometimes threatened when reference is obscured by a vagueness of terms. Both singular terms and general terms can be vague. A singular term naming a physical object can be vague concerning the boundaries of that object in space-time: "Insofar as it is left unsettled how far from the summit of Mount Rainier one can be and still count as on Mount Rainier, 'Mount Rainier' is vague" (WO, 126). A general term will commonly be vague in two ways: (a) with respect to the various boundaries of all of its objects, and (b) as to the inclusion or exclusion of marginal objects. "Thus take the general term 'mountain': it is vague on the score of how much terrain to reckon into each of the indisputable mountains, and it is vague on the score of what lesser eminences to count as mountains at all" (WO, 126).

As a general rule vagueness does not disturb the truth values of the sentences in which vague words occur, and, therefore, paraphrase is not usually necessary. However, sometimes the truth value of a sentence does depend upon settling the vagueness of some constituent term. When such cases become important, as they might for example in law, they create pressure for new verbal conventions, for a changed trend of usage that resolves the vagueness in one way or another to the satisfaction of the truth value of the containing sentence. "Thus take the question of biggest fresh lake. Is Michigan-Huron admissible, or is it a pair of lakes? Here the briefest reflection on likely criteria will issue in a favorable verdict" (WO, 128).

Communication sometimes fails when reference is frustrated by ambiguity of terms. "The striking thing about . . . ambiguous terms

. . . is that from utterance to utterance they can be clearly true or clearly false of one and the same thing, according as interpretative clues in the circumstances of utterance point one way or another. This trait, if not a necessary condition of ambiguity of a term, is at any rate the nearest we have come to a clear condition of it" (WO, 131). For example, 'light' is ambiguous when predicated of dark feathers: 'Dark feathers are light'. This proposed partial criterion of ambiguity is used by Quine as a means for differentiating terms that are truly ambiguous from terms that are merely general; thus: "Take 'hard' said of chairs and questions. As remarked, ambiguity may be manifested in that the term is at once true and false of the same things. This seemed to work for 'light', but it is useless for 'hard'. For can we claim that 'hard' as applied to chairs ever is denied of hard questions, or vice versa?" (WO, 130). Obviously, Quine expects his reader to answer 'No' to this question—his point being that the word 'hard' has a single inclusive sense and is, therefore, not ambiguous but is merely general, in the sense of being true of some very unlike things.

Turning, now, from the ambiguity of terms, one might extend "the notion of ambiguity beyond terms to apply to particles—notably 'or', with its proverbial inclusive and exclusive senses—and even to syntax" (WO, 134). Thus, recalling from §1.3 our discussion of the categorematic and syncategorematic uses of adjectives in attributive position, we might say that attributive position is syntactically ambiguous as between the truly attributive use of an adjective and a syncategorematic use. "The same may be said of predicative position; for 'The violinist was poor' can mean that he was impoverished or that he played poorly" (WO, 134). However, the most notable of the *syntactical ambiguities* is that of pronominal reference: "And Satan trembles when he sees/The weakest saint upon his knees" (from P.E.B. Jourdain, *The Philosophy of Mr. B*rtr*nd R*ss*ll*, Chicago and London, 1918; cited in WO, 135). The problem here can be easily solved by paraphrasing the second line of the poem as 'The weakest saint upon the weakest saint's knees'. When the antecedent of a troublesome pronoun is a *definite* singular term (in this case, a singular description), we can usually supplant the pronoun with that definite singular term and thereby produce a paraphrase that eliminates the ambiguity and the pronoun. However, when the antecedent of the troublesome pronoun is an *indefinite* singular term, a more drastic and artificial sounding paraphrase is called for; thus: " 'A lawyer told a colleague that he thought a client of his more critical of himself than of any of his rivals' " (WO, 135) can be paraphrased, and ambiguities eliminated, with the aid of variables, as " 'A lawyer *x* told a colleague *y* that *x* [or *y*?] thought a client *z* of *y* [or *x*?] more critical of *z* [or *y*? or *x*?] than of any of *z*'s [or *y*'s? or *x*'s?] rivals' " (WO, 136).

Another notable kind of ambiguity has to do with the *scope* of indefinite singular terms. In order to understand what Quine means by 'scope', consider the following:

(1) If any member contributes he gets a poppy,

and

(2) If every member contributes, I'll be surprised.

The first sentence asserts of each member that if he contributes, he will receive a poppy. The second sentence, however, does not make the corresponding assertion of every member that if he contributes, I'll be surprised. Rather, (2) says that I expect less than unanimous contributions. "The contrast between (1) and (2) brings out the idea of the scope of an indefinite singular term. The scope of 'any member' in (1) is (1) in its entirety, whereas the scope of 'every member' in (2) is just 'every member contributes' " (WO, 138). As a rule, 'any' takes maximum scope, and 'every' takes minimum scope.

Unlike (1) and (2), the scope of the indefinite singular term in the following sentence is ambiguous:

(3) I believe he saw a letter of mine.

If the scope of 'a letter of mine' in (3) is taken to be 'he saw a letter of mine', then the whole sentence applies 'I believe' to the self-contained sentence 'he saw a letter of mine'. According to this interpretation the whole sentence amounts to the claim that I believe (merely) that he did not miss all my letters. On the other hand, if the scope of 'a letter of mine' is taken to be the whole sentence, including 'I believe', then the whole sentence amounts to the claim that there are one or more specific letters of mine, which I believe he saw. Similarly:

> If in 'Each thing that glisters is not gold' we take the scope of the indefinite singular term 'each thing' as the whole sentence, we have a falsehood: a sweeping denial of goldhood with respect to glistering things. If we take the scope rather as 'each thing that glisters is gold', and so reckon 'not' as an outside operator governing the whole, we have the truth that Shakespeare intended. (WO, 139; *note omitted*).

As a means for dealing with this matter of the ambiguity of the scope of indefinite singular terms, Quine recommends that we exploit the 'such that' construction: "Representing the indefinite singular term as '*b*' and its scope as ' . . . *b* . . .', we may sum the method up in this maxim: rewrite the scope ' . . . *b* . . .' as '*b* is such that . . . it . . .'" (WO, 140). This way of displaying scope is essentially a matter of getting the indefinite singular term into the position of the grammatical subject of a predication which is its scope, and thereby reducing the question of scope to the question of spotting a subject's predicate. The point of the 'such that' is merely that it enables us to convert anything we might want to say about the indefinite singular term '*b*' into a single complex predicate 'such that . . . it . . .', attributable to *b*. For example, (1) becomes

(4) Each member is such that if he contributes he gets a poppy,

and (2) becomes

(5) If each member (is such that he) contributes, I'll be surprised.

A further kind of failure of reference attributable to ambiguity, and one which is central to Quine's program of paraphrasing, concerns the positions of singular terms. This kind of failure of reference is explained by Quine's doctrines of *referential opacity* and *referential transparency*: "in sentences there are positions where the term is used as a means simply of specifying its object, or purporting to, for the rest of the sentence to say something about, and there are positions where it is not" (WO, 141–42). For example, the position of 'Tully' in (6) is such that 'Tully' serves to designate a person, but the position of 'Tully' in (7) is not such a position:

(6) Tully was a Roman,

(7) 'Tully was a Roman' is trochaic.

When a singular term is used in a sentence purely to specify its object, as is 'Tully' in (6), and the predicate is true of the object, then certainly the sentence will remain true when any other singular term designating the same object is substituted for the original singular term. "Here we have a criterion for what may be called *purely referential position*: the position must be subject to the *substitutivity of identity*" (WO, 142; *note omitted*). Contrariwise, to demonstrate that a position is *not* purely referential (or, nonreferential), we need only show that the substitution of one co-designative term for another in a true sentence produces a false sentence. For example, to show that the position of 'Tully' in (7) is not purely referential, we need only substitute 'Cicero' for 'Tully', which yields the falsehood

(8) 'Cicero was a Roman' is trochaic.

(7) is true because the linguistic expression named therein—i.e., the words appearing between the single quotation marks in (7)—has the property of being trochaic. And, even though (8) is the product of re-placing 'Tully' in (7) with its co-designate 'Cicero', nevertheless, (8) turns out to be false because, unlike (7), the linguistic expression named in (8)—i.e., the words appearing between the single quotation marks in (8)—does not have the property of being trochaic. In short, the position of 'Tully' in (7) is not purely referential.

As (6) illustrates, a purely referential position is the position of singular terms under predication. Thus, 'purely referential position' is defined relative to predication. However, purely referential position is a concept that can be extended to apply also to positions of singular terms relative to other singular terms that contain them. The principle of substitutivity of identity will serve in connection with containment within singular terms, as it did in connection with predication, as a cri-terion of purely referential position. But, whereas the principle of sub-stitutivity of identity in predication said that the containing sentence keeps its *truth value* when the contained singular term is supplanted by any other singular term having the same referent, the principle in con-nection with singular terms says that the containing singular term keeps its *reference* when the contained singular term is so supplanted. Take, for example, "Tully was a Roman"; this is a singular term nam-ing the expression inside the quotation marks. The position of 'Tully', a singular term within the singular term "Tully was a Roman," can be shown to be a nonreferential position by merely substituting 'Cicero' for 'Tully', thereby yielding "Cicero was a Roman" which, again, is a singular term, but "Cicero was a Roman" ≠ "Tully was a Roman"; these two quotations are names of *different* linguistic expressions. Quotation will always give rise to nonreferential positions, i.e., quota-tion is a construction that lacks referential *transparency* and is, there-fore, an *opaque* construction. But, since quotation can always be sup-planted by spelling,[6] nonreferential positions that arise from quotation

6. The point here is that the convention adopted concerning the use of single quotation marks (namely, that they be regarded as forming singular terms naming the expressions contained inside the quotation marks) has the undesirable effect of obscur-

are best regarded as mere surface appearances, which can be circum-
vented by a change in notation. Also, there are cases where not purely
referential positions of singular terms can be eliminated by paraphrase.

Quine seems to use the terms 'referential position' and 'nonreferential position' to talk about *positions* of singular terms within constructions or modes of containment, and the terms 'referential transparency' and 'referential opacity' to talk about the *constructions* or
modes of containment. But, in the end, these are perhaps just two ways
of talking about the same thing, since Quine calls "a mode of containment Φ referentially transparent if, whenever an occurrence [i.e., the
position] of a singular term t is purely referential in a term or sentence
ψ (t), it is purely referential also in the containing term or sentence
Φ (ψ (t))" (WO, 144).

Clearly, all of the modes of containment afforded by truth-functional connectives are, by this criterion, referentially transparent. For
example: 'Plato' occurs purely referentially in 'Plato was a philosopher'; 'Aristotle' occurs purely referentially in 'Aristotle was a philosopher'; and they both continue to occur purely referentially in the truth-
functional compound 'Either Plato was a philosopher or Aristotle was
a philosopher'; hence, disjunction is referentially transparent. Similarly, general terms predicatively used can be viewed as grammatical
constructions or modes of containment: they are modes of containment
of the subject singular terms in the sentences. As such, "they are referentially transparent; for this is simply to say . . . that the subject position in a predication is purely referential" (WO, 144–45).

Of particular interest to Quine is the ambiguity of belief constructions (e.g., '*a* believes *p*') with regard to their being either transparent
or opaque, depending upon whether one understands 'believes' as a
genuine relative term, or not. For example, suppose (9) is true:

(9) Tom believes that Cicero denounced Catiline.

Suppose further that Tom does not know that Cicero and Tully are the
same person. We therefore could expect Tom to deny that Tully de-

---

ing the referential position of 'Tully' in "Tully was a Roman" simply because 'Tully'
and 'Cicero' have different shapes. To circumvent this incidental problem and to dis-
pel the apparent opacity, we can avoid the use of single quotation marks and, instead,
spell out

tee–yu–ell–ell–wye–space–doublye–ay–ess–space–ay–space–ar–oh–em–ay–en

by using these names of the letters found in "Tully was a Roman." Now the spelling of
'Cicero' can be substituted for the spelling of 'Tully'.

nounced Catiline. If, in the face of Tom's denial of 'Tully denounced Catiline', we were prepared both to affirm (9) and to deny 'Tom believes that Tully denounced Catiline', then the position of 'Cicero' in (9) is being regarded as not purely referential (or nonreferential). But, the position of 'Cicero' in 'Cicero denounced Catiline' is purely referential. Hence, 'believes', as just construed, is not a genuine relative term, and the belief construction is opaque.

On the other hand, there is a way of construing belief constructions as referentially transparent. In the opaque sense of belief considered above, Tom's denial of 'Tully denounced Catiline' serves to show that he does not believe that Tully denounced Catiline, even while he believes that Cicero did, but "in the transparent sense of belief . . . Tom's earnest 'Cicero denounced Catiline' counts as showing that he does believe that Tully denounced Catiline, despite his own misguided verbal disclaimer" (WO, 145). This latter way of construing belief constructions regards 'believes' as a genuine relative general term, relating Tom and Cicero, while the former way of construing belief constructions relates Tom to no man. In short, 'Cicero' has purely referential position in (9) or it does not, according as 'believes' is taken transparently or not, and that is to say, whether it is construed as a genuine relative general term or not.

In defining 'purely referential position' Quine employs the criterion of substitutivity of identity, but since *indefinite* singular terms do not designate objects, classes of objects, or anything else, the criterion of substitutivity of identity and therefore purely referential position apply thus far only to *definite* singular terms. Nevertheless, what is being tested for reference are positions within constructions, and indefinite singular terms can be put into those positions. Thus

(10) The commissioner is looking for the dean

and

(11) The commissioner is looking for someone

differ from each other in that (10) has the position after 'looking for' occupied by a definite singular term (a singular description), while (11) has the same position occupied by an indefinite singular term. Another difference is the referential/nonreferential characters of these positions. The position of 'the dean' in (10) can be taken as referential or as nonreferential depending on whether 'looking for' is taken as a genuine relative general term or not. However, the position of 'someone' in (11) must be taken as purely referential, if proper sense is to be made of it, for if (11) is true, then there must be someone for whom the commissioner is looking, even if that person remains undesignated. Thus, any designation of that person that is substituted for 'someone' in (11) would continue to make (11) true. "To put the point paradoxically, indefinite singular terms need referential position because they do not refer" (WO, 147).

Indefinite singular terms can also find their way into belief constructions; such, for example, is 'someone' in (12):

(12) Ralph believes that someone is a spy.

In *Word and Object* Quine argues that such belief constructions as (12) suffer from an ambiguity of the scope of the contained indefinite singular term (*see* WO, 147). For example, depending on whether the scope of 'someone' in (12) is taken narrowly, or broadly, (12) becomes, respectively, either

(13) There is someone whom Ralph believes to be a spy,

or

(14) Ralph believes there are spies.

Quine calls the sense of 'believes' evidenced in (13) the *relational* or *de re* sense, and the sense of 'believes' evidenced in (14) the *notional* or *de dicto* sense (*see* QPA, 185–86). The respective senses of (13) and (14) are expressed perspicuously by (15) and (16):

(15) $(\exists x)$ (Ralph believes that x is a spy),
(16) Ralph believes that $(\exists x)$ (x is a spy).

(15) asserts that Ralph believes of *some particular individual* that he is a spy, while (16) asserts merely that Ralph believes there are spies. The position of the indefinite singular term in (16), i.e., of the variable 'x', can be taken as purely referential or as nonreferential; (16) makes sense either way. However, things are otherwise with (15): the position of the indefinite singular term in (15), i.e., of the variable 'x', must be understood transparently, if proper sense is to be made of (15). In short, belief must be taken transparently to make proper sense of (15), though it can be taken either way for (16). Hence the ambiguity of (12).

There is a problem, however, with construing (12) in the manner of (15). Imagine that Ralph has noticed a man in a brown hat behaving in such a manner that Ralph believes he is a spy. Imagine also that Ralph has seen at times a certain gray-haired gentleman jogging on the beach. Suppose that Ralph is unaware that the men are one and the same. Can we say of *this man*, that Ralph believes him to be a spy? Quine thinks we are faced with difficulties no matter how we answer this question. If we answer in the affirmative, then we find ourselves accepting a conjunction of the type

(17) *w* sincerely denies ' . . . ' and *w* believes that . . .

as true, with one and the same sentence in both blanks; for instance:

(18) Ralph sincerely denies 'the gray-haired man is a spy' and Ralph believes that the gray-haired man is a spy.

(18) and the like are not outright contradictions, but they are oddities which must be accepted as the price for saying things like (15). An additional and stronger reason for rejecting the transparent interpretation of belief is that its acceptance commits the believer to believing literally everything (*see* WO, 148–49).

On the other hand, if we answer in the negative, we would thereby be ruling simultaneously that

(19) Ralph believes that the man in the brown hat is a spy,

and

(20) Ralph does not believe that the man seen at the beach is a spy,

which is tantamount to denying any relationship between Ralph and some particular individual. In other words, we would no longer be regarding (15) in the *relational* or *de re* sense. Moreover, we would no longer be construing (15) transparently, and, therefore, the quantifier of (15), '$(\exists x)$', would no longer serve to bind the variable, 'x', inside the now opaque belief construction. What is Quine's response to this dilemma?

In *Word and Object* Quine contends that "in general what is wanted is not a doctrine of transparency or opacity of belief, but a way of indicating, selectively and changeably, just what positions in the contained sentence are to shine through as referential on any particular occasion" (WO, 149). The technique that Quine devised in response to this need simply amounts to adopting the convention of localizing the failure of transparency in the 'that' of 'believes that' and in the 'to' of 'believes to', and not in the 'believes'. Following this convention, both 'Cicero' and 'Catiline' occur nonreferentially in

(21) Tom believes that Cicero denounced Catiline;

'Cicero' occurs purely referentially while 'Catiline' occurs nonreferentially in

(22) Tom believes Cicero to have denounced Catiline;

'Catiline' occurs purely referentially while 'Cicero' occurs nonreferentially in

(23) Tom believes Catiline to have been denounced by Cicero;

and both 'Cicero' and 'Catiline' occur purely referentially in

(24) Tom believes Cicero and Catiline to be related as denouncer and denounced.

According to this convention 'believes that' is unequivocally opaque, but we may paraphrase selectively to alter the purely referential and nonreferential positions as we please. Further, the convention can be generalized to apply to all expressions of propositional attitude of which 'believes that' is only one example; others are 'says that', 'wishes that', 'endeavors that', 'urges that', 'fears that', 'is surprised that', and so forth. But if 'believes that' is unequivocally opaque, then (15) and its kind must be renounced as bad formulations which involve an illicit pronominal (or variable) cross-reference from inside an opaque construction to an indefinite singular term (or quantifier) outside.

Quine's rejection of (15) as a paraphrase of (13) does not mean that Quine—in *Word and Object*—also rejects the idea that (12) is ambiguous. Rather, his attitude in *Word and Object* is the same as in his earlier paper, "Quantifiers and Propositional Attitudes" (1956). There he claims there is a vast difference between (13) and (14), for if Ralph is like most of us, (14) is true and (13) is false; hence the ambiguity of (12). With an eye to preserving the distinction between (13) and (14), but without relying on (15) as a paraphrase of (13), Quine recommends paraphrasing (13) somewhat along the lines of (25):

(25) $(\exists x)$ (x is believed by Ralph to be a spy).

Here, unlike (15), thanks to the convention of localizing the opacity in 'to' instead of in 'believes', the quantifier does not attempt to bind a variable in an opaque construction, i.e., there is no cross-reference from inside an opaque construction to a quantifier outside.

More recently however, in "Intensions Revisited" (1977), Quine *does* reject his earlier point of view regarding the ambiguity of (12). In this later essay he contends that the distinction between (13) and (14) is *vacuous*, whereas, before, he claimed it was *vast*. In other words, Quine's current view is that sentences like (13) are meaningless, as they stand, apart from some context. Ralph cannot be said to believe *simpliciter* that some unspecified person is a spy; he can only be said to believe that the man in the brown hat is a spy, or the man at the beach is a spy, or that some other designated individual is a spy. This change of Quine's mind resulted in part from his realization that "the notion of knowing or believing who or what someone or something is, is utterly dependent on context. Sometimes, when we ask who someone is, we see the face and want the name; sometimes the reverse. Sometimes we want to know his role in the community. Of itself the notion is empty" (IR, 10; *note omitted*). The upshot of this is that (25) must be renounced right along with (15), for both were suggested paraphrases of (13), which itself must now be renounced on grounds of its meaninglessness. In short, Quine no longer thinks—as he did in *Word and Object* and in "Quantifiers and Propositional Attitudes"—that (12) is ambiguous. Furthermore, not only does he now renounce *all* relational or *de re* belief, he renounces *all de re* or quantified propositional attitudes generally.

A complete account of how Quine attempts to handle belief constructions must await later discussions of explication and the objects of the propositional attitudes. For the present, our topic is the irregularities and indeterminacies of reference in English, and the role simple paraphrase plays in their elimination; and there is one more kink in the referential apparatus of English to be smoothed out, namely, constructions containing *opaque verbs*. Take, for example,

(26) Ernest is hunting lions.

One is tempted, at first, to paraphrase (26) as

(27) $(\exists x)$ (x is a lion and Ernest is hunting x).

(27) is true just in case there is a lion (or lions) that Ernest is hunting; if there is no lion (or lions), then (27) is false. But there is an opaque sense of 'is-hunting' expressed by (26), which makes (26) true even when there are no lions in the vicinity of Ernest's hunt. The point is more vivid with

(28) Ernest is hunting unicorns

and

(29) $(\exists x)$ (x is a unicorn and Ernest is hunting x).

(28) may be true in the opaque sense, while at the same time (29) is false, supposing of course that the universe contains no unicorns.

The generalized convention for localizing opacity in certain particles, together with a catalogue of propositional attitudes such as those already mentioned, can be of help in analyzing ambiguous terms like 'is-hunting'; for example, we can paraphrase (26) as

(30) Ernest is endeavoring that some lion is such that Ernest shoots it,

or as

(31) Some lion is such that Ernest is endeavoring that Ernest shoots it.

These two paraphrases supplant 'is-hunting' with the propositional attitude 'is endeavoring that . . . shoots', and our convention localizes the opacity of this expression in the first 'that' of (30), and in the second 'that' of (31). (The 'that' of 'such that' is unaffected by our convention, as the 'such that' construction is invariably transparent.) (31), however, is a bad formulation for just the same reason that (15) was: there is a pronominal cross-reference from inside an opaque construction to a 'such that' outside. (30) also has a problem in that 'Ernest' occurs both as purely referential (first occurrence) and as nonreferential (second occurrence). However, (30) can be further paraphrased as

(32) Ernest is endeavoring (-to-cause) himself to shoot a lion.

In (32) 'Ernest' occurs only referentially, while 'lion' occurs nonreferentially in the opaque 'to shoot a lion', if we agree to localize the opacity in 'to' of (32). However, in

(33) Ernest is endeavoring (-to-cause) himself and a certain lion to be related as shooter and shot

both 'Ernest' and 'lion' occur in purely referential positions. Consequently, (32) exemplifies the opaque sense of the verb 'is-hunting' of (26), while (33) exemplifies its transparent sense. The formalization of (32) is '$(\exists x)$ (x is Ernest and x is endeavoring (-to-cause) himself to shoot a lion)' or '$(\exists x)$ (Fx and Gx)', while the formalization of (33) is '$(\exists x)$ $(\exists y)$ (x is Ernest and y is a lion and x is endeavoring-to-cause x and y to be related as shooter and shot)', or '$(\exists x)$ $(\exists y)$ (Fx and Ly and

Gxy)'; and, while the truth of the former does not depend upon the existence of lions, the truth of the latter does.

This concludes our account of Quine's discussion of the indeterminacies and irregularities of reference and of simple paraphrase. We have seen that certain vaguenesses and ambiguities of reference that pervade everyday usage, and threaten successful communication, can be eliminated by techniques of paraphrase. This was especially evident in the simple cases of ambiguous pronominal reference (cf. the saint's knees and the lawyer's client, and the like). However, it is not so evident that communication is served (in any straightforward manner) by paraphrasing 'Ernest is hunting lions' as 'Ernest is endeavoring (-to-cause) himself and a (certain) lion to be related as shooter and shot': this paraphrase may be accurate, but the motivation behind so extreme a paraphrase is unlikely to be the desire to facilitate communication in the marketplace.

I do not wish to saddle Quine with any kind of hard and fast distinction between what I am calling simple paraphrase and explication generally so-called; indeed, I see no philosophical importance attaching to the distinction. But it must be admitted, too, that while some paraphrasing activity is motivated by a desire to facilitate communication, some is not. Other motives include the clarification of concepts, the facilitating of deductions, and the clarification of ontic commitments. To be sure, it is possible that in some paraphrases more than one of these concerns may coincide, but they need not. And, in those cases where a paraphrase contributes nothing toward facilitating communication in any straightforward sense, I am inclined to think that the activity of simple paraphrase, so common to ordinary discourse, has been left behind (*see* WO, 157–58).

§3.5.1.2   *Explication as elimination*

We are now in a position to examine the third and final phase of Quinian analysis—the philosophical activity of explication. As was noted in §3.4 in connection with his attack on analyticity and synonymy, Quine recognizes several types of definitional activity, each of which results in a different kind of definition. Three of these are lexical definitions, conventional definitions, and explications. Lexical definitions arise when the lexicographer, as an empirical scientist, glosses one term with another, for example, 'bachelor' as 'unmarried man', on the basis "of his belief that there is a relation of synonymy between those forms, implicit in general or preferred usage prior to his own work"

(TDE, 24). Conventional definitions, on the other hand, do not rely upon preexisting synonymies for here the definiendum becomes synonymous with the definiens simply because the definiens has been created expressly for the purpose of being synonymous with the definiendum. Thus, conventional definitions merely amount to the "conventional introduction of novel notations for purposes of sheer abbreviation" (TDE, 26). In explication, however, "the purpose is not merely to paraphrase the definiendum into an outright synonym, but actually to improve upon the definiendum by refining or supplementing its meaning" (TDE, 25). Quine refers to Carnap as an advocate of the method of explication, citing the passage in *Meaning and Necessity* where Carnap says:

> The task of making more exact a vague or not quite exact concept used in everyday life or in an earlier stage of scientific or logical development, or rather of replacing it by a newly constructed, more exact concept, belongs among the most important tasks of logical analysis and logical construction. We call this the task of explicating, or of giving an *explication* for, the earlier concept; this earlier concept, or sometimes the term used for it, is called the explicandum; and the new concept, or its term, is called the explicatum of the old one. . . .
>
> Generally speaking, it is not required that an explicatum have, as nearly as possible, the same meaning as the explicandum; it should, however, correspond to the explicandum in such a way that it can be used instead of the latter.[7]

As a paradigm example of this kind of definitional activity, Quine cites the explication of the notion of an ordered pair:

> [An ordered pair is] a device for treating objects two at a time as if we were treating objects of some sort one at a time. A typical use of the device is in assimilating relations to classes, by taking them as classes of ordered pairs. The father relation becomes the class of just those ordered pairs which, like ⟨Abraham, Isaac⟩, have a male and one of his offspring as their respective components. (WO, 257; *notes omitted*)

But there is a difficulty with the notion of an ordered pair: Just what kind of object is an ordered pair? This question is not one to be

7. Rudolf Carnap, *Meaning and Necessity* (Chicago: The University of Chicago Press, 1947), pp. 7–8; *note omitted*.

answered by appealing to observation. Rather, it is a linguistic problem to be settled by appealing to explication. The problem just is that the expression 'ordered pair' and expressions like '$\langle x, y \rangle$' are *defective nouns*, similar to 'sake' in the respect of "not [being] at home in all the questions and answers in which we are accustomed to imbed terms at their full-fledged best" (WO, 258). However, these expressions, unlike 'sake', cannot be dismissed as irreferential fragments of some containing phrase (viz. 'sake' in 'for the sake of'). For as it happens, the notion of an ordered pair was introduced into mathematics, subject to the single postulate

(1) If $\langle x, y \rangle = \langle z, w \rangle$ then $x = z$ and $y = w$,

for the purpose of assimilating relations to classes, as classes of ordered pairs. And, therefore, ordered pairs must be objects on a par with other objects as members of classes. In short, the problem is that for the purposes of theory we need ordered pairs as objects, but the expression 'ordered pair' does not have the linguistic status of a term (i.e., 'ordered pair' is a defective noun). Our task, thus, is to explicate 'ordered pair' by introducing an expression that can be used for 'ordered pair' in every relevant context, but one that is also a full-fledged term "marking out" a category of appropriate objects, i.e., objects meeting the requirements of (1). Thus the task of explicating 'ordered pair' reduces to the task of "systematically fixing upon some suitable already-recognized object, for each x and y, with which to identify $\langle x, y \rangle$. The problem is a neat one, for we have in (1) a single explicit standard whereby to judge whether a version is suitable" (WO, 258). In fact, there are several acceptable explications—relative to (1)—of the notion of ordered pair. "The earliest, put forward by Wiener in 1914, ran (nearly enough) as follows: $\langle x, y \rangle$ is identified with the class $\{\{x\}, \{y, \wedge\}\}$, whose members are just (*a*) the class $\{x\}$, whose sole member is x, and (*b*) the class $\{y, \wedge\}$, whose sole members are y and the empty class" (WO, 258). A later and better known explication of ordered pair is due to Kuratowski in which $\langle x, y \rangle$ is identified with $\{\{x\}, \{x, y\}\}$. Both of these explications meet the requirements of (1), and are therefore acceptable, even though they conflict with each other on other grounds. This divergence need not concern us, however. Our only concern (for the present) is that the explication we choose should meet the requirements of (1), which guarantee the similarity of function between the notion of an ordered pair and our explication of it. There may be a great many other respects in which the notion of an ordered pair and our explication of it differ, but this does not affect our analysis, for we have not claimed the explicatum and the explicandum (to use Carnap's terminology) to be synonymous. The same point can be made in connection with competing explications. Neither Wiener's nor Kuratowski's explication claims to be the uniquely correct analysis of an ordered pair. Nor does either claim to be synonymous with the notion of ordered pair, or even with each other. All that is being claimed is that where the original notion of ordered pair was defective and perplexing, these explications of it (in well known terms of classes) are not; and, further, both explications serve functions paralleling those of the original notion relevant to the purposes for which the original was needed. According to Quine:

> A similar view can be taken of every case of explication: *explication is elimination*. We have, to begin with, an expression or form of expression that is somehow troublesome. It behaves partly like a term but not enough so, or it is vague in ways that bother us, or it puts kinks in a theory or encourages one or another confusion. But also it serves certain purposes that are not to be abandoned. Then we find a way of accomplishing those same purposes through other channels, using other and less troublesome forms of expression. The old perplexities are resolved. (WO, 260)

More correctly, perhaps, the old perplexities are *dissolved*, "for when explication banishes a problem it does so by showing it to be in an important sense unreal; viz., in the sense of proceeding only from needless usages" (WO, 260; *note omitted*). Explication shows how these usages can be avoided in favor of ones that engender no such problems. Thus the problem posed by our original question 'What kind of object is an ordered pair?' is "dissolved by showing how we can dispense with ordered pairs in any problematic sense in favor of certain clearer notions" (WO, 260).

Such, then, in general, is the nature of explication. Yet, there is one feature of explication that the example of ordered pairs oversimplifies, namely, the task of determining the function of the original expression that the explicatum is supposed to parallel. In the case of the troublesome 'ordered pair' the relevant function was atypically clear in the form of (1). So there seem to be two steps involved in the construction of an explication: (a) recognition, of a particular useful function of the original expression and (b) recognition or construction of some alternative expression that has a parallel function but is not encumbered by the needless usages of the original. However, there is something unsettling about describing the activity in this way, for it suggests that the function of the original expression must be well enough understood to begin with in order to recognize or construct another expression suitable for serving the "same" relevant function. But, if one can clearly recognize one usage among others of the original expression that serves a particular purpose, then why bother to provide another expression to serve that purpose? Quine's answer to this is, I think, vaguely contained in the following quotation:

> [In philosophical analysis or explication] we do not claim to make clear and explicit what the users of the unclear expression had unconsciously in mind all along. We do not expose hidden meanings, as the words 'analysis' and 'explication' would suggest; we supply lacks. We fix on the particular functions of the unclear expression that make it worth troubling about, and then devise a substitute, clear and *couched in terms to our liking*, that fills those functions. Beyond those conditions of partial agreement, dictated by our interests and purposes, any traits of the . . . [explicatum] come under the head of "don't-cares." (WO, 258–59; *my emphasis*)

It would seem from this quotation that when we bother to explicate a term (or concept), our aim is not only to eliminate needless usages that obscure or otherwise hinder the usage of the original term (or concept) we have focused on; we also aim at *couching the explicatum in terms to our liking*. By saying that an explicatum is to be couched in terms to our liking, Quine does not mean just any terms one pleases—at least not if Quine is doing the explicating. Rather, he means terms that are amenable to the aims of regimentation, i.e., terms that conform to the thesis of extensionality. So there seem to be in Quine's case two criteria, not one, for evaluating the acceptability of any particular explication: one is that the explicatum be capable of serving the desired function of the original; the other is that the terms of the explicatum be subject to the principle of extensionality.

§3.5.1.3 *Regimentation*

We have already noted that explication is elimination—the elimination of needless usages—and we are now ready to appreciate Quine's program of eliminating various of the terms, auxiliaries, and constructions isolated by grammatical analysis (re: §1.3). These terms, auxiliaries, and constructions are eliminated by successive applications of explication, which culminate in the production of a canonical notation containing no constructions (modes of containment) other than predication, truth functions, and either universal or existential quantification, and no singular terms other than variables, and no occurrences of general terms other than in predicative position. Let us examine Quine's eliminations but let us also keep in mind Quine's remark that

> Where the objective of a canonical notation is economy and clarity of elements, we need only to show how the notation *could* be made to do the work of all the idioms to which we claim it to be adequate; we do not have to use it. Notations of intermediate richness can be less laborious to use, and different forms have advantages for different purposes. So, reassured that we are in no way compromising our freedom, we can be uncompromising in our reductions. (WO, 161–62)

Following Quine, we can begin the program of eliminating or reducing the terms and constructions of English by requiring that indefinite singular terms be held to subject position. And, as Quine recommends, we can "standardize their manner of occurrence a bit further, insisting specifically that they occur always followed by a predicate of the form 'is an object x such that . . . x . . .'" (WO, 162). Accordingly,

(1) John has something

becomes

(2) Something is an object x such that John has x.

Notice, again, that the 'that' of 'such that' is transparent—unlike the 'that' and 'to' of expressions of propositional attitude.

Further, we can dispense with almost the entire category of indefinite singular terms: "The essential forms of indefinite singular terms reduce thus to 'every F' and 'some F' (in the sense of 'a certain F'), where 'F' stands for any general term in substantival form" (WO, 162). Thus, 'A lion is hungry' becomes 'Some lion is hungry.' In fact, this whole class of indefinite singular terms (i.e., 'some F') can be reduced further to the one indefinite singular term 'something'. Adopting the convention for standardizing the occurrence of indefinite singular terms, we get 'Something is an object x such that x is a lion and x is hungry'. As an abbreviation for 'Something is an object x such that' we can write '$(\exists x)$' which is, of course, the existential quantifier and is usually read 'something x is such that'. Thus, in the canonical notation 'A lion is hungry' becomes '$(\exists x)$ (x is a lion and x is hungry)'. Similar remarks apply to the singular terms classified as occurrences of the form 'every F': 'Each lion eats meat' becomes 'Every lion eats meat'. This whole class of indefinite singular terms (i.e., 'every F') can be reduced to 'everything'. Then, per our convention, we get 'Everything is an object x such that if x is a lion then x eats meat'. And, as an abbreviation for 'Everything is an object x such that' we can write '(x)', the universal quantifier, which can be read 'everything x is such that'. In this way the referential work of the entire class of indefinite singular terms can be handled by 'something' and 'everything', which never occur except followed by 'is an object x (or y, etc.) such that'. And, even these two surviving indefinite singular terms can be reduced to one by the equivalence of '$(\exists x)$' and 'not (x) not'.

Indefinite singular terms aside, another reduction which we can effect is that of demonstrative singular terms to singular descriptions. We recall from §1.3 that singular descriptions are degenerate cases of demonstrative singular terms (i.e., 'this' or 'that' was replaced by 'the' and the gesture indicating spatio-temporal extent was dropped). Thus we can explicate 'this (or that) apple' as 'the apple here (there)'. "This use of the indicator words 'here' and 'there' as general terms attributively adjoined to 'apple' depends on pointing just as did the use of 'this' or 'that': no less and no more" (WO, 163).

Singular descriptions share a feature with some other kinds of singular terms, namely, the feature of being built upon general terms. Thus, class names like 'dogkind' are formed by suffixing '-kind' to general terms in substantival form or by prefixing 'the class of' to pluralized substantivals: thus 'the class of dogs'. Another kind of singular term built upon general terms is the attribute name, e.g., 'blueness'. These terms are formed by suffixing '-ness' or '-ity' to general terms in adjectival form and by inflecting infinitively or gerundively a general term in verbal form: thus 'to be a dog'. Also, there are relation names like 'nextness', 'giving', etc. Just as we standardized the occurrences of indefinite singular terms and the predicates following them, we can also standardize the occurrences of the four kinds of definite singular terms just mentioned and their predicates. Thus, the singular description becomes 'the F', or

(3) The object x such that . . . x . . . .

The class name (or class abstraction) becomes 'the class of F', or

(4) The class of objects x such that . . . x . . . .

The attribute name (or attribute abstraction) becomes 'to be an F', or

(5) To be an object x such that . . . x . . . .

And the relation name (or relation abstraction) becomes

(6) To be objects x and y such that . . . x . . . y . . . .

Also, just as 'Something is an object x such that' and 'Everything is an object x such that' were conventionally defined by '$(\exists x)$' and '(x)', respectively, so those portions of (3)–(6) prior to the first ellipses can be abbreviated as '$(\imath x)$', '$\hat{x}$', 'x' and 'xy'. Further, just as '$(\exists x)$' and '(x)' are variable binding operators attaching to sentences to produce sentences, for example '$(\exists x)$ (. . . x . . .)' and '(x) (. . . x . . .)', so these four variable binding operators attach to sentences to produce singular terms. Thus, we can write '$(\imath x)$ (. . . x . . .)', '$\hat{x}$ (. . . x . . .)', '$x[$ . . . x . . . $]$', and '$xy[$ . . . x . . . y . . . $]$' in place of (3)–(6). These latter two expressions are abstraction notations for *intensions*:

> monadic intensions, or attributes, and dyadic intensions, or relations. In the same spirit we might adopt simply the brackets without prefix to express abstraction of medadic (O-adic) intensions, or propositions; thus '[Socrates is mortal]' would amount to the words 'that Socrates is mortal', or 'Socrates's being mortal', when these are taken as referring to a proposition. (WO, 164–65)

However, even these five classes of definite singular terms will admit of reduction. Thus, (4), the class name, can be reduced to a singular description by explicating '$\hat{x}$ (. . . x . . .)' as:

(7) $(\imath y)$ (x) $(x \in y$ if and only if . . . x . . . $)$.

For example, the class name 'the class of dogs', or '$\hat{x}(Dx)$', can be explicated as the singular description 'the object y is such that everything (which) is an object x (is) such that x is a member of (the object) y if and only if (the object) x is a dog', or '$(\imath y)$ (x) $(x \in y$ if and only if $Dx)$'. This singular description uniquely determines its object of reference, y, by claiming that objects which are members of (the class) y are all and only those objects which comprise the extension of the general term 'is a dog'. The extension of a general term is the class of all those objects of which the term is true, and the description claims that the members of (the class) y and the members of the class which constitutes the extension of 'is a dog' are the same members. And, since two classes are identical if and only if they contain the same members (viz., $(x = y)$ if and only if $(z) [(x \in z)$ if and only if $(y \in z)])$, the class y and the extension of 'is a dog' are identical. So the singular description uniquely specifies the same (extensional) object as the class name and thereby serves a parallel function of the class name.

However, this method of explication just used to eliminate class names will not work for eliminating intensional abstraction. For, unlike classes, two attributes are not regarded as identical simply because both are possessed by all and only the same objects, nor are two relations regarded as identical simply because they relate all and only the same objects. Thus, for example, the attribute name 'to be an object x such that x has doghood' cannot be eliminated by explicating it as the singular description

(8) $(\imath y) (x) (x$ has y if and only if x has doghood$)$,

which can be read as 'the object y is such that everything (which) is an object x (is) such that x has (the object) y if and only if (the object) x has doghood'. But (8), unlike (7), does not uniquely specify its object of reference, since merely claiming that only the same objects have y and have doghood does not clinch the identity of y and doghood. This does not mean, however, that intensional abstraction cannot be explicated. Indeed, it can, and in all three forms: attribute names, relation names, and proposition names. However, before these explications can be introduced we need to examine some prefatory moves of regimentation. For example, we need to see how 'purely referential position' can be defined for variables, and we need to examine some of the more rudimentary explications of singular terms.

In §3.5.1.1 we defined 'purely referential position' for *definite singular terms* relative to predication and relative to other definite singular terms by reference to the criterion of the substitutivity of identity. Then, since *indefinite singular terms* can occupy the same positions, we extended the definition to cover them also. Thus, derivatively, we can speak of variables in referential position even though, unlike definite singular terms, they do not name (nor even purport to name).

However, it should be pointed out that the substitutivity criterion can be trained upon the variables directly, without prior talk of definite singular terms, for the substitutivity of identity can be stated with variables as a quantified conditional:

(9) (x) (y) (if $x = y$ and . . . x . . . then . . . y . . .).

In this conditional ' . . . x . . .' stands for the sentences in which 'x' is said to have purely referential position. This ability to define 'purely referential position' independently of singular terms is of some import since Quine plans eventually to eliminate from the most austere form of the canonical notation all singular terms (other than variables), including names, singular descriptions, intensional abstractions, time, indicator words, and algebraic expressions. But, at the same time, referential position will be retained. These singular terms are eliminated because of the kinks they bring to logical theory. Let us examine some of these kinks or problems so that we might better appreciate the explication, and therefore elimination, of these terms.

In the sentence 'Pegasus is a winged horse' it would appear that the name 'Pegasus' occupies purely referential position, since it enjoys the position of a singular term under predication. However, the whole idea behind purely referential position is connected with the notion that terms that occupy such a position are used purely to specify their objects for the rest of the sentence to say something about. And, for those of us who know that 'Pegasus' fails to specify an object, it seems clearly mistaken to grant the status of purely referential position to 'Pegasus' in 'Pegasus is a winged horse'. Furthermore, if 'Pegasus' fails to specify an object, then the sentence 'Pegasus is a winged horse' is neither true nor false; it is said to suffer a truth value gap. Therefore, definite singular terms that lack objects threaten the intelligibility of purely referential position, and they enter predications that appear to be either true or false but are, in fact, neither.

These problems might be settled by different measures than the elimination from the canonical notation of singular terms other than variables, but this issue is aggravated by one more consideration, namely, the multifarious extranotational considerations that figure in determining whether a particular expression refers or not. Since *knowing* that 'Pegasus' does not refer to an object varies from person to person, a canonical notation that allows such expressions the status of termhood is burdened with making notational stipulations relative to each user of the notation. For the sake of simplifying our logical theory, a better measure seems to be the wholesale elimination of these troublesome expressions. This is especially true in light of the uniform manner available for regimenting all singular terms other than variables to predicative position. Where 'a' is a singular term other than a variable, and ' . . . a . . .' is any sentence containing 'a' in purely referential position, we can, by the substitutivity of identity, i.e. by (9), obtain

(10) (x) (if $x = a$ and . . . x . . . then . . . a . . .),

which is equivalent, by elementary quantification theory, to

(11) If $(\exists x)$ $(x = a$ and . . . x . . .) then . . . a . . . .

Conversely, we may obtain

(12) If . . . a . . . then $(\exists x)$ $(x = a$ and . . . x . . .);

for, if . . . a . . . then $a = a$ and . . . a . . . . (11) and (12) combine to show that ' . . . a . . .' is equivalent to '$(\exists x)$ $(x = a$ and . . . x . . .)', which contains 'a' only in the position of ' $= a$'. This demonstration shows that purely referential occurrences of singular terms other than variables can be got down to the type of ' $= a$' (*see* WO, 178). Thus, the same singular terms that gave problems in connection with purely referential position and in connection with truth value gaps (e.g. 'Pegasus') can be maneuvered into a standard position: ' $=$ Pegasus'. ' $=$ Pegasus', taken as a whole, is, in effect, a predicate and thus a general term; and general terms do not raise the problems just noted with singular terms. "What suggests itself is that ' $=$ Pegasus', ' $=$ mama', ' $=$ Socrates', etc. be parsed anew as indissoluble general terms, no separate recognition of singular terms 'Pegasus', 'mama', 'Socrates', etc. being needed for other positions" (WO, 178–79). Quine's general explanation of this move is as follows:

The equation '$x = a$' is reparsed in effect as a predication '$x = a$' where ' $= a$' is a verb, the 'F' of 'Fx'. Or look at it as follows. What was in words 'x is Socrates' and in symbols '$x = $ Socrates' is now in words still 'x is Socrates', but the 'is' ceases to be treated as a separate relative term '$=$'. The 'is' is now treated as a copula which, as in 'is mortal' and 'is a man', serves merely to give a general term the form of a verb and so suit it to predicative position. 'Socrates' becomes a general term that is true of just one object, but general in being treated henceforward as grammatically admissible in predicative position and not in positions suitable for variables. It comes to play the role of the 'F' of 'Fa' and ceases to play that of the 'a'. (WO, 179)

This reparsing of names as general terms depends upon the theorem of confinability explained above, i.e., upon the theorem confining singular terms to the position of 'a' in '$= a$'. But, since the theorem only applies to purely referential uses of terms, what bearing, it may be asked, does this method have on sentences like 'Pegasus is a winged horse', where the name 'Pegasus' does not refer? Well, 'Pegasus is a winged horse' can be paraphrased as '$(\exists x)$ (x is Pegasus and x is a winged horse)' in which 'is Pegasus' is reparsed as a general term, which is true of nothing, and thus the sentence is always false. So the problems of the intelligibility of purely referential position and of truth value gaps can be eliminated in one systematic stroke. We should remind ourselves, however, that our explication does not make a synonymy claim. The explicatum is an acceptable paraphrase as long as it fulfills the needs for which the explicandum was required and as long as it is consistent with the aims of regimentation (i.e., the thesis of extensionality). However, if the paraphrase "happens incidentally to produce sense where the original suffered a truth-value gap and so was wanted for no purpose, we may just let the added cases turn out as they will. . . . Such waste cases, . . . don't cares, are a frequent feature of good paraphrases" (WO, 182).

Singular descriptions, like names, sometimes suffer truth value gaps. Thus, if the sentence ' . . . x . . .' of a description '$(\imath x)$ (. . . x . . .)' is fulfilled by more than one object x or by none, then any sentence that contains the description in referential position can be neither true nor false and, therefore, suffers a truth value gap. Elimination of singular descriptions in favor of some construction that does not suffer truth value gaps is desirable. In order to see how this is possible, compare the identity

(13) $y = (\imath x)$ (. . . x . . .)

with the quantification

(14) (x) (. . . x . . . if and only if $x = y$).

[(14) may be abbreviated as ' . . . y . . . and y only'.] Presumably, if either (13) or (14) is true of an object y, then both are. However, if (13) is not true of one object y (which could happen if there were no object y fitting the description, or if there were more than one object y fitting the description), then it is merely innocent of truth value, rather than false. On the other hand, under those same conditions (14) would be false. So explicating (13) as (14) has the logically desirable effect of filling all of the truth value gaps of (13) with falsity. Thanks to the theorem of confinability of singular terms, which allows us to limit the occurrences of any singular terms other than variables to occurrences as right-hand members of equations (e.g., ' = Pegasus'), and thanks to our ability to paraphrase existence sentences like 'Pegasus exists' as '($\exists$x) (x is Pegasus)', we can easily eliminate *all* occurrences of singular descriptions in favor of quantifications. "Where the term is '($\imath$x) (. . . x . . .)', we have thereafter only to paraphrase the equations and the existence sentence away by paraphrasing 'y = ($\imath$x) (. . . x . . .)' as ' . . . y . . . and y only', . . . and '($\imath$x) (. . . x . . .) exists' as '($\exists$y) (. . . y . . . and y only)'" (WO, 184).

Another class of singular terms to be explicated is the class of algebraic type terms like '$x + y$'. Terms of this type can be reduced to descriptions by adopting an appropriate relative term in place of each algebraic operation.

> For example, to get rid of ' + ' we adopt a triadic relative term 'Σ' and reckon 'Σwxy' as true when and only when $w = x + y$; thenceforward we can render anything of the form '$a + b$', however complex the terms represented by 'a' and 'b', as '($\imath$w) Σwab'. What this reduction amounts to is a reparsing of the ' = ' and ' + ' of '$w = x + y$' as a simple triadic relative term; the 'Σ' is only for vividness. (WO, 184)

Other instances of algebraic expression can be dealt with in the same way.

Let us return now to the problem of explicating intensional abstraction. Instead of viewing the brackets '[ ]' of propositional abstraction as an operator that applies to a sentence to form a singular term and then viewing ' = ' of '$a = [p]$' as a relative term that applies to the two singular terms 'a' and '$[p]$' to form a sentence, we can, following the pattern established for the algebraic expressions, reparse ' =[ ]' as an irreducible operator that applies outright to 'a' and 'p' to form a sentence '$a =[p]$'. This operator, ' =[ ]', can be written for vividness as 'O', so that '$a = [p]$' becomes 'aOp'; then the old '$[p]$' comes out as '($\imath$w) (wOp)'. Attribute abstraction can be dealt with similarly by "reparsing '$a = x [. . . x . . .]$' as formed by an irreducible two-place variable-binding operator in the fashion 'aO_x (. . . x . . .)'; then the old 'x[. . . x . . .]' comes out as '($\imath w$) (wO_x(. . . x . . .))'. Similarly for the abstraction of relations" (WO, 185). This treatment of the constructions of intentional abstraction is part of Quine's program for reducing singular terms to variables. However, this treatment can be avoided altogether by not recognizing the various forms of intentional abstraction as genuine singular terms in the first place, and it is this latter approach which Quine ultimately opts for.

There is but one further type of singular term, other than variables, which remains to be explicated and eliminated. These are the indicator words, and we shall discuss them when we talk about the canonical notation and tense. Right now, we shall turn our attention to general terms and to their confinement to predicative position.

Where canonical notation is relaxed, leaving unanalyzed components like 'is eating' or 'is next to', etc., usually depends upon the purpose at hand. Typically, however, what remains unanalyzed has the form of a general term. Moreover, this residual general term regularly ends up in predicative position. Witness, for example, the confinement of the general terms to predicative position in the following paraphrases:

(15) I now have a dog,
     ($\exists x$) (x is a dog and I now have x);

(16) Every dog barks,
     (x) (if x is a dog then x barks);

(17) Paul and Elmer are sons of colleagues,
     ($\exists x$) ($\exists y$) (Paul is son of x and Elmer is son of y and x is a colleague of y);

(18) I now hear lions,
     ($\exists x$) (x is a lion and I now hear x and ($\exists y$) ($y \neq x$ and y is a lion and I now hear y)).

Occurrences of general terms in singular terms like the singular description 'the F' and the attribute name 'to be an F' are likewise resolved into predicative position in '($\imath x$) (Fx)' and '$x[Fx]$'. Some types of occurrences of general terms like 'F of b' (e.g., 'brother of Abel') and 'FG' (e.g., 'red ball') can be reduced to constructions where the composite general terms can be dissolved. Thus '(F of b)x' becomes 'Fxb' and '(FG)x' becomes 'Fx and Gx', where the components end up in predicative position. Similar moves can be made for the forms '(F and G)x' and '(F or G)x', viz. 'Fx and Gx' and 'Fx or Gx'.

There remain, however, composite general terms that are not reducible to their components, for example, the application of an adverb or syncategorematic adjective to a general term, and juxtaposed substantives. The component parts of these composite terms do not reduce to predicative position, but the whole term at which paraphrasing leaves off does. For example, '*x* is a mere child' cannot be reduced to '*x* is a mere and *x* is a child', but 'is a mere child' can nevertheless be confined to predicative position as an unanalyzed whole. "In brief the point is that the only canonical position of a general term is predicative position, whatever the term's uncanonical substructure" (WO, 175).

Another move that contributes to theoretical simplicity is explicating tense distinctions by relying on indicator words. We may conveniently hold to the grammatical present as a form but treat it as temporally neutral, dropping all other tenses. Thus " 'I will not do it again' becomes 'I do not do it after now', where 'do' is taken tenselessly and the future force of 'will' is translated into a phrase 'after now', comparable to 'west of here' " (WO, 170). Time is thus treated on a par with space. In fact, Quine conceives of time as a dimension of physical objects. Physical objects (which are discussed in detail in §3.5.2.2) are, more or less, four-dimensional slices of space-time, and "are not to be distinguished from events or, in the concrete sense of the term, processes. Each comprises simply the content, however heterogeneous, of some portion of space-time, however disconnected and gerrymandered" (WO, 171; *note omitted*).

In the canonical notation, tense is to be eliminated in favor of such temporal qualifiers as 'now', 'then', 'before *t*', 'at *t*', 'after *t*', and these only when needed. "We are to think of *t* as an epoch of any desired duration and any desired position along the time axis. Then, where *x* is a spatiotemporal object, we can construe '*x* at *t*' as naming the common part of *x* and *t*" (WO, 172; *note omitted*). Thus, 'at' is similar to the juxtaposition that forms the singular term 'red wine', for 'at' is best conceived as a juxtapositive particle joining terms for physical objects and terms for epochs, just as 'red wine' is a term formed (attributively) by juxtaposition of an adjectival and a general term, true of that portion of the world which is red at wine. The other elements of these tense constructions can be analyzed in various ways. For example, we can treat the indicator words 'now' and 'then' on par with 'I' and 'you' as singular terms. "Just as the temporary and shifting objects of reference of 'I' and 'you' are people, those of 'now' and 'then' are times or epochs. 'I now' and 'I then' mean 'I at now', 'I at then'; the custom just happens to be to omit the 'at' here, as in 'red wine' " (WO, 173; *note omitted*). Thus we have indicator words on our hands as singular terms occurring in explications of demonstrative singular terms as singular descriptions (e.g., 'this apple' as 'the apple here'), as explications of tensed verbs (e.g., 'I heard a lion' as 'I hear a lion then'), and occurring randomly in occasion sentences (like 'John is yawning now'), and in standing sentences (like 'John is here'). These indicator words can impair deductions, for when contextual cues are lacking, indicator words, with their transiency of reference, can give rise to fallacies of equivocation. Thus, their explication and, therefore, elimination is desirable. Let us examine the steps that can be taken in this regard.

When we reduced demonstrative singular terms like 'this apple' to singular descriptions like 'the apple here', we, of course, introduced indicator words in the explication—in this case the indicator word 'here'. However, when we explicated singular descriptions as quantifications, the indicator word became an irreducible part of the general term ' = the apple here'. The case is similar, if more complex, for indicator words that are introduced in connection with eliminating tensed verbs from the canonical notation. For example, 'I heard a lion' becomes 'I hear a lion at t'. 'lion at t' is to be understood, according to Quine, as a singular term true of that part of space-time which is both lion and epoch. However, it is a singular term preceded (in this case) by the indefinite particle 'a', which means that 'a lion at t' is to be regarded as an indefinite singular term which is reducible to 'some lion at t' and, thus, to the form 'some F'. Therefore, the indicator word 'then', which we initially introduced to eliminate the tensed verb 'heard', is first construed as a definite singular term, then as an indefinite singular term, and, finally, as a general term. The process of explication is something like the following:

(a) I heard a lion then.   (tensed verb: 'heard')
(b) I hear (tenselessly)   (indicator word: 'then')
    a lion then.
(c) I hear (tenselessly)   (singular term: 'lion-at-t')
    a lion-at-t.
(d) I hear (tenselessly)   (indefinite singular term: 'a-lion-
    a-lion-at-t.   at-t')
(e) I hear (tenselessly)   (reduction of indefinite singular
    some F.   term to general term)
(f) I hear (tenselessly)   (confinement of general term to
    something x such   predicative position)
    that Fx.

There are other indicator words naming spatiotemporal objects—unlike 'now' and 'then'—which need not be explicated as singular terms like 'lion at *t*' before being parsed as general terms. Such terms can be parsed directly as relative general terms predicable of times (or epochs). For example, the construction '*x* is eating *y* before *t*' straightaway becomes '$(\exists u)$ (*u* is before *t* and *x* at *u* is eating *y*)'.

Indicator words occurring in occasion sentences and standing sentences at large offer no special problems when they occur as general terms, for they can be regarded merely as irreducible particles of those terms. However, when they occur as singular terms, it can happen that the contextual cues are insufficient to fix the objects of their reference. When this happens in the communication situation we often ask for clarification in the form of additional specifications. So if the indicator word 'then' is not contextually clear in 'Bob testified then', we can require that 'then' be explicated by a more specific singular term, for example, by the singular description 'the twenty-fifth day of June, 1980'. Of course, this description may then, by the methods explained, be confined to predicative position as a general term.

This way of treating indicator words is part of Quine's general method of eternalizing sentences—a procedure designed to fix the truth of a sentence absolutely. As was noted in §2.2.1, Quine regards a sentence to be a repeatable sound pattern, or repeatedly approximable norm. Nor is truth a trait of mere sentences; it is a trait of a sentence for a person at a time. Thus, if the sentence

(19) Tom opened the door then

is believed true by some person at some time, then there must be, no matter how inadequately singled out, some particular Tom and some particular door at issue. The sentence can be eternalized by supplying Tom's surname, address, and other details, and by specifying where the door is and what time is intended. Any standing sentence can become an eternal sentence "when times, places, or persons concerned are objectively indicated rather than left to vary with the references of first names, incomplete descriptions, and indicator words" (WO, 193–94). This technique, of course, is not intended to take the place of explicating tensed verbs from the sentences of the canonical notation. Rather, it is to be used in conjunction with it.

This concludes our discussion of Quine's recommendations for eliminating all singular terms other than variables from the most austere version of his canonical notation. As we have seen, he recommends that simple singular terms (such as proper names) be reparsed as general terms; he recommends that demonstrative singular terms, class names, proposition names, attribute names, relation names, and algebraic-type terms, be explicated as singular descriptions. These singular descriptions are, in turn, to be explicated as quantifications wherein the only terms are variables and general terms (confined to predicative position). Further, he recommends that indicator words be explicated as quantifications, or, in some cases, directly as general terms. "Thus evidently nothing stands in the way of our making a clean sweep of singular terms altogether, with the sole exception of the variables themselves" (WO, 185; *note omitted*).

If Quine's recommendations were followed, then it would be possible to limit the basic constructions of the developing canonical notation to just three: predication (composed of general terms and variables, sometimes quantified, sometimes not), universal quantification (or existential quantification), and truth functions (reducible to one: Scheffer's stroke, ' $\downarrow$ ', or 'neither . . . x . . . nor . . . y . . . '). Nevertheless, it is very important to realize that "none of the eliminations of singular terms . . . eliminated objects" (WO, 192). For example, when we explicate sentences like 'Pegasus exists' as '($\exists x$) (x is Pegasus)', and sentences like 'Tom is tall' as '($\exists x$) (x is Tom and x is tall)', the objects, if any, referred to by 'Pegasus' and 'Tom' in the original sentences are likewise being referred to by the quantifiers in their paraphrases. In particular, earlier, when we reconstrued the expression '$a = [p]$' as being formed by applying the irreducible operator ' = [ ]' (abbreviated by 'O') to 'a' and to 'p' outright (viz., 'aOp') instead of 'a' and '[p]' being related by a relative term ' = ', we did not thereby eliminate the proposition [p] from the inhabitants of the universe alluded to in the 'everything' and 'something' of '(x)' and '($\exists x$)': "The object x concerned in the notation 'xOp' that supplanted '$x = [p]$' is still the proposition [p], nameless though it be forevermore." Similar remarks hold for attributes and relations: they all remain (if they ever were) within the range of values of the bound variables of the relevant quantifications, despite the fact that they are now nameless.[8]

8. Quine has been persistently misunderstood by critics on this point. As he has rightly pointed out (cf. WO, 192 n.1), one source of this misunderstanding is a confusion over the meaning of the expression 'values of the variables of quantification.' Some readers misinterpret the phrase to mean 'singular terms' rather than 'objects designated by singular terms' (actually, the range of values may even include more things than are nameable). This misinterpretation leads them to the erroneous conclusion that

Since Quine finds the admission of intensional objects such as propositions, attributes, and relations into the range of values of the bound variables of quantification an unwelcome event, for reasons to be given below, he recommends that we withdraw our earlier recognition of proposition abstraction, attribute abstraction, and relation abstraction, as singular terms. In doing so, of course, we unburden ourselves of the tedious business of paraphrasing '$[p]$', '$x[\ldots x \ldots]$', and '$xy [\ldots x \ldots y \ldots]$'as the descriptions '$(\imath w) (wOp)$', '$(\imath w) (wO_x (\ldots x \ldots))$', and '$(\imath w) (wO_{xy} (\ldots x \ldots y \ldots))$', and, eventually, as quantifications. But this withdrawing of recognition of the singular-term status for proposition abstraction, attribute abstraction, and relation abstraction can be exercised only if we are also willing and able to rid the universe of intensional objects. e.g., propositions, attributes, and relations. This is exactly what Quine desires. His justification for eliminating intensional objects is predicated upon two lines of argumentation. First, he issues a battery of persuasive arguments contending that the needs for which intensional objects have been posited are either false needs or else needs which can be fulfilled by positing less objectionable entities, i.e., entities that are readily identified and individuated. For example, the needs for propositions that have arisen in connection with discussions of translation, synonymy, truth, modal logics, meanings, and objects of the propositional attitudes are, according to Quine, false needs stemming from misconceptions and confusions regarding these topics. Moreover, some of the legitimate philosophical needs for objects can be met by sentences instead of propositions, general terms instead of attributes, and ordered pairs instead of relations. Second, Quine argues that intensional objects cannot be individuated—that is, there is no acceptable principle of individuation, no acceptable principle of identity, for intensional objects. (These two lines of argument will be taken up in §3.5.1.5, §3.5.1.6, and §3.5.1.7.)

§3.5.1.4   *Quinian analysis*

We have seen in the preceding pages what the nature of explication is and the role explication plays in the regimentation of English. The

---

the elimination of singular terms other than variables is an elimination of *values of the variables of quantification*, and hence of objects. This misunderstanding appears to be the basis for the charge made by some of Quine's critics that his program of paraphrase is trivial or even silly because it makes ontic decisions purely an arbitrary matter of grammar.

three phases of Quinian analysis—grammatical analysis (§1.3), simple paraphrase (§3.5.1.1), and explication (§3.5.1.2)—combine to constitute a program of regimentation issuing forth a canonical notation that is composed only of predication, quantification, truth functions, variables, and general terms (§3.5.1.3):

> What thus confronts us as a scheme for systems of the world is that structure so well understood by present-day logicians, the logic of quantification or calculus of predicates. . . . (WO, 228)

> It is in spirit a philosophical doctrine of categories, except that it is peculiarly relative in its import. Of itself it sets no limits to the vocabulary of unanalyzed general terms admissible to science. But it sets limits to the ways of deriving complex predicates . . . from those undictated components. It is a doctrine that limits what can be said of things to (*a*) such "prime traits" or general terms as may be expressly admitted severally on merits beyond this doctrine's purely relativistic concerns, and (*b*) such "derivative traits" as can be formulated in those primary terms with help of predication, quantification, and truth functions alone. It delimits what counts as scientifically admissible construction, and declares that whatever is not thus constructible from given terms must either be conceded the status of one more irreducibly given term or eschewed. The doctrine is philosophical in its breadth, however continuous with science in its motivation. (WO, 228–29)

One of the primary functions of such a canonical notation is that of serving as a means for making perspicuous the ontic commitments of a theory. All one would have to do in order to become clear about what reference is being made by the terms of any theory is to paraphrase (explicate) the sentences of the theory into the symbols of the canonical notation. So if a true sentence of a particular theory of psychology, say, contained the expression 'mind', and if, when paraphrased into the canonical notation, the sentence remained true only if we admitted minds as objects within the range of values of the bound variables of the new sentence, then and only then can we say: (a) the expression 'mind' is to be looked upon as a general term, (b) the theory of which the sentence is a part is committed to the existence of minds as objects, and (c) anyone maintaining that the sentence is true would ipso facto be committed to the existence of minds as objects. It is in this sense that the canonical notation serves as a criterion for determining the ontological commitments of a theory; it serves as a means for making clear what a theory says there is.

According to Quine, the central question of ontology, 'What exists?', is more clearly stated as the question 'What is there?'. In a way, this is another instance of explication, for the purpose of supplanting 'exists' in the original formulation of the question with a term (e.g. 'is') having a relevant, partial, parallel function is to eliminate needless philosphical usages that have become associated with 'exists' but not with 'is'. The move is a welcome one for it evades the philosophical gambit of claiming that 'exists' is used in various senses in 'Quine exists', 'Pegasus exists', 'Number exists', etc. (cf. WTI).

The task of answering this question of what there is belongs both to the scientist and to the philosopher, but the philosopher's task is the more general. Given physical objects, the scientist is the one to decide whether there are wombats and unicorns. Similarly, given classes, or numbers, or whatever objects mathematicians need, it is up to mathematicians to say whether in particular there are any even prime numbers, etc. However, the philosopher's task deals with the more general question of whether there are physical objects, classes, numbers, etc. His "is the task of making explicit what had been tacit, and precise what had been vague; of exposing and resolving paradoxes, smoothing kinks, looping off vestigial growths, clearing ontological slums" (WO, 275). And it is no secret, at this point, as to how the philosopher is to go about his task: he applies the methods of Quinian analysis to everyday language, regimenting its terms and constructions to yield a canonical notation of the appropriate austerity. And, adhering to this notation, the objects which the philosopher admits are just those objects which he recognizes as belonging to the universe of values over which the bound variables of quantification are considered to range. "Such is simply the intended sense of the quantifiers '(x)' and '$(\exists x)$': 'every object x is such that', 'there is an object x such that'. The quantifiers are encapsulations of these specially selected, unequivocally referential idioms of ordinary language" (WO, 242).

In a sense, the canonical notation is useful in settling the "form" that a theory may take but not its "content." Here I am thinking of "form" in the sense of "grammatical form." The "content" (i.e., the objects and the predicates—the ontology and ideology) of the theory is dependent upon how particular sentences of the theory are paraphrased into the canonical notation. For example, if certain sentences are paraphrased in such ways that the values of the bound variables of the paraphrases range over propositions, attributes, relations, numbers, and classes, then the "content" of the theory includes propositions, attributes, relations, and the like as objects. Obviously, the problem of how to paraphrase a given sentence into the canonical notation is not settled by reference to the canonical notation alone. The canonical notation only settles the "form" of the constructions that paraphrases must take; it does not also establish the range of the values of the bound variables of the paraphrases. (Strictly speaking, the canonical notation settles more than the form of acceptable constructions. It also settles the logic of a theory by restricting inferences from one sentence to another to just those allowable by the theory of truth functions and quantification.) Thus the question for the philosopher, once he has a canonical notation at his disposal, is: on what independent grounds can competing paraphrases be adjudicated? That is, assuming our discourse includes sentences containing the defective noun 'sake', how can we decide whether these sentences should be paraphrased such that the values of the bound variables range over sakes as objects? Should

(1) July 4th is celebrated for the sake of patriotism

be paraphrased as

(2) $(\exists x)\ (\exists y)\ (x$ is July 4th and x is celebrated for y and y is the sake of patriotism),

or as

(3) $(\exists x)\ (x$ is July 4th and x is celebrated for the sake of patriotism)?

The problem of whether to admit sakes as objects is clarified by making *semantic ascent*. This is the technique of talking about *words* rather than about any *objects* allegedly denoted by the words. Thus, instead of debating whether sakes are objects or not in order to determine which paraphrase is desirable, the philosopher can ask whether the expression 'sake' occurs in the discourse of the theory as a full-fledged term or not—hence the shift from the talk of objects to the talk of words. The question of treating sakes as objects is thus reduced (or so it seems) to the question of treating 'sake' as a term. However:

> Even a superficially termlike occurrence is no proof of term-hood, failing systematic interplay with the key idioms generally. Thus we habitually say 'for the sake of', with 'sake'

> seemingly in term position, and never thereby convict our-
> selves of positing any such objects as sakes, for we do not
> bring the rest of the apparatus to bear: we never use 'sake' as
> antecedent of 'it', nor do we predicate 'sake' of anything.
> 'Sake' figures in effect as an invariable fragment of a preposi-
> tion 'for the sake of', or 'for 's sake'. (WO, 236)

We may be perceived, therefore, to have posited sakes as objects only
when we have brought 'sake' into suitable interplay with the whole
distinctively objectificatory apparatus of the language of the theory: articles and pronouns and the idioms of identity, plurality, and predication—or, in the canonical notation, quantification. To paraphrase (1)
as (2) is to accord 'sake' the status of a full-fledged term, which it is
not ordinarily. Therefore, the better paraphrase of (1) seems to be (3),
which relegates 'sake' to the position of an irreducible nonreferential
particle of a prepositional phrase.

However, as we have already seen in connection with the defective
noun 'ordered pair', failure of full-fledged termhood is *not* a sufficient
reason for the wholesale relegating of such expressions to the status of
particles rather than terms. On the contrary, Quine took steps to ensure
that 'ordered pair' was accorded all of the dignities of a term when he
explicated it by recourse to classes. Consequently, there must be another standard that comes to bear upon the business of determining
which defective nouns are to be paraphrased in the manner of 'ordered
pair'. This other standard is what Quine calls *utility for theory* or *systematic efficacy*. In short, the doctrine is a pragmatic one, which emphasizes the utility of treating an expression in the one way rather than
in the other. And, while no evident purpose is served by treating 'sake'
as a term, certain purposes are served by treating 'ordered pair' as
a term (e.g., explicating relations as ordered pairs). The question
whether to treat an expression as a term or as a particle is indeed a
"question whether to give it general access to positions appropriate to
general terms, or perhaps to singular terms, subject to the usual laws of
such contexts. Whether to do so may reasonably be decided by considerations of systematic efficacy, utility for theory" (WO, 236–37).

We have now examined, in some detail, the method of Quinian analysis. We first looked at the anatomy of the method and found it con-
sisted of three closely related activities: grammatical analysis (§1.3),
simple paraphrase (§3.5.1.1), and explication (§3.5.1.2). Further, we
found that the method facilitated the regimentation of everyday lan-

guage (or, more specifically, English) into the form of a purely extensional canonical notation consisting of quantifiers, truth functions, variables, and predicates (§3.5.1.3): Quinian analysis is the *means* of
regimentation and the canonical notation is the *product* of regimentation. In addition to examining the anatomy of the method, we inquired
into the *motivation* behind its construction and also into the *utility* of
its product. We found that the motivating force behind Quinian analysis is, in particular, the desire to rid everyday English of anomalies and
conflicts implicit within its referential apparatus—anomalies and conflicts which tend to hinder communication, cripple deduction, obfus-
cate ontic commitments, and confound the construction of theories
generally—and is, in general, the desire to construct an extensional
language adequate for the purposes of science. Also, we found that the
utility of the product of Quinian analysis, the canonical notation, lay in
its propensity to facilitate deductions and to clarify concepts, as well as
in its ability to make clear the ontic commitments of theories about the
world—i.e., of scientific and philosophical theories about what there
is. So much for Quinian analysis; let us now turn to the promised
examination of Quine's arguments in favor of dispensing with intensional objects.

§3.5.1.5 *Propositions*

Quine has isolated four apparent needs that have prompted philosophers to posit *propositions*: (1) the need for translational constants; (2)
the need for constants of philosophical analysis; (3) the need for truth
vehicles; and (4) the need for objects of the propositional attitudes. He
contends that none of these apparent needs justifies the positing of
propositions.

§3.5.1.5.1 *As translational constants*

Propositions have sometimes been posited as entities that facilitate or
justify the translation of the sentences of one language *uniquely* into
sentences of another language. Thus, 'Il pleut' is uniquely translatable
as 'It is raining' because both sentences express (somehow) the *same*
proposition.

However, Quine thinks it a mistake to believe that the notion of propositions as shared meanings (or objectively valid translation relations)
adds any clarity to our understanding of the enterprise of translation.
The truth is that in translating from scratch, all one has to go on is the
observed behavior of the speakers in question. And, as we noted in

connection with the discussion of radical translation, the totality of verbal dispositions is compatible with alternative sentence-to-sentence translations so different from one another that translations of standing sentences under two such systems can differ in point of truth value. The positing of propositions only serves to obscure the fact that this indeterminacy can occur: "The notion of proposition seems to facilitate talk of translation precisely because it falsifies the nature of the enterprise. It fosters the pernicious illusion of there being a uniquely correct standard of translation of eternal sentences" (WO, 208). Were it not for the indeterminacy of translation "we could hope to define in behavioral terms a general relation of sentence synonymy suited to translational needs, and our objection to propositions themselves would thereby be dissipated" (WO, 207). Insofar, then, as Quine's rejection of propositions as translational constants turns upon the indeterminacy of translation, it also turns upon the naturalistic-behavioristic conception of language, since, as we noted earlier, the indeterminacy of translation itself is a natural consequence of the NB conception of language.

§3.5.1.5.2   *As constants of philosophical analysis*

Quine argues that it is no less a mistake to suppose that the notion of propositions as shared meanings clarifies the paraphrastic enterprise of philosophical analysis. "On the contrary, . . . synonymy claims would generally be out of place in such connections even if the notion of synonymy as such were in the best of shape" (WO, 208). Quine is making two points about what he calls philosophical analysis: (1) because of the indeterminacy of translation there is no hope in the various instances of philosophical analysis of finding *analysanda* and *analysantia* that necessarily express the same proposition; (2) usually the philosophical analysis of some statement or concept is motivated by some ambiguity, vagueness, or other bothersome trait of the *analysanda* that is not wanted carried over into the *analysantia*. In short, for Quine, philosophical analysis (or explication) is not a quest for synonymy. Rather, in his view, explication is elimination—elimination of bothersome traits of expressions and constructions. Hence there is no need to posit propositions as shared meanings in order to explain the nature of philosophical analysis.

Judging from Quine's remark last quoted, he would maintain his view of philosophical analysis as explication even if synonymy were made behaviorally respectable. Thus, it cannot be claimed that Quine's view of philosophical analysis, insofar as it shuns synonymy, does so

for reasons of indeterminacy. In short, it cannot be claimed that explication is based on the NB conception of language. Nevertheless, if the
NB conception of language is true, and as a result the indeterminacy
thesis is true, then any program of philosophical analysis that did seek
synonymous *analysanda* and *analysantia* would be misguided.

§3.5.1.5.3   *As truth vehicles*

Propositions have sometimes been introduced as truth vehicles. One
reason for this is that it is felt that sentences (even declarative sentences) are not the kind of things that are true or false. What kind of
things are true or false, then? A typical analysis of the matter goes like
this: Take the declarative sentence 'That is my book'. Now this sentence token is just so many marks on paper, and marks on paper are
neither true nor false. However, marks on paper can have a meaning.
The meaning of the sentence type (of which the above token is an instance) is roughly: the book in question belongs to the speaker. Is this
meaning, then, what is true or false? No, for suppose that Tom utters
the sentence in question while pointing to his Plato volume, and suppose also that John utters the sentence in question while pointing to the
same volume. Let us suppose further that the Plato volume belongs to
Tom, and not to John. Since both Tom and John uttered tokens of the
same type, thereby expressing the same meaning (namely, the book in
question belongs to the speaker), but what Tom said was true and what
John said was false, and since a particular truth vehicle — whatever its
precise nature turns out to be — cannot be at the same time both true
and false, it follows that what is true or false are not meanings. Both
Tom and John used tokens of the same type, with a single meaning, to
make different assertions; the difference between the two occasions of
utterance must lie, therefore, in what each *asserted*. It is this notion of
assertion that we can identify with the proposition, the thing that is the
bearer of truth and falsity.[9]

Now this analysis can be simplified and made more plausible in
one motion if we do away with talking of the meanings of sentences
like 'That is my book' and just talk of the meanings of eternal sentences, i.e., sentences whose indicator words have been replaced by
names, dates, times, places, and whose verbs are read as tenseless.
Thus, Tom's utterance of 'That is my book' and John's utterance of it

9. This fairytale analysis comes in large part from *Logic: A Comprehensive Introduction* by Samuel D. Guttenplan and Martin Tamny (New York: Basic Books Inc.,
1971), pp. 12f.

would be eternalized *differently* and would, therefore, have different meanings, and these meanings are what the previous analysis called assertions or propositions. We simply do not recognize meanings (of declarative sentences) now, apart from the propositions themselves. On either analysis, however, the proposition and not the sentence is the truth bearer. But perhaps we can simplify and clarify matters further still:

> instead of appealing here to propositions, or meanings of eternal sentences, there is no evident reason not to appeal simply to the eternal sentences themselves as truth vehicles. If we undertake to specify the proposition "expressed" by the utterance of some non-eternal sentence, e.g. 'The door is open', on some particular occasion, we do so by bracketing some eternal sentence that means the proposition; thus we have had to compose an appropriate eternal sentence anyway, and we could as well stop there. (WO, 208)

Quine's recommendation that we stop with the eternal sentence presupposes that we have a specifiable way of expanding the utterance of noneternal sentences into eternal ones. To put the matter vaguely, this procedure would be much like the activity of paraphrasing ordinary language into logical symbols. The method is patently pragmatic: If a paraphrase can be made to serve the purpose in the logic for which the ordinary language expression was wanted, then the paraphrase is adequate—there is no claim of synonymy. Similarly, "the eternal sentence will be one that the original speaker could have uttered in place of his original utterance in those original circumstances without detriment, so far as he could foresee, to the project he was bent on. I need hardly say that there is scope here for refinement, but let it not be supposed that acquiescence in talk of expressed propositions provides it" (WO, 208).

§3.5.1.5.4   *As objects of propositional attitudes*

Propositions have sometimes been introduced as objects of the attitudinal verbs. For example, in 'Tom believes that Cicero denounced Catiline', what Tom is said to believe is the object, presumably a proposition, expressed by 'that Cicero denounced Catiline'. Quine's proposal in this quarter is simply to deny that there are any objects of the attitudinal verbs, propositions or otherwise. Verbs like 'believes that' are construed by Quine as constituting a new lexical category in the formal language of science, which he calls *attitudinatives* (*see* PL,

32). The attitudinatives attach grammatically to sentences to form not names of objects, e.g., propositions, but, rather, they form predicates. So in 'Tom believes that Cicero denounced Catiline' the singular term 'Tom' is predicatively attached to the general term 'believes that Cicero denounced Catiline' which, in turn, is composed of the attitudinative 'believes that' and the sentence 'Cicero denounced Catiline'. Belief constructions as well as other attitude constructions do not designate objects of any sort; they are simply predicates which may or may not be truly predicated of objects (like Tom). So, the sentence 'Tom believes that Cicero denounced Catiline' is true, if, and only if, Tom is in fact included in the extension of the predicate 'believes that Cicero denounced Catiline.'

Why does Quine take the apparently extreme position of denying the existence of the objects of the propositional attitudes (viz. beliefs, fears, wishes, hopes, etc.)? Ostensibly the problem lies with the individuation of the purported objects: the beliefs, the wishes, the fears, etc. Deeper down, the problem is the indeterminacy of translation. The intentionalist could argue that when it comes down to translating the Martian's 'gavagai' there is really no indeterminacy involved. We merely translate 'gavagai' as 'rabbit' if, and only if, the Martian is disposed to *apply* 'gavagai' to all of the things he *believes* to be rabbits. So, from the intentionalist's point of view there is a uniquely correct matter of fact to translation after all. However, the problem with this approach is, according to Quine, that 'apply' and 'believes' are just as behaviorally indeterminate as 'gavagai' is. To support his case Quine draws upon R. M. Chisholm's development of (Franz) Brentano's thesis which asserts that intentional idioms are not reducible to behavioral terms: "Evidently, then, the relativity to non-unique systems of analytical hypotheses invests not only translational synonymy but intentional notions generally. Brentano's thesis of the irreducibility of intentional idioms is of a piece with the thesis of indeterminacy of translation" (WO, 221).

It would seem, then, that there is something of an option here for the theorist:

> One may accept the Brentano thesis either as showing the indispensability of intentional idioms and the importance of an autonomous science of intention, or as showing the baselessness of intentional idioms and the emptiness of a science of intention. My attitude, unlike Brentano's, is the second. To accept intentional usage at face value is . . . to postulate trans-

lation relations as somehow objectively valid though indeterminate in principle relative to the totality of speech dispositions. Such postulation promises little gain in scientific insight if there is no better ground for it than that the supposed translation relations are presupposed by the vernacular of semantics and intention. (WO, 221)

§3.5.1.6 *Attributes and relations*

"The strictures against propositions apply with equal force to *attributes* and *relations*" (WO, 209; *my emphasis*). Just as propositions were posited as the meanings of eternal closed sentences (i.e., sentences containing no free variables), so attributes and relations might be looked upon as posited meanings of eternal open sentences (sentences containing one or more free variable); open sentences which, for each choice of values of their free variables, take on truth values independent of speaker and occasion. However, the objection to propositions on the matter of individuation applies unchanged to attributes and relations. In the case where propositions were wanted as truth vehicles, it was possible to get by without positing propositions and in their place to use eternal closed sentences. Similarly, for some of the purposes for which attributes and relations might be posited we can in their stead talk simply of open sentences and general terms. Also, we can dispense with attributes and relations as objects of the propositional attitudes.

There are further uses of attributes and relations which have no analogues among propositions. Some of these uses are important and cannot be met by merely talking of open sentences and general terms. But these further purposes for which attributes and relations are wanted are well served by classes and ordered pairs, respectively, which are like attributes and relations except for their identity conditions.

For the most part, Quine's worry with propositions, attributes, and relations is in connection with their individuation: How do we know when we have one proposition and when we have two? How do we know when one attribute or relation is different from, or identical with, some other attribute or relation? But, at a deeper level Quine's claim is stronger, for it asserts that because these idioms are *behaviorally indeterminate* there are no answers to these questions. Here, again, it is Quine's commitment to the NB conception of language which lies at the bottom of his rejection of propositions, attributes, and relations. This same commitment is the basis for his rejection of modal logic.

§3.5.1.7 *Modal logic*

Quine is very much opposed to the project of developing a logic of the so-called logical modalities 'Necessarily . . .' and 'Possibly . . .'. "Used as a logical modality, 'necessarily' imputes necessity unconditionally . . . as an absolute mode of truth; and 'possibly' denies necessity, in that sense, of the negation" (WO, 195). The grounds of Quine's opposition to modal logic (in the sense of the logical modalities just explained—modal logic in the "strict" sense, as Quine sometimes calls it) are four: (a) modal logic resulted from and is perpetuated by a conflation of use and mention; (b) unrestricted quantification into modal contexts is nonsensical; (c) restricted quantification into modal contexts results in a total collapse of modal distinctions; and (d) the cost of making quantified modal logic intelligible is acceptance of an untenable metaphysical doctrine of essentialism. Let us examine each of these points against the intelligibility of modal logic, in turn.

§3.5.1.7.1 *Conflating use and mention*

There are three points concerning modal logic and confusion over use and mention which Quine makes; they are: (a) "modern modal logic was conceived in sin: the sin of confusing use and mention" (RPM, 177); (b) "modal logic does not require confusion of use and mention" (RPM, 179); and (c) "confusion of use and mention engenders an irresistible case for modal logic" (RPM, 179). Quine's first point is historical: Modal logic was begun by C. I. Lewis in 1918. According to Lewis, sentences beginning with 'necessarily' were to be regarded true if and only if those contained sentences were, themselves, analytic. For example, the truth of the sentence

(1) Necessarily 9 > 4

is explained by saying

(2) '9 > 4' is analytic.

It is doubtful that Lewis would ever have started this if Whitehead and Russell, who followed Frege in defending Philo of Megara's version of 'If p then q' as 'Not (p and not q)', had not made the mistake of calling the Philonian construction "material implication" instead of the material conditional. Lewis protested that a material implication so defined would have to be not merely true but analytic in order to qualify as implication properly so-called. Such was his account of "strict implication."

> 'Implies' and 'is analytic' are best viewed as general terms, to be predicated of sentences by predicative attachment to names (e.g. quotations) of sentences. In this they contrast with 'not', 'and', and 'if-then', which are not terms but operators attachable to the sentences themselves. Whitehead and Russell, careless of the distinction between use and mention of expressions, wrote 'p implies q' (in the material sense) interchangeably with 'If p then q' (in the material sense). Lewis followed suit, thus writing 'p strictly implies q' and explaining it as 'Necessarily not (p and not q)'. Hence his development of a modal logic of 'necessarily' as an operator on sentences. (WO, 196)

In short, Whitehead and Russell should not have written

(3) p implies q

but, rather,

(4) 'p' implies 'q',

thereby properly indicating that 'p' and 'q' are being *mentioned* and not used; and that 'implies' is a *general term* joining singular terms to form a sentence and *not* a sentence-forming *operator* on sentences. Their failure to state the matter properly contributed to the misidentification of 'implies' with 'if-then'. And, insofar as the material conditional, 'not (p and not q)', was offered as an explication of 'if-then', it also appeared as being offered as an explication of 'implies'. But, as Lewis correctly perceived, the material conditional is inadequate as an explication of 'implies'. Unfortunately though, from Quine's perspective, Lewis's remedy carried over the same confusion of use and mention found in Whitehead and Russell. Despite all this, however, such a modal logic does not require for its conception that one become confused about the use and mention of expressions—Quine's second point, (b). But, and this is Quine's third observation, (c), when it comes to *accepting* modal logic as a legitimate undertaking, it might very well help if one did confuse the use and mention of expressions, for the arguments produced in favor of modal logic typically turn upon such confusions (*see* RPM, 177–79).

§3.5.1.7.2   *Unrestricted quantification into modal contexts*

If one is content to explicate sentences like (1) of §3.5.1.7.1 as sentences like (2) of §3.5.1.7.1, and if one is willing to accept the notion of analyticity (which, of course, Quine is not), then why is there any need for modal logic? Why not just add 'is analytic' to the lexicon of predicates, truly predicable only of analytic statements? Apparently, the answer to this is that one wants to be able to quantify into modal contexts and this would be impossible to do with sentences like (2) of §3.5.1.7.1, since quotation is an opaque construction. But is it any the more legitimate to quantify into modal contexts? Quine argues that it is not. Consider the following two sentences:

(1) Necessarily 9 > 4,

(2) Necessarily the number of major planets > 4.

Quine maintains that in any plausible interpretation (1) is true and (2) is false. And, since the only difference between (1) and (2) is that '9' occurs in (1) where 'the number of major planets' occurs in (2), and "since 9 = the number of major planets, we can conclude that the position of '9' in (1) is not purely referential and hence that the necessity operator is opaque" (WO, 197; *note omitted*). In short, quantifications like

(3) (*x*) Necessarily (*x* > 4)

are senseless; the quantifier outside the opaque context cannot bind a variable inside the opaque context. *Unrestricted* quantification into modal contexts simply does not make sense.

§3.5.1.7.3   *Restricted quantification into modal contexts*

Illustrations of opacity, such as the one given above, depend on there being objects that can be specified in different ways that are not necessarily equivalent, so that some traits are entailed with necessity under one specification of an object, but not under another specification of it. It would seem, then, that if we were to exclude all such objects from the universe of objects available as values of the variables of quantification, then we could thereby dispose of the objection to quantifying (unrestrictedly) into modal contexts. "Thus we can legitimize quantification into modal position by postulating that whenever each of two open sentences uniquely determines one and the same object *x*, the sentences are equivalent by necessity" (WO, 197). However, the adoption of this postulate restricting the range of the values of the bound variables has two undesirable if not disastrous consequences. The first is that all identities are necessary identities, which is rather odd, to say the least. The second is that every true sentence is necessarily true, and since the converse of this (i.e., every necessarily true sentence is true) also holds, it follows that modal distinctions collapse, since it would then be the case that any sentence is true if, and only if, it is necessarily true. Consequently, neither what I am calling unrestricted quantification nor restricted quantification can be implemented systematically in modal contexts. Must modal logic be given up, then?

§3.5.1.7.4   *Essentialism*

There may yet be hope for the modal logician. Clearly, the modal logician cannot adopt the postulate suggested in §3.5.1.7.3, for if he does, then all modal distinctions collapse. So the only option available, other than abandoning modal logic altogether, is to somehow work out a modified version of unrestricted quantification. According to Quine, the metaphysical view of essentialism affords just such an opportunity. Essentialism is the view that "an object, of itself and by whatever name or none, must be seen as having some of its traits necessarily and others contingently, despite the fact that the latter traits follow just as analytically from some ways of specifying the object as the former traits do from other ways of specifying it" (RM, 155). On the basis of this metaphysical doctrine, the modal logician can argue, for instance, that the number designated by '9' and by 'the number of major planets' is, of itself and independently of how it is specified, something that necessarily, not contingently, exceeds 4. Quantification into modal contexts goes through, then, despite the situation illustrated by 'Necessarily 9 > 4' and 'Necessarily the number of planets > 4'. It goes through, that is, so long as we can distinguish the essential from the accidental properties of things. Quine sees difficulties in this quarter:

> Perhaps I can evoke the appropriate sense of bewilderment as follows. Mathematicians may conceivably be said to be necessarily rational and not necessarily two-legged; and cyclists necessarily two-legged and not necessarily rational. But what of an individual who counts among his eccentricities both mathematics and cycling? Is this concrete individual necessarily rational and contingently two-legged or vice versa? Just insofar as we are talking referentially of the object, with no

special bias toward a background grouping of mathematicians as against cyclists or vice versa, there is no semblance of sense in rating some of his attributes as necessary and others as contingent. Some of his attributes count as important and others as unimportant, yes; some as enduring and others as fleeting; but none as necessary or contingent. (WO, 199)

So the acceptance of modal logic, according to Quine, depends upon also accepting a metaphysical doctrine of essentialism. But essentialism is not a doctrine that Quine can accept, given his commitment to the NB conception of language. That conception of language has led Quine to the view that what objects there are, together with their properties, is a question to be settled only relative to some theoretical framework that itself is underdetermined by experience; moreover, it is a question to be settled only relative to some translation of that theory into the canonical notation. "Relative to a particular inquiry, some predicates may play a more basic role than others, or may apply more fixedly; and these may be treated as essential" (IR, 10). But the notion of objects having essential or contingent properties in some absolute sense is, for Quine, an unintelligible metaphysical view. Consequently Quine has no use for modal logic. We may now turn our attention to the other aspect of Quine's commitment to the theses of the unity of science: physicalism.

§3.5.2 *Physicalism*

Briefly stated, physicalism is the view that whatever traits of reality are worthy of the name can be described, if at all, in terms of objective physical-state predicates. A contrary view is phenomenalism, the doctrine that statements about physical objects can be completely analyzed into statements about actual and possible sense data and logico-mathematical auxiliaries. Quine qualifies as a physicalist according to the above characterization of that view, and he has never been a phenomenalist in the sense just explained. At one time in his career, however, Quine flirted with a lesser form of phenomenalism. In some of his essays of the late 1940s and early 1950s—notably, "On What There Is" (1948), "Identity, Ostension, and Hypostasis" (1950), and "Two Dogmas of Empiricism" (1951)—Quine manifested a certain tolerance for what might be called *mitigated phenomenalism*.

In those essays he characterized the importation of physical posits into our conceptual scheme as a matter of mere convenience. Their purpose was to systematize and simplify an already intelligible (even if perhaps chaotic) stream of immediate experience. At the same time he vehemently denied that all talk about physical objects could be reduced to talk about actual and possible sense data and logico-mathematical auxiliaries. Moreover, he suggested that the phenomenalistic conceptual scheme, as opposed to the physicalistic one, is the *literal truth* about the world; physical objects were, therefore, fictions.

Quine in 1981 still believes that the importation of physical objects into our conceptual scheme is justified, ultimately, on the ground of their contributing systematic efficacy to our overall theory of the world. But he now rejects the part of his earlier view that accorded *literal truth* to the phenomenalistic conceptual scheme. The pivotal essay in this regard appears to be "On Mental Entities" (1953). In that piece Quine declared unequivocally "that it is a *mistake* to seek an immediately evident reality, somehow more immediately evident than the realm of external objects" (OME, 225; *my emphasis*). This remark compares favorably with a passage found in the clearly physicalistic section one of *Word and Object*, where Quine explained: "There is every reason to inquire into the sensory or stimulatory background of ordinary talk of physical things. The *mistake* comes only in seeking an implicit sub-basement of conceptualization, or of language" (WO, 3; *my emphasis*). Moreover, the arguments that Quine put forth in section one of *Word and Object* in support of this claim merely flesh out the bones of the arguments adumbrated seven years earlier in "On Mental Entities."

After "On Mental Entities" appeared in 1953, Quine published "The Scope and Language of Science" (1954) and "Posits and Reality" (1960). (This latter essay was actually "written about 1955 for the beginning of *Word and Object*, but eventually superseded" [PR, 246]). These three essays are early unambiguous expressions of Quine's commitment to physicalism, or, conversely, of his rejection of mitigated phenomenalism.

In the remainder of this section, I shall examine Quine's arguments against mitigated phenomenalism (§3.5.2.1) and inquire into what 'physicalism' means for Quine (§3.5.2.2). In doing so, I shall again broach the topics of naturalism, systematic efficacy, ontology, and ideology, among others.

§3.5.2.1   *The brief against phenomenalism*

As noted above, Quine never has been a phenomenalist in the sense of one who believes that all talk about physical objects can be reduced to talk about sense data and logico-mathematical auxiliaries. We have already reviewed his objections to any such program of reductionism (re: §3.4). Against that program he argued that the ideal of reductionism was ill-begotten, since it was born of an illegitimate understanding of the way individual sentences of theories relate to the world, namely, the view that every sentence of a theory has a unique set of confirming and infirming experiences associated with it. The true picture of that relation is rather, according to Quine, the holistic one; and, as we have seen, holism reduces reductionism to relativity. But this argument leaves intact the view that I have referred to as mitigated phenomenalism, the view that the sense data of which the phenomenalist speaks are the literal truth about the world, and that physical objects are therefore mere fictions. How has Quine argued against this view since 1953?

In general, the arguments and considerations that Quine levels against this form of phenomenalism add up to the claim that sense data "are neither adequate in lieu of physical objects nor helpful in addition to them" (WO, 239). Sense data are inadequate *in lieu of* physical objects in the following respects and for the following reasons. (a) Language learning requires physical objects: "Each of us learns his language from other people, through the observable mouthing of words under conspicuously intersubjective circumstances" (WO, 1). Sense data could not be used in lieu of physical objects in any realistic account of language learning. (b) A closely related point is that talk of subjective sense qualities is largely a derivative idiom, derived from talk of physical objects: "When one tries to describe a particular sensory quality, he typically resorts to reference to public things—describing a color as orange or heliotrope, a smell as like that of rotten eggs" (WO, 1). More generally:

> Even the terms which we have come to regard as strictly and immediately sensory, like 'red', are obviously objective in reference in the first instance: we learn the word 'red' by being confronted with an external object which our parent calls red. . . . When, at a certain stage of epistemological sophistication, we transfer the word 'red' to an alleged datum of immediate subjective sense experience, we are doing just what we do when we say we have a sinking sensation: I feel *as if* I were really, externally falling, and I feel *as if* I were really confronted by an external red object." (OME, 225)

(c) The quest for sense data is both prompted by and guided by a prior acceptance of physical objects: "Impressed with the fact that we know external things only mediately through our senses, philosophers from Berkeley onward have undertaken to strip away the physicalistic conjectures and bare the sense data" (WO, 1–2). But, according to Quine, the insight which motivated this quest for sense data, namely, the insight that we can know external things only through impacts on our nerve endings, "is itself based on our general knowledge of the ways of physical objects—illuminated desks, reflected light, activated retinas" (WO, 2). Furthermore, the quest is guided by the same kind of general knowledge, for as we try to isolate the sense data from the physicalistic conjectures "we find ourselves depending upon sidelong glances into natural science" (WO, 2). For example, "we may hold that the momentary data of audition are clusters of components each of which is a function of just two variables, pitch and loudness; but not without knowledge of the physical variables of frequency and amplitude in the stimulating string" (WO, 2). (d) Typical sense datum accounts of memory are inadequate: Memories are typically construed by sense datum theorists as being present, faint copies of past sense data. But such an account will not do, for even if it fits some memories, it clearly does not fit the overwhelming majority. For example, when we remember, say, the surface of a desk, we do not remember it "as a color patch extending across the lower half of the visual field; what we remember is *that* there was a desk meeting such-and-such approximate specifications of form and size in three-dimensional space. Memory is just as much a product of the past positing of extra-sensory objects as it is a datum for the positing of past sense data" (OME, 224). (e) More generally, the view that the stream of immediate experience is composed exclusively of fleeting sense data is false. Just as a person's memories are largely the product of past conceptualizations, so too one's immediate experience is largely the product of his present purposes and past conceptualizations: "immediate experience simply will not, of itself, cohere as an autonomous domain. References to physical things are largely what hold it together" (WO, 2). According to Quine:

> The contribution of reason cannot be viewed as limited merely to conceptualizing a presented pageant of experience and positing objects behind it; for this activity reacts, by selection and emphasis, on the qualitative make-up of the pageant itself in its succeeding portions. *It is not an instructive oversimplification, but a basic falsification, to represent cognition as a discern-*

ment of regularities in an unadulterated stream of experience.
Better to conceive the stream itself as polluted, at each suc-
ceeding point of its course, by every prior cognition. (OME,
224; *my emphasis*)

(a)–(e) being the reasons why sense data are inadequate in lieu of
physical objects, we may now inquire into the reasons that Quine gives
for thinking sense data are not helpful *in addition to* physical objects.
The points Quine urges in this connection are two: (f) Sense data are
not needed in addition to physical objects as means for reporting illusions and uncertainties, and (g) they are not needed to account for our
knowledge or discourse of physical objects themselves. With respect
to (f), "one might claim that such purposes are adequately met by a
propositional-attitude construction in which 'seems that' or the like is
made to govern a subsidiary sentence about physical objects" (WO,
235). Thus (for example), of a straight stick partially emersed in a
transparent beaker of water, one could say 'It *seems that* the stick is
bent' without admitting a special object of illusion, for the subsidiary
sentence is indeed about a physical object, namely, the straight stick.
With respect to (g), Quine argues "that the relevance of sensory stimulation to sentences about physical objects can as well (and better) be
explored and explained in terms directly of the conditioning of such
sentences or their parts to physical irritations of the subject's surfaces"
(WO, 235). The central point is that "nothing is clarified, nothing but
excess baggage is added, by positing intermediary subjective objects
of apprehension anterior to the physical objects overtly alleged in the
spoken sentences themselves" (WO, 235).
    What all of these points add up to is an application by Quine of his
general principle of systematic efficacy or utility for theory. Physical
objects have utility for theory; in fact, "in a contest for sheer systematic utility to science, the notion of physical object still leads the field"
(WO, 238; *note omitted*). On the other hand, sense data, since they
neither suffice to the exclusion of physical objects nor are needed in
addition to physical objects, lack utility for theory; and, as a consequence, they have no place in a theory of knowledge.
    Quine's repudiation of sense data is of a piece with his naturalism,
i.e., his rejection of the quest for a first philosophy that is somehow
epistemologically firmer than science, upon which science itself can be
based. The connection between these two is brought out clearly in the
following passage from "On Mental Entities":

The crucial insight of empiricism is that any evidence for science has its end points in the senses. This insight remains valid, but it is an insight which comes *after* physics, physiology, and psychology, *not before*. Epistemologists have wanted to posit a realm of sense data, situated somehow just me-ward of the physical stimulus, for fear of circularity: to view the physical stimulation rather than the sense datum as the end point of scientific evidence would be to make physical science rest for its evidence on physical science. *But if with Neurath we accept this circularity, simply recognizing that the science of science is a science, then we dispose of the epistemological motive for assuming a realm of sense data.* (OME, 225–26; *my emphasis*)

Besides these arguments against mitigated phenomenalism, which are based upon the principle of systematic efficacy (i.e., the in-lieu-of arguments and the in-addition-to arguments), and the argument from naturalism, Quine uses a paradigm case argument. The paradigmatic contexts for the learning of the terms 'reality' and 'evidence' are those contexts involving the presumption of physical objects. Consequently, despite the realization that physical objects are posited (unconsciously, of course) in the course of organizing our responses to stimulation, it does not follow that they are, therefore, "unreal" and that sense data are what is "real" (i.e., that physical objects are *mere* fictions and sense data are the *literal truth* about what there is). At least it does not follow if one refrains from shifting standards of reality by equivocating on 'real'. "The familiar material objects may not be all that is *real*, but they are admirable examples" (WO, 3; *my emphasis*). Similarly, it does not follow from the fact that the only "evidence" that we have for the existence of physical objects is that their assumption helps to organize our experience that we, therefore, have *no* "evidence" for their existence, except, again, on pain of equivocation, this time on 'evidence'. The correct conclusion to draw is, rather, that the systematic efficacy of the positing of physical objects *just is* the evidence for their existence: "We can continue to recognize . . . that molecules and even the gross bodies of common sense are simply posited in the course of organizing our responses to stimulation; but the moral to draw from our reconsideration of the terms 'reality' and 'evidence' is that posits are not *ipso facto* unreal" (PR, 251).

§3.5.2.2 *Quine's brand of physicalism*

As we noted in §3.5.2, since about 1953 Quine has been an avowed physicalist in the sense of being one who believes that reality can be fully described, if at all, exclusively in terms of physical-state predicates. In this section, I inquire more precisely into what Quine understands by this doctrine and what he regards to be its more important philosophical consequences. Quine has recently published two essays, "Facts of the Matter" (1977) and "Whither Physical Objects" (1976), in which he addresses himself to these very topics.

In "Facts of the Matter" Quine propounds four versions of the thesis of physicalism; they are:

(P_1) There is no difference in the world without a difference in the positions or states of bodies.

(P_2) There is no change without a change in the positions or states of bodies.

(P_3) There is no difference in the world without a difference in the number, or arrangement, or trajectories of atoms.

(P_4) There is no difference in matters of fact without a difference in the fulfillment of the physical-state predicates by space-time regions.

Each of these successive formulations of the thesis of physicalism is intended to be an improvement, in one way or another, over its predecessor.

(P_1) asserts that there is no difference *in the world* without a difference in the positions and states of bodies. The import of the phrase 'in the world' excludes any differences between abstract objects such as those of mathematics. In other words, there could be differences between two sets, or two numbers, or two functions, without there being any corresponding differences in the positions and states of bodies. But is not the admission of the existence of such abstract objects a repudiation of physicalism? No; the physicalist, in Quine's sense, does not insist on an exclusively corporeal ontology. Rather, what he cares to stress is that bodies are *fundamental* to nature, in the sense declared by (P_1).

(P_2) is an improvement over (P_1) in that (P_1) could be viewed as being vacuously true if it is understood as merely saying that there is no difference in the physical world without a difference in the positions and states of bodies. (P_2) is not susceptible to this vacuity, since it is less likely to be construed as narrowly as (P_1). In fact, some philosophers would find (P_1) true and (P_2) false if (P_1) were construed as being about the physical world and (P_2) were construed as being about both the physical world and the mental world, for such philosophers might believe that changes in mental states, or some such changes, do not require any corresponding physical changes. So (P_2) is likely to be construed more broadly than is (P_1), and it is to be preferred to (P_1) for that reason. Also, (P_2) still excludes abstract objects from consideration, since abstract objects are changeless.

Nevertheless, contrary to the unnamed mentalistic philosophers alluded to above, the physicalist will regard (P_2) as applying to *all* changes, including any so-called mental changes. In fact, this is the main thrust of the doctrine of physicalism: "If a man were twice in the same physical state, then, the physicalist holds, he would believe the same things both times, he would have the same thoughts, and he would have all the same unactualized dispositions to thought and action. Where positions and states of bodies do not matter, there is no fact of the matter" (FM, 162).

However, this application of physicalism to mental life should not, Quine cautions, be regarded as a reductionist doctrine of the sort sometimes imagined:

> It is not a utopian dream of our being able to specify all mental events in physiological or microbiological terms. It is not a claim that such correlations even exist, in general, to be discovered; the groupings of events in mentalistic terms need not stand in any systematic relation to biological groupings. What it does say about the life of the mind is that there is no mental difference without a physical difference. Most of us nowadays are so ready to agree to this principle that we fail to sense its magnitude. It is a way of saying that the fundamental objects are the physical objects. It accords physics its rightful place as the basic natural science without venturing any dubious hopes of reduction of other disciplines. (FM, 163; *note omitted*)

Furthermore:

> If there is no mental difference without a physical difference, then there is pointless ontological extravagance in admitting minds as entities over and above bodies; we lose nothing by applying mentalistic predicates directly to persons as bodies,

much in the manner of everyday usage. We still have two species of predicates, mental and physical, but both sorts apply to bodies. Thus it is that the physicalist comes out with an ontology of just physical objects, together with sets or other abstract objects of mathematics; no minds as additional entities. (FM, 163)

Actually, the dictum 'no mental difference without a physical difference' tells us nothing until the expression 'physical difference' is given some content. Similarly, the two versions of the thesis of physicalism which we have examined, (P_1) and (P_2), likewise remain inadequate until the expression 'states of bodies', which occurs in them, is given some content. In short, we must say what to count as states of bodies.

In his discussion of this question in "Facts of the Matter," Quine points out that one of the primary motivations of physics over the centuries has been the specification of just what is to count as a physical difference, a physical trait, a physical state. For example, in primitive atomic theory, with its uniform atoms, the macro bodies of our primordial conceptual scheme give way to micro bodies—atoms. According to this theory, any physical difference is a difference in the number, or arrangement, or trajectories of the component atoms. Physicalism on these terms is the thesis (P_3): There is no difference in a world without a difference in the number, or arrangement, or trajectories of atoms.

However, this expression of the physicalist's thesis, (P_3), is no longer adequate, since the uniform atoms of primitive atomic theory have long since given way to a confusing array of elementary particles characteristic of modern nuclear theory. Moreover, "there are indications that the utility of the particle model, the extrapolation of the primordial body into the very small, is now marginal at best. A field theory may be more to the point: a theory in which various states are directly ascribed in varying degrees to various regions of space-time" (FM, 164). In short, physics began with the macro bodies of our primordial conceptual scheme, then posited micro bodies on analogy with these, then further subdivided these micro bodies into their subatomic particles, and now would eschew these subatomic particles in favor of space-time regions.

Actually, the evolution of the ontology of physics can be taken further: "By identifying each space-time point with a quadruple of real or complex numbers according to an arbitrary system of coordinates, we can explain [i.e., explicate] the space-time regions as sets of quadruples of numbers" (FM, 164). But this is not the end of the matter either, for numbers, themselves, can be explicated in terms of set theory, indeed, in terms of pure set theory which is devoid of concrete objects. All that is needed is the empty set, set of the empty set, set of the set of the empty set, etc. This "brave new ontology" (FM, 164) is something of an irony, however:

> As physicalists we have welcomed bodies with open arms. Ungrudgingly we opened the way to other physical objects too, however ill shaped and loosely knit [for example, all the world's sugar, scattered though it is, and atoms, and subatomic particles, unobservable though they be], for at worst they were kinfolk. On the other hand the mathematical objects attained the ontological scene only begrudgedly for services rendered [i.e., because they brought with them to our theory simplicity and fecundity]. A way of dispensing with them and making do with a strictly physical ontology would have been exceedingly welcome, whereas the opposite reduction did not appeal to us.
>
> It is ironical, then, that we at length find ourselves constrained to this anti-physical sort of reduction from the side of physics itself. It is this I have wanted to bring out. Bodies were best, but they needed to be generalized to physical objects for reasons that rested on physical concerns: we wanted to provide designata for mass terms, and we wanted to accommodate physical processes or events. Physical objects, next, evaporated into space-time regions, but this was the outcome of physics itself. Finally the regions went over into pure sets; still, the set theory itself was there for no other reason than the need for mathematics as an adjunct to physical theory. *The bias is physical first and last, despite the airiness of the ontology.* (WPO, 502–3; *my emphasis*)

Despite this "ontological debacle" (WPO, 503; *see also* FM), Quine's fourth specification of the thesis of physicalism, (P_4), is left unscathed, for it is stated *not* in terms of states of bodies but in terms of physical vocabulary: There is no difference in matters of fact without a difference in the fulfillment of the physical-state predicates by space-time regions. The language in question is the language of science: "there are the truth functions, the quantifiers and their variables, and a lexicon of predicates. The variables now range over the pure sets. The predicates comprise the two-place mathematical predicate '$\in$' of set membership and, for the rest, physical predicates. These will serve to ascribe physical states to space-time regions, each region being a set of quadruples of numbers" (FM, 165).

Physical states may be ascribed outright, or they may be ascribed quantitatively. An example of the former would be 'Fx' where 'F' stands in place of a one-place predicate, say, 'red', and the variable 'x' ranges over sets of quadruples of numbers; an example of the latter would be 'Fxy' where 'F' stands in place of a two-place predicate, say, 'the temperature in degrees Kelvin of the region . . . is . . . ' and the variable 'x', again, ranges over sets of quadruples of numbers and the variable 'y' ranges over single real numbers measuring the quantitative state. "Also there may be polyadic predicates ascribing relations, absolute or quantitative, to pairs of regions, or to triples, or higher. In any event the lexicon of physical predicates will be finite, such being the way of lexica" (FM, 166).

Quine recognizes that this formulation of the thesis of physicalism, (P_4), is unfinished. The system of coordinates that must be used for determining the sets of quadruples of numbers remains to be specified, and, more importantly, there is the matter of specifying the lexicon of physical-state predicates. But this latter task is one of the major historical tasks of physics itself, namely, the ascertaining of a minimum catalogue of elementary states such that there is no change without a change in respect to them. Insofar as physics is incomplete in this sense, Quine has no choice but to leave his formulation of physicalism incomplete.

An important point to be made in connection with the ontological debacle—the physicalist's repudiation of physical objects in favor of an ontology of pure sets—is

> that this triumph of hyper-Pythagoreanism has to do with the values of the variables of quantification, and not with what we say about them. It has to do with *ontology* and not with *ideology*. The things that a theory deems there to be are the values of the theory's variables, and it is these that have been resolving themselves into numbers and kindred objects—ultimately into pure sets. The ontology of our system of the world reduces thus to the ontology of set theory, but our system of the world does not reduce to set theory; for our lexicon of predicates and functors will stand stubbornly apart. (WPO, 503; *my emphasis*).

Taking all of this in philosophical stride, Quine suggests that the proper reaction to this ontological debacle is to attach "less importance to mere ontological considerations than we used to do. We might come to look to pure mathematics as the locus of ontology as a matter of course, and consider rather that the lexicon of natural science, not the ontology, is where the metaphysical action is" (WPO, 503–4; *note omitted*).

This brings to a close our survey of some of the contributions that Quine has made toward the realization of the ideals of the unity of science movement. The method of Quinian analysis has yielded a purely extensional language, which prescribes the form and logic of our overall theory of the world but not its content (i.e., it does not prescribe a list of admissible predicates). The list of admissible predicates (the theory's ideology) is largely a matter of the historical development of science itself—hence the incompletability of Quine's doctrine of physicalism. As for the ontology of our overall theory of the world, Quine has lately, but tentatively, settled on an ontology of pure sets. I say *tentatively*, for as Quine takes pains to emphasize, it is science as it is currently being practiced that calls for the postulation of sets in the first place. And it is quite possible that as science continues to develop, sets may go by the board in favor of some other ontological posit(s).

§3.6 *Philosophy of science*

The final aspect of Quine's philosophy with which we shall concern ourselves is philosophy of science. Actually, it could be plausibly argued that we have been concerning ourselves with Quine's philosophy of science all along. This is especially true inasmuch as I have used the epistemological question of how we could acquire our (scientific) theory of the world as the exegetical locus of my entire essay, and as I have presented Quine's philosophy as a systematic attempt to articulate an answer to this question *within the confines of science (or the scientific spirit) itself*. A few general points about Quine's view of the nature of theory construction in science yet need making, or are worth remaking.

Quine regards scientific theories as networks of sentences that are both underdetermined by and holistically related to experience:

> The totality of our so-called knowledge or beliefs, from the most casual matters of geography and history to the profoundest laws of atomic physics or even of pure mathematics and logic, is a man-made fabric which impinges on experience only along the edges. Or, to change the figure, total science is

like a field of force whose boundary conditions are experience.
A conflict with experience at the periphery occasions readjust-
ments in the interior of the field. Truth values have to be re-
distributed over some of our statements. Reëvaluation of some
statements entails reëvaluation of others, because of their logical interconnections—the logical laws being in turn simply
certain further statements of the system, certain further elements in the field. Having reëvaluated one statement we must
reëvaluate some others, which may be statements logically
connected with the first or may be the statements of logical
connections themselves. But the total field is so underdetermined by its boundary conditions, experience, that there is
much latitude of choice as to what statements to reëvaluate in
the light of any single contrary experience. No particular experiences are linked with any particular statements in the interior
of the field, except indirectly through considerations of equilibrium affecting the field as a whole. (TDE, 42–43)

Another point worth making is that Quine's view of science is pro-
vocatively pragmatic. It is so because it contains both a radical tendency as well as a conservative tendency. The radical tendency issues
from Quine's *instrumentalism*: "As an empiricist I continue to think of
the conceptual scheme of science as a tool, ultimately, for predicting
future experience in the light of past experience. Physical objects are
conceptually imported into the situation as convenient intermediaries
—not by definition in terms of experience, but simply as irreducible
posits comparable, epistemologically, to the gods of Homer" (TDE,
44; *note omitted*). The conservative tendency issues from Quine's
commitment to *realism*:

> For my part I do, qua lay physicist, believe in physical objects
> and not in Homer's gods; and I consider it a scientific error to
> believe otherwise. But in point of epistemological footing the
> physical objects and the gods differ only in degree and not in
> kind. Both sorts of entities enter our conception only as cul-
> tural posits. The myth of physical objects is epistemologically
> superior to most in that it has proved more efficacious than
> other myths as a device for working a manageable structure
> into the flux of experience. (TDE, 44)

These seemingly contrary forces at work in Quine's view of science have provoked one commentator to remark that Quine's view of

science *vacillates* between instrumentalism and realism.[10] But Quine's view of science does not really vacillate between instrumentalism and realism. Rather, Quine embraces a pragmatism which accommodates both without conflict. Quine has written:

> To call a posit a posit is not to patronize it. . . . Everything to which we concede existence is a posit from the standpoint of a description of the theory-building process, and simultaneously real from the standpoint of the theory that is being built. Nor let us look down on the standpoint of the theory as make-believe; for we can never do better than occupy the standpoint of some theory or other, the best we can muster at the time. (WO, 22)

To appreciate how all of this fits together coherently, we need to begin at the beginning, with learning theory. We said in §1.2 that, for Quine, learning is a matter of acquiring a repertoire of habits. Equipped with innate standards of perceptual similarity and with traces of episodes with their reciprocal enlivening effect, and motivated by pleasure and pain, human organisms (and others) take to learning. Perceptually similar salient features of episodes, along with their pleasures and pains, all encoded (somehow) in the traces, are associated into kinds. The fundamental learning mechanism involved is extrapolation, or simple induction:

> An individual's innate similarity standards undergo some revision, of course, even at the common-sense level, indeed even at the subhuman level, through learning. An animal may learn to tell a cat from an owl. The ability to learn is itself a product of natural selection, with evident survival value. An animal's innate similarity standards are a rudimentary *instrument* for prediction, and then learning is a progressive refinement of that *instrument*, making for more dependable prediction. (NNK, 71; *my emphasis*)

Many similarities of episodes will go unnoticed or unheeded, but the ones promoting the interests and aims of the organism will ordinarily come to stand out and be acted upon.

10. Cf. J. J. C. Smart, "Quine's Philosophy of Science," in *Words and Objections, Essays on the Work of W. V. Quine*, ed. D. Davidson and J. Hintikka (Dordrecht-Holland: D. Reidel Publishing Company, 1969), pp. 8f.

When language, a social instrument as well as a social art, comes on the human scene, it does so as the acquisition of further habits. Sounds become encoded in traces as salient features of episodes right along with other sensory input. Early language learning is ostensive: heard words are associated directly with other information of the episodes which constitute the similarity bases underlying the correct usages of the words. Eventually language grows into "a vast and bewildering . . . conceptual or linguistic apparatus, the whole of natural science. Biologically, still, it is like the animal's learning about cats and owls; it is a learned improvement over simple induction by innate similarity standards. It makes for more and better prediction" (NNK, 71).[11]

This "ponderous linguistic structure, fabricated of theoretical terms linked by fabricated hypotheses, and keyed to observable events here and there" (NNK, 71) stands as a remarkable improvement over simple induction as a means for anticipating experience. But there is a price to be paid for this advance. In acquiring habits by simple induction over instances, if some anticipated experience fails to materialize, that very habit will wither. But now, with the hypothetico-deductive method in full force, when some expected or predicted event implied by some part of a theory fails to materialize, there is a choice to be made as to how to revise the theory so that such false predictions will not be made in the future. That there is a choice here is a consequence of the fact that the language of theory goes beyond observation sentences to include sentences that are not directly linked to observation and that can be learned only by dint of irreducible leaps of analogy.

When we attempt to construct or revise a theory, there will be great latitude in the range of possible hypotheses. This latitude is what constitutes the radical element of instrumentalism: we can tell a story (i.e., posit, or make hypotheses) about Homer's gods or physical objects. But Quine's instrumentalism is not a license for a fantasyland either. The hypotheses we invent must be plausible. As Quine sees it, there are six virtues of plausible hypotheses: conservatism, modesty, simplicity, generality, refutability, and precision (cf. WB, chaps. 6 and 7).

When Quine says that a hypothesis should be *conservative*, he

11. The reference to cats and owls is an allusion to the point, just made by Quine on p. 71 of "The Nature of Natural Knowledge," that visual resemblance is a poor index of kinship: certain owls have evolved so as to resemble cats or monkeys in appearance.

means that it should be consistent with as many of our presently held beliefs as possible. In the context of revising a theory, Quine sometimes calls this the *maxim of minimum mutilation*. Suppose, for example, that a theory (or a part thereof) implies (i.e., predicts) some observation that does not materialize (viz., a false pegged observation conditional). If we chose not to discount this failure as a mistake in measurement, or as an illusion, or the like, then we must recognize that part of the theory that implied this false sentence is itself false— but the mere failure does not tell us *where* the theory is false. The idea of conservatism is to fasten on the minimum amount of theory for revision—divide and conquer, as Quine says in *The Web of Belief*. A graphic instance of this would be the case where we attempt to salt our food but, despite our most vigorous efforts, no salt comes out of the shaker. We could explain this by hypothesizing that the shaker is empty, or that the salt inside is wet, or that salt is lighter than air, or that salt doesn't conform to the law of falling bodies, etc. Surely, however, the maxim of minimum mutilation dictates that once we have thus divided our hypotheses, the ones to conquer (i.e., to reject) are the latter two hypotheses, rather than either of the former. Conservatism dictates we adopt the minimum revision of our beliefs in the face of change. Moreover, "conservatism is rather effortless on the whole, having inertia in its favor. But it is sound strategy too, since at each step it sacrifices as little as possible of the evidential support, whatever that may have been, that our overall system of beliefs has hitherto been enjoying" (WB, 67).

Modesty is a virtue of hypotheses that is closely akin to conservatism. Quine distinguishes two varieties of modesty, the logical and the humdrum: "One hypothesis is more modest than another if it is weaker in a logical sense: if it is implied by the other, without implying it. . . . Also, one hypothesis is more modest than another if it is more humdrum: that is, if the events that it assumes to have happened are of a more usual and familiar sort, hence more to be expected" (WB, 68). The idea here is to bring in a big myth only if a small myth will not do the job. For example, suppose that while hiking in the mountains we narrowly escape a terrible avalanche. Upon regaining our composure, we might hypothesize that the avalanche was merely a fortuitous (if untimely) act of nature or we might hypothesize that some person set the avalanche in motion. If avalanches are common in the area but people aren't, then modesty favors the former hypothesis.

Quine emphasises that there is no need to draw a sharp line

between conservatism and modesty—the one can grade off into the other. Nevertheless, there remain grades of modesty still to choose among even though conservatism—compatibility with previous beliefs—is achieved to perfection; for a modest hypothesis and an immodest hypothesis might both be compatible with all previous beliefs.

Modesty can also grade off into *simplicity*. Simplicity is another virtue of plausible *hypotheses*, but simplicity is even more valued as a virtue of scientific *theories*:

> There is a premium on simplicity in the hypotheses, but the highest premium is on simplicity in the giant joint hypothesis that is science, or the particular science, as a whole. We cheerfully sacrifice simplicity of a part for greater simplicity of the whole when we see a way of doing so. (WB, 69)

Exactly what simplicity is, Quine is not sure. He thinks it is subjective and closely linked to our innate standards of perceptual similarity. Whatever it is, it has survival value for the species, for it plays a major role in the formation of our expectations about the course of future experiences.

The plausibility of a hypothesis also depends on its degree of *generality*. Requiring a hypothesis to be general is a way of guarding against ad hoc hypotheses, a way of ensuring that hypotheses will not be confirmed by mere coincidences. Also, generality is required of a hypothesis if it is to lend itself to being tested repeatedly, at different times and places, under slightly different conditions.

Simplicity and generality are wanted together in a hypothesis. One without the other would be rather useless: A simple hypothesis without generality would lack applicability; a general hypothesis without simplicity would be unwieldy. Nevertheless, there is a certain give and take between simplicity and generality: "When a way is seen of gaining great generality with little loss of simplicity, or great simplicity with no loss of generality, then conservatism and modesty give way to scientific revolution" (WB, 75).

The fifth virtue of plausible hypothesis is *refutability*: There must be some conceivable event (or events) that would suffice to refute the hypothesis. If this requirement is not met, then the hypothesis implies nothing and is, therefore, confirmed by nothing; it is vacuous. But Quine cannot lean very heavily on this virtue since his holism also claims that *any* hypothesis can be retained, come what may.

The final virtue of plausible hypotheses is *precision*. The more precise a hypothesis is, the more strongly it is confirmed by each of its successful predictions. Precision comes mainly with the utilization of quantitative measurement. However, explication of terms can also be a means for introducing precision into hypotheses.

Regarding Quine's instrumentalism, we can say that he sees science as an instrument for predicting future experience and for explaining past experience. Beyond conforming to experience, the hypotheses of science must measure up to the six virtues of plausibility just surveyed. Even with these constraints, however, science is underdetermined by experience. Different systems of science could, Quine insists, be built on the same experiential (i.e., observational) base—hence the radical tendency of Quine's pragmatism.

On the conservative side is Quine's realism—the view that the objects posited in scientific theories, including the so-called theoretical entities, are real. The issue here is subtle. Quine has said that the criterion for settling what the objects of a theory are is membership in the range of values of the bound variables of the theory: to be is to be the value of a bound variable. He has also said that it makes no sense to say what the objects of a theory are beyond saying how to interpret or reinterpret that theory in another. These claims express the essence of his doctrine of ontological relativity, i.e., the doctrine of the relativity of the real. Such a doctrine appears to be more in tune with his instrumentalism than with his realism. However, there is a further consideration, namely, that the current physical theory, despite its being underdetermined by experience in principle, is the *best* theory presently available of what is real: "Unlike Descartes, we own and use our beliefs of the moment, even in the midst of philosophizing, until by what is vaguely called scientific method we change them here and there for the better" (WO, 24–25). The key consideration here is Quine's naturalism, his rejection of the ideal of a first philosophy somehow prior to science: "Neurath has likened science to a boat which, if we are to rebuild it, we must rebuild plank by plank while staying afloat in it" (WO, 3). Thus, for Quine, epistemology is only science self-applied.

> Science tells us that our data regarding the external world are limited to the irradiations of our bodily surfaces, and then science asks how it is that people manage from those data to project their story about the external world—true though the story is. 'Posit' is a term proper to this methodological facet of sci-

ence. To apply the term to molecules and wombats is not to deny that these are real; but declaring them real is left to other facets of science, namely physics and zoology. (RS, 293–94)

So realism is conservative because the science of a time settles, for that time, what there is in the world: "Within our own total evolving doctrine, we can judge truth as earnestly and absolutely as can be; subject to correction, but that goes without saying" (WO, 25).

What makes Quine's pragmatism provocative, I said, is its inclusion of both radical and conservative tendencies. It is just here, in this doctrine of relative realism, that the provocation is greatest. It is so because it opposes a stubborn tendency to think that Quine cannot have it both ways: either science is inventing myths or it is discovering true reality. But I think this is more of a stubborn tendency than a reasoned view. The tendency is spawned by an uncritical acceptance of a vaguely discernible thing-in-itself. According to this tendency, theories closer to the true reality are less mythical and more factual. The truth of a theory is, then, somehow a measure of its approximation to this ultimate reality. This is an intuitively persuasive picture of the matter, and it stubbornly resists Quine's alternative and, I think, more enlightened view (*see* WO, 23).

§3.7 *Summary and conclusions*

My position throughout has been that Quine's philosophy is best understood as a systematic, uniquely empiricistic, attempt to provide an answer to the question of how one could acquire his unified theory of the world. I have tried to sketch the systematic character of Quine's philosophy by emphasizing its naturalistic-behavioristic basis, and in particular, by explaining how the NB conception of language (i.e., a naturalistic view of language and a behavioral theory of meaning), once adopted and seriously adhered to, provides the framework (i.e., the constraints) within which the bulk of Quine's system develops. My argument has been that if one adopts Quine's genetic strategy together with the NB conception of language and the view that scientific theories are essentially linguistic structures, then one is led to see that science is underdetermined by experience to some extent insofar as theoretical language goes beyond observation sentences. Further, the theories of science will be viewed as holistically related to experience: not every sentence of such theories will possess its own unique empirical meaning. And, if there is underdetermination (in Quine's strong sense of the term) and holism, then there will be indeterminacy of translation and inscrutability of reference. Furthermore, inscrutability when sufficiently generalized becomes the doctrine of ontological relativity. Also, holism entails the rejection of the analytic-synthetic distinction, and, of course, of reductionism. Synonymy goes by the board, too, and, with it, meanings, propositions, attributes, and relations; from a behavioristic point of view, they all suffer from a lack of individuation. Modal logic must be given up as well. And, finally, underdetermination and holism lead to Quine's pragmatic philosophy of science.

Quine's philosophy is *empiricistic* despite his rejection of the empiricistic dogmas of the analytic-synthetic distinction and epistemological reductionism, for as we noted in §1.1, he still adheres to two cardinal tenets of empiricism: (1) whatever evidence there is for science (or theory) is sensory evidence, and (2) all inculcation of meanings of words must rest ultimately on sensory evidence. Another yardstick for measuring the extent to which a philosopher is an empiricist is whether he denies the possibility of a priori synthetic knowledge—which, of course, Quine does. In fact, Quine even denies the possibility of a priori analytic knowledge, for he rejects the notion of analyticity. In *Language, Truth and Logic*, A. J. Ayer maintained (erroneously) that there were only two possible positions for an empiricist to take regarding the truths of geometry, mathematics, and logic: the empiricist may claim these truths to be inductive generalizations (e.g., J. S. Mill), or he may claim they are analytic (e.g., Ayer). Quine rejects both of these alternatives, opting instead for a *third* empiricistic position, namely, that such truths are one and all synthetic (there being no analytic truths), which puts him on Mill's side against Ayer, but also that these truths are not empirical generalizations, which puts him on Ayer's side against Mill. The statements of geometry, mathematics, and logic are true, according to Quine, because of the systematic efficacy that these disciplines bring to our overall theory of the world.

So by either or both of these two measurements—all scientific knowledge and all cognitive meaning rest ultimately on sensory experience and the denial of the existence of a priori knowledge—Quine comes out an empiricist. And yet, what makes Quine's empiricism unique is not just the rejection of the two dogmas of the old empiricism; more to the point is his naturalism, his rejection of a first philosophy as a desideratum. Quine has recognized that the philosophical skeptic's challenge to science springs from within science itself. The argument from illusion, of which skeptics are so fond, makes sense only because illusion itself makes sense; but illusion makes sense only because of a prior acceptance of physical objects. Recognition of this fact goes a long way toward relieving the new epistemologist of the impossible burden of propounding a first philosophy, a long way, that is, toward establishing enlightened empiricism.

Chapter 4. The defense

§4.1 *Defending Quine's naturalistic-behavioristic conception of language*

A question of some importance for Quine's philosophy is whether Quine's theory of language learning is defensible. As we have seen, his theory is rooted in the conviction that language is learned by social emulation and social feedback (i.e., the naturalistic-behavioristic thesis). In explaining the learning of observation sentences this conviction is highly plausible. There the salience of the relevant nonverbal stimuli is clearly an intersubjectively appreciable feature of the learning situation, and the psychological mechanism involved does appear to closely approximate the stimulus-response model. In short, Quine's account of how observation sentences could be learned by direct conditioning seems to be on pretty firm ground.

When Quine's discussion of language learning moves away from talk about learning some observation sentences by direct conditioning to talk about learning most other sentences by analogic synthesis (i.e., to talk about learning new sentences by building them from learned parts by analogy with the way those parts have previously been seen to occur in other sentences), his theory becomes both more problematic and more speculative, for the stimuli involved in analogic synthesis are not always obvious, and the psychological mechanisms, unlike direct conditioning, are obscure and little understood. Consequently, there is room for debate over the precise nature of the innate psychological mechanisms responsible for the acquisition of the greater part of language. For example, are the principles involved in learning most of language merely specialized instances of some very general principles of learning that are equally applicable in nonlinguistic contexts, or are they highly specialized principles, unique to the linguistic context, and not at all comparable, say, to induction, generalization, abstraction, etc.? In particular, does the behavior of others in the speech community actually mold the verbal behavior of the child into social conformity, as Quine suggests: "Different persons growing up in the same language are like different bushes trimmed and trained to take the shape of identical elephants. The anatomical details of twigs and branches will fulfill the elephantine form differently from bush to bush, but the overall outward results are alike" (WO, 8)? Or, does the behavior of others in the speech community set a highly specialized, innate language acquisition device into operation, without affecting the manner of its functioning to any great extent?

The contemporary linguist-philosopher Noam Chomsky has championed a theory of language acquisition opposed to Quine's along the lines of the alternative suggested above. In short, Chomsky has painted a picture of language acquisition that is centered around a postulated innate mechanism of language learning of an essentially nonbehavioristic character. Chomsky's view has had a tremendous impact. Many students are under the mistaken impression that Chomsky has totally refuted any kind of behavioristic account of language learning. Consequently, a brief survey of Chomsky's theory, highlighting some of its more controversial claims, may help us to better appreciate the viability of Quine's alternative view.

§4.2   *Chomsky's innateness hypothesis*

Chomsky's "innateness hypothesis" (with respect to language learning) is the view that one of the faculties of the mind common to the human species is a faculty of language. This faculty of language serves as a sensory system for the preliminary analysis of linguistic data and as a schematism that determines, quite narrowly, a certain class of grammars. Each grammar is a theory of a particular language specifying formal and semantic properties of a potentially infinite array of sentences. These sentences, each with its particular structure, constitute the language generated by the grammar. The languages generated by such grammars are those which can be acquired in the normal way. The language faculty, when appropriately stimulated (i.e., when exposed to a linguistic environment at the propitious time and for sufficient duration), will construct a grammar. The person knows the language generated by the constructed grammar. This knowledge is used

by a competent speaker-hearer to understand what is heard and to produce discourse as an expression of thought within the constraints of the
internalized principles, in a manner appropriate to situations as these
are conceived by other mental faculties, free of stimulus control.

Our purpose here is to examine the evidence Chomsky uses to support his innateness hypothesis of language acquisition in order to see
whether such evidence refutes Quine's behavioristic theory of language
acquisition. Before pursuing this matter, however, we must consider a
few more relevant details of Chomsky's theory. First, it should be
noted that Chomsky's theory pertains to physiologically normal children who experience routine socialization patterns in a linguistic environment. The emphasis upon physiologically normal children is important because Chomsky thinks that the innate capacity for language
learning is a species-specific property (i.e., a property belonging only
to members of the human species and only to those members of the
species who are physiologically normal) and is genetically inherited.
The emphasis upon normal socialization patterns in a linguistic environment is important because Chomsky thinks the activation of the
innate language acquisition device requires verbal stimulation before
the age of puberty (approximately). Also, it should be pointed out that
Chomsky is not claiming that the innate language faculty (even when
appropriately stimulated) is *alone* responsible for the normal child's
acquisition (or use) of language. Chomsky claims, rather, that the innate language faculty is only one factor (but a very necessary one)
among many factors that play roles in the child's acquisition (and use)
of language. Chomsky makes the point this way:

> In the case of language-acquisition . . . it must be emphasized
> that the model I am suggesting can at best only be regarded as a
> first approximation to a theory of learning, since it is an instan-
> taneous model and does not try to capture the interplay be-
> tween tentative hypotheses that the child may construct, new
> data interpreted in terms of these hypotheses, new hypotheses
> based on these interpretations, and so on, until some relatively
> fixed system of competence is established. I think that an in-
> stantaneous model is a reasonable first approximation, but this,
> as any other aspect of research strategy, must ultimately be
> evaluated in terms of its success in providing explanations and
> insight.[1]

1. Noam Chomsky, *Language and Mind*, enlarged ed. (New York: Harcourt
Brace Jovanovich, Inc., 1968), pp. 187–88.

The evidence Chomsky musters in support of the innateness hypothesis is varied. It can be divided very generally into three groups of observations: (1) those pertaining to the general conditions of language learning (or "primary linguistic data" as Chomsky calls them), (2) those pertaining to nonhuman communication systems versus human language, and (3) those pertaining to certain alleged universal features of generative grammars that have been constructed in the field of linguistics.

§4.2.1   *Primary linguistic data*

It certainly must be admitted that the speech a child hears around him is limited, fragmentary, and full of imperfections. Children learn a first language in a relatively short span of time, at an early age, and well before their general intellectual faculties are much developed. The child who learns a first language thus seems to perform a remarkable feat, for in "internalizing" the grammar of the languge being spoken around him, he does something very close to constructing (subconsciously, of course) a theory of that language. Furthermore, different individuals in the same speech community develop essentially the same language. From these observations Chomsky concludes that language acquisition is explicable *only* on the assumption that these individuals employ highly restrictive principles that guide the internalization or construction of their grammars. And, since it is obvious that humans are not innately disposed to learn one natural language rather than some other, it is equally obvious that the system of principles that they employ in language learning (and language use) must be a species property. In other words, powerful constraints must be operative restricting the variety of human languages.

Quine could certainly agree with most of Chomsky's observations concerning the general conditions of language learning. Indeed, Quine makes much of the fact that theories (and languages) are underdetermined by experience. This condition is the basis for the central question of epistemology, as Quine sees it, namely, how do we explain the torrential output (theory) on the basis of the meager input (experience).

Also, Quine has expressed agreement (*see* LP, 56) with Chomsky's characterization of the minimum requirements to be met by any theory advanced to explain language acquisition in the face of these facts, namely, Chomsky's claim that "we must attribute to the organism, as an innate property, a structure rich enough to account for the fact that the postulated grammar is acquired on the basis of the given conditions of access to data; second, we must not attribute to the organism a structure so rich as to be incompatible with the known diversity of languages." [2] Thus there seems to be little or no real disagreement between Quine and Chomsky over the characterization of the primary linguistic data: both agree that language is underdetermined by experience and that the child possesses an innate language readiness. The disagreement between Quine and Chomsky occurs when it comes time to characterize the required innate structure: Quine rejects what he takes to be Chomsky's irreducibly mentalistic posits, and Chomsky rejects what he takes to be Quine's unreasonable, behavioristic restrictions.

To conclude, it seems clear that Chomsky's argument in favor of an innate language acquisition device of the specific character he has in mind, when based solely on the consideration of primary linguistic data, is inconclusive. Despite the fact that language acquisition is underdetermined by experience and that it is acquired by normal children in a fairly short span of time, language may, nevertheless, be acquired without the use of innate mechanisms of this specific character.

§4.2.2   *Sui generis properties of language*

Regarding the second group of observations mentioned above upon which he bases his innateness hypothesis, Chomsky claims that all known animal communication systems operate on one or the other of two principles. One of these principles is what he calls the *principle of the speedometer*. Animals operating on this principle can produce "a potentially infinite, in fact in principle continuous, set of signals as output in response to a continuous range of stimuli." [3] The other principle of animal communication systems is the *principle of strict finiteness*. A system based on this principle "consists of a finite number of signals, each produced under a fixed range of stimulus conditions." [4] Whether infinite (as in the case of the speedometer principle) or finite (as in the case of the strict finiteness principle), the acquisition and use of animal communication systems are, in principle, explainable in terms of conditioning.

Human language differs qualitatively from animal systems "in that it is in principle an infinite discrete system rather than a continuous system or a strictly finite system of signals, and that it is related to stimuli not by the mechanism of stimulus control, but by the much

2. Ibid., p. 170.

3. Noam Chomsky, "Knowledge of Language," *The London Times Literary Supplement*, 1968, p. 523.

4. Ibid.

more obscure relation of appropriateness." [5] Thus, for Chomsky, knowing a language is more than possessing a repertoire (infinite or finite) of dispositions to verbal behavior keyed to stimuli. Rather, knowing a language is a matter of mastering "a set of rules and principles that determine an infinite, discrete set of sentences, each of which has a fixed form and a fixed meaning or meaning-potential." [6] This system of rules and principles is the generative grammar internalized by the child in learning his first language. Chomsky would have us believe that the acquisition of this kind of grammar, which is potentially capable of generating an infinite set of discrete (i.e., novel) sentences and is a peculiarly human achievement, is explicable *only* on the assumption that humans are biologically endowed with an innate faculty of language acquisition.

The combinatorial productivity, however, which Chomsky cites as one of the *sui generis* properties of human language, may in fact be less than that. Man has developed this device to a remarkable extent, but Quine reports that Premack's chimpanzee has acquired this same ability within modest limits. "It would thus appear that combinatorial productivity in language affords no sharp line between man and beast. Man may plume himself on having been the first to develop a combinatorially productive language, but the ability to learn it may be more widespread" (MVD, 85).

As for the other alleged *sui generis* property, the freedom of human language from stimulus control, even behaviorists like B. F. Skinner recognize that verbal behavior needs no environmental support. But the fact that speech is unpredictably spontaneous is insufficient of itself to justify Chomsky's innateness hypothesis, for according to Quine:

> Animal drives are still at work behind the torrent of human speech, but they are seldom clearly to be traced. Even if in our verbal output we differ from Premack's chimpanzee only in degree and not in kind, still it is this overwhelming difference of degree that invites the mentalistic accounts of verbal behavior. The torrent of words is seen as a manifestation of the speaker's inner life beyond animal drives. (MVD, 85–86)

In conclusion, Chomsky's claims—(1) that human language is, for reasons having to do ultimately with the genetic uniqueness of Homo

5. Ibid.
6. Ibid.

sapiens, qualitatively different from animal communication systems in that human languages have a recursive property that animal communication systems do not and cannot have, and (2) that human languages are free from stimulus control whereas animal communication systems are not—are both highly debatable.

§4.2.3   *Linguistic universals*

Consider now the third source of support for Chomsky's innateness hypothesis, namely, claims regarding certain alleged features of generative grammars. Chomsky thinks that there exist some features of generative grammars that are universal, although he has not as yet been able to demonstrate this conclusively. It is tacit knowledge of these linguistic universals that largely constitutes the child's (idealized) innate language acquisition device. Particular assumptions about linguistic universals may pertain to any of the three components of a generative grammar, i.e., to syntactic, semantic, or phonological components, and to interrelations among the three components. In general, however, any such universals will fall into one of three classifications: substantive universals, formal universals, and universal constraints.

A theory of *substantive universals* claims that items of a particular kind in any language must be drawn from a fixed class of items. Chomsky gives hypothetical examples of such universals pertaining to the three components of a generative grammar, but one example pertaining to the syntactic component will suffice for our purposes. It might be suggested, for example, that the study of generative grammar warrants the conclusion that "certain fixed syntactic categories (Noun, Verb, etc.) can be found in the syntactic representations of the sentences of any language and that these provide the general underlying syntactic structure of each language."[7] Such syntactical categories are hypothetical examples of substantive linguistic universals.

It is possible, however, to look for linguistic universals of a more abstract sort. Whereas substantive universals concern the vocabulary for the description of language, *formal universals* involve rather the character of the rules that appear in grammars and the ways in which they can be interconnected. For example, it might be suggested that the syntactic component of the grammar for any possible human language must contain transformation rules.

---

7. Noam Chomsky, *Aspects of the Theory of Syntax* (Cambridge, Mass.: M.I.T. Press, 1965), p. 28.

A third sort of linguistic universal is called *universal constraints*. If particular sorts of grammatical rules are never found in human languages, then one might conjecture that there are universal constraints on the form of grammatical rules.

> For example, some claim that there is a universal constraint against moving material in or out of a conjunctive structure. In English, one cannot pluck *old men* out of the conjunction *old men and women*, so as to derive **old men are loved by my father and women* or **they are loved by my father and women* from *my father loves old men and women* by transformations which are acceptable if they move the *whole* conjunction. If this were generally true, then the *constraint* would be universal.[8]

If we follow Quine, we must conclude that this third source of support for Chomsky's innateness hypothesis, namely, the belief in linguistic universals, is illusory. The problem is that the kinds of grammatical observations relied upon to identify the various so-called linguistic universals characteristically go beyond all possible behavioral evidence. In other words, claims like 'language *L* has the grammatical categories of subject and predicate' typically involve the utilization of grammatical hypotheses that, by their very nature, can never be confirmed or refuted by anything in the behavior of the speakers of *L*. Quine puts the point as follows:

> To make proper sense of the hypothesis that the subject-predicate construction is a linguistic universal, we need an unequivocal behavioral criterion of subject and predicate. It is not enough to say that if we take these and these as subjects and those and those as predicates then there are ways of so handling the rest of the language as to get general English translations. The trouble is that there are extensionally equivalent grammars. Timely reflection on method and evidence should tend to stifle much of the talk of linguistic universals. (MRCLT, 109)

In a word, the problem with the evidence used to support the postulation of linguistic universals is that it is typically behaviorally indeterminate, and therefore susceptible to the indeterminacy of translation.

---

8. Justin Leiber, *Noam Chomsky: A Philosophical Overview* (New York: St. Martin's Press, 1975), pp. 121–22. The asterisks preceding the italicized sentences indicate that those sentences are *irregular*. See p. 28 of Leiber's book for a discussion of the difference between irregular and merely unusual sentences.

In summary, it appears that the three major sources of support for Chomsky's innateness hypothesis, namely, the primary linguistic data argument, the *sui generis* argument, and the linguistic universal argument, are all less than conclusive. More to the point, they do not conclusively refute Quine's alternative behavioristic account of language learning. However, standing quite apart from these arguments is a recent attempt by Chomsky, found for the most part in his *Reflections on Language*, to establish that with respect to doctrines concerning the study of language there are, in effect, two Quines: there is the Quine of 1960, and there is the Quine of 1969 onward (I shall at times refer to these, respectively, as Quine-I and Quine-II), and that these two Quines are not only inconsistent with each other but that Quine-II has almost completely abandoned the behaviorism of Quine-I.

§4.3   *Is Quine-I inconsistent with Quine-II?*

According to Chomsky, Quine-I's position is characterized by three claims: (1) a language is a fabric of sentences variously associated to one another and to nonverbal stimuli by the mechanism of conditioned response; (2) language is learned by association of sentences with sentences, association of sentences with stimuli, and analogic synthesis; (3) learning also involves a quality space with built-in distance measures which can be determined experimentally.[9]

The position of Quine-II, according to Chomsky, is characterized by the claims that (1) the mechanism of conditioning is insufficient to explain all of language learning; (2) generative grammar is what mainly distinguishes language from subhuman communication systems; (3) there are as yet unknown innate structures in addition to mere quality space that are needed in language learning to get the child over the hump that lies beyond ostension or conditioning; (4) any innate mechanisms of language aptitude, however elaborate, would be welcomed if they can be made intelligible and plausible.[10]

As Chomsky sees it, there is no way to reconcile the two Quines:

> If conditioning is insufficient to explain language learning (1969) then a language is not a fabric of sentences and stimuli associated by conditioned response (1960), and sentences are not "learned" by the three mechanisms of 1960. If generative

9. Cf. Noam Chomsky, *Reflections on Language* (New York: Pantheon Books, Random House, Inc., 1975), pp. 198–99.
10. Ibid., p. 199.

grammar is the essential defining characteristic of human language, then, again, the earlier account can be dismissed, since a generative grammar can [not] be described . . . as a fabric of sentences and stimuli associated by conditioning. . . . If innate mechanisms of arbitrary complexity are permissible, so long as conjectures are eventually made sense of in terms of external observations, then there is no reason to assign any special place to dimensional structures such as a "quality space," nor to structures determined by differential conditioning and extinction tests.[11]

As I see it, however, these conflicts between Quine-I and Quine-II, which Chomsky alleges, are more apparent than real. Consider the first alleged inconsistency. If Chomsky is claiming that Quine's 1969 position is that not all of language learning is explicable in terms of conditioned response, Chomsky is rendering a true account, for Quine-II says:

> Conditioned response does retain a key role in language-learning. It is the entering wedge to any particular lexicon, for it is how we learn observation terms (or, better, simple observation sentences) by ostension. Learning by ostension is learning by simple induction, and the mechanism of such learning is conditioning. But this method is notoriously incapable of carrying us far in language. (LP, 57)

But is this 1969 position inconsistent with Quine's 1960 characterization of a language as a fabric of sentences variously associated to one another and to nonverbal stimuli by the mechanism of conditioned response *and* with his 1960 account of how sentences are learned? I shall argue that it is not, and, further, that Chomsky's belief to the contrary is based, at least in part, on a misunderstanding of Quine's 1960 account of how sentences are learned.

To begin with, consider Chomsky's remarks concerning the methods of sentence learning discussed by Quine in *Word and Object*:

> The *first* method is association of sentences with sentences; the *second* association of sentences with stimuli. These *two* methods would, it is true, lead to a fabric of associated sentences and stimuli. But there is a *third* method that is left rather ob-

11. Ibid., pp. 199–200.

scure in *Word and Object*, namely, learning of sentences by what . . . [Quine] calls "analogic synthesis". I quote in full his discussion of this notion: 'It is evident how new sentences may be built from old materials and volunteered on appropriate occasions simply by virtue of analogies. Having been directly conditioned to the appropriate use of "Foot" (or "This is my foot") as a sentence, and "Hand" likewise, and "My foot hurts" as a whole, the child might conceivably utter "My hand hurts" on an appropriate occasion, though unaided by previous experience with that actual sentence.' . . .

Suppose that the sentence "My hand hurts" is "learnt" in this manner, and consider now the assumption that a language is a fabric of sentences associated by the mechanism of conditioned response. Then the sentence "My hand hurts" in the given example is associated to the complex containing "foot", "My foot hurts", and "hand" by the mechanism of conditioned response. To say this would be to deprive the notion of "conditioned response" of its strict meaning, or anything resembling this meaning. The responses and stimuli entering into the relationship of "conditioning" need not even appear together. Of course, until the notion of "analogic synthesis" is given content, the theory is vacuous.[12]

Chomsky's point in this passage seems to be that the methods of learning sentences by associating sentences with sentences and by associating sentences with nonverbal stimuli (the "first" and "second" methods) would indeed lead to a fabric of associated sentences and stimuli, but the "third" method, analogic synthesis, deprives the notion of conditioned response of anything like its strict meaning; consequently, to say of a language containing sentences learned by analogic synthesis that it is characterizable as a fabric of sentences associated by the mechanism of conditioned response is either false (if 'conditioned response' is taken in its strict sense) or vacuously true (if 'conditioned response' is taken in some unspecified sense).

But, of course, Quine does not propose *three* methods for learning sentences in *Word and Object*, but only two: direct conditioning (or ostension) and analogic synthesis. Contrary to Chomsky's interpreta-

---

12. Chomsky, "Knowledge of Language," pp. 523–24, *my emphasis*.

tion, analogic synthesis is not a "third" method in addition to direct conditioning and association of sentences with sentences; analogic synthesis *is* the associating of sentences with sentences. Consider what Quine says in the paragraph immediately following the 'My hand hurts' example cited by Chomsky:

> But think how little we would be able to say if our learning of sentences were strictly limited to those two modes: (1) learning sentences as wholes by a direct conditioning of them to appropriate non-verbal stimulations, and (2) producing further sentences from the foregoing ones by analogical substitution as in the preceding paragraph. The sentences afforded by mode (1) are such that each has its particular range of admissible stimulatory occasions, independently of wider context. The sentences added by (2) are more of the same sort—learned faster thanks to (2), but no less capable of being learned in mode (1). Speech thus confined would be strikingly like bare reporting of sense data. (WO, 9)

A page later Quine goes on to say:

> Mode (2) above is already, in a way, an associating of sentences with sentences; but only in too restrained a way. Further inter-verbal associations are required which provide for the use of new sentences without tying them, even derivatively, to any fixed ranges of non-verbal stimuli. (WO, 10)

Now the first thing to notice in all this is that Quine describes the learning of 'My hand hurts' as a case of *analogical substitution*. It is an instance of learning a sentence by means of a substitutional transformation rule that was itself gleaned, we may conjecture along Quinian lines, by virtue of a perceived grammatical analogy between 'hand' and 'foot': 'hand' may be substituted for 'foot' in 'My foot hurts' under a certain fixed range of nonverbal stimuli. In *The Roots of Reference* Quine-II conjectures instances of learning sentences by means of transformation rules of this kind as well as by means of transformation rules that are decidedly *not* of the substitutional kind. Quine's generic term for all such *modes* of sentence learning is 'analogic synthesis'. All cases of analogical substitution thus count as cases of analogic synthesis, but not vice versa, since not all cases of analogic synthesis are substitutional in character.

A second thing to notice is that in Quine's example, 'My hand

hurts' is not only associated with a prompting range of nonverbal stimuli, but also with the previously acquired sentences 'My foot hurts',
'Foot', and 'Hand'. Nevertheless, it could have been learned without
the aid of these other sentences; it could have been learned as an unstructured whole, directly conditioned to the appropriate range of nonverbal stimuli. In short, it could have been learned via mode (1), just
as the other sentences of the example were presumed to have been
learned. Chomsky has so misunderstood the import of this last point
that he has written that Quine in *Word and Object*

> seems to imply that the process of analogical synthesis is the-
> oretically dispensable, simply serving to speed matters up. . . .
> Therefore, we can perhaps conform to his intentions by totally
> disregarding this process, and considering the knowledge [of
> language] attained by a long-lived adult using only the first two
> methods instead of the knowledge [of language] attained by a
> young child who has used all three. . . . Noting further that a
> child of nine and a man of ninety share knowledge of language
> in fundamental respects . . . it would seem, further, that little
> is lost in omitting 'analogical synthesis' from consideration en-
> tirely, even for the young child. *Assuming that this interpreta-*
> *tion of Quine's remarks is correct*, we derive support for the
> conclusion that he regards a language as a *finite* network of as-
> sociated sentences, some associated also to stimuli, since this
> is just the structure that would arise from the two postulated
> mechanisms of language learning with substantive content.[13]

Chomsky goes on to note that this interpretation of Quine-I's remarks
on sentence learning is inconsistent with a truism that Quine-I himself
explicitly accepts, namely, that a language is an *infinite* set of sentences. Chomsky does not perceive this inconsistency as a *reductio ad
absurdum* of his interpretation of Quine's remarks on the methods of
sentence learning.

A third thing to notice is that Quine claims the 'My hand hurts'
example *is* an instance of the association of sentences with sentences.
Hence Chomsky's differentiation of the association of sentences with
sentences (the "first" method) and analogic synthesis (the "third"
method) raises suspicions about how Chomsky is construing 'associa-

13. Noam Chomsky, "Quine's Empirical Assumptions," in *Words and Objections, Essays on the Work of W. V. Quine*, ed. D. Davidson and J. Hintikka (Dordrecht-
Holland: D. Reidel Publishing Company, 1969), pp. 56–57, *my emphasis*.

tion of sentences with sentences'. (He seems to be thinking of the association of *whole* sentences with *whole* sentences.)

Fourth, Quine's remark that the association operative in the 'My hand hurts' example is *too restrained* is intended to underscore the fact that the newly acquired sentence was learned in association with other sentences that, as we have already noted, were all assumed to have been learned previously by direct conditioning. This being the case, the newly acquired sentence will have its particular range of nonverbal stimulatory occasions, just as though it, too, had been learned by being directly conditioned to a fixed range of nonverbal stimuli.

Fifth, when Quine adds that *further interverbal associations are required*, etc., he is not introducing some new, "third" method of learning sentences. Rather, he is simply saying that the 'My hand hurts' example by no means exhausts the resources of analogic synthesis (i.e., analogic synthesis is comprised of many *modes* of sentence learning). Quine then immediately proceeds to supply examples of sentences that occur as responses to verbal stimuli, as in instances of interrogation, for example, 'Red' said in response to 'What color will you have?', and examples of sentences that are prompted as responses to nonverbal stimuli but that require "the verbal network of an articulate theory . . . to link the stimulus with the response" (WO, 11) as when "someone mixes the contents of two test tubes, observes a green tint, and says 'There was copper in it'" (WO, 10–11). But these additional cases are noteworthy not because they represent a "third" method of learning sentences but because they exemplify cases of the association of sentences with sentences of a more interesting and productive kind than was exemplified in the 'My hand hurts' example. It is such instances of interverbal association as these that allow us to rise above the level of phenomenalistic reporting by constructing sentences that, unlike 'My hand hurts', cannot be tied, even derivatively, to any fixed ranges of nonverbal stimuli.

One last bit of textual evidence supports the view that Quine recognizes only *two* general methods for learning sentences:

> Not that all or most sentences are learned as wholes. Most sentences are built up rather from learned parts, by analogy with the way in which those parts have previously been seen to occur in other sentences which may or may not have been learned as wholes. What sentences are got by such analogical synthesis, and what ones are got directly, is a question of each individual's own forgotten history. (WO, 9; *note omitted*)

In summary, I think a close reading of the relevant passages of *Word and Object*, when compared with Chomsky's interpretation of those passages, will reveal that Chomsky has misunderstood the number and character of the methods Quine discusses for learning sentences.

Suppose, as I believe, that in the passages in question in *Word and Object* Quine proposed only *two* methods for learning sentences: ostension and analogic synthesis. Suppose, further, that analogic synthesis *is* the associating of sentences (and/or their parts) with other sentences (and/or their parts) in multifarious ways. Now recall Chomsky's admission that the association of sentences with sentences and the association of sentences with nonverbal stimuli would lead to a fabric of associated sentences and stimuli. Should we conclude from all this that Chomsky's first inconsistency charge (namely, that Quine-II's admission that conditioning is insufficient to account for all of language learning is inconsistent with both Quine-I's account of language learning *and* his characterization of language as a fabric of associated sentences and stimuli) has, therefore, been answered? I think it is pretty clear that we should not, for when Chomsky admitted that the association of sentences with sentences and the association of sentences with nonverbal stimuli would indeed lead to a fabric of associated sentences and stimuli, he apparently had in mind the association of *whole* unstructured sentences with other *whole* unstructured sentences and the association of *whole* unstructured sentences with nonverbal stimuli, a phenomenon that he apparently finds intelligible; not so, analogic synthesis, however. In other words, there is still the outstanding matter of Chomsky's denial of the intelligibility of the premise that analogic synthesis *is* a matter of association or conditioning.

Let us recall, specifically, Chomsky's complaint concerning Quine's notion of analogic synthesis. He claimed that analogic synthesis deprived the notion of conditioned response of its "strict" meaning, or anything resembling that meaning, since the responses and the stimuli entering into the alleged relationship of conditioning need not even appear together. Consequently, to say of a language containing sentences learned by analogic synthesis that it is characterizable as a fabric of sentences associated by the mechanism of conditioned response is either false (if 'conditioned response' is taken in its strict sense) or vacuously true (if 'conditioned response' is taken in some other unspecified sense).

The heart of Chomsky's complaint seems to be that if the (strict) notion of conditioning is to be meaningful, then in any particular case of conditioning the relevant stimuli and response must occur together, and in the 'My hand hurts' example the stimuli and response do not occur together. Consequently, if the 'My hand hurts' example is a typical instance of analogic synthesis, which we may confidently suppose it is since it is the only detailed instance Quine provides in the whole of *Word and Object*, then, Chomsky thinks, it is fair to conclude that analogic synthesis is not a (strict) case of conditioning and a language containing sentences learned by analogic synthesis cannot therefore meaningfully be characterized as a fabric of sentences associated by the mechanism of conditioned response.

However, even if we assume with Chomsky that his strict notion of conditioned response is the only acceptable one, why should we assume further with him that the relevant stimuli and response do not occur together in the 'My hand hurts' example? There is, after all, the presence of the prompting nonverbal stimulus, namely, the hurting hand. And, although it is highly implausible to suppose that while the child's hand is hurting he says aloud or even to himself 'My foot hurts', 'Foot', and 'Hand', so that the throbbing hand and all of the relevant sentences of the example are nearly present at once, it is not implausible to suppose that there are some physiological structures, which underlie the conditioning of the other sentences of the example to nonverbal stimuli, that *are* present. No one is claiming that the association is a conscious matter, nor even that it could always be made a conscious matter. Perhaps Quine could have stated the matter more accurately if he had said that the utterance of 'My hand hurts' (the response) is associated not with the *sentences* 'My foot hurts', 'Foot', and 'Hand', but with their respective dispositions to be uttered, or with their respective dispositions to be assented to when queried—in other words, to certain (present) physiological states of the utterer of 'My hand hurts' along with, of course, the hurting hand. Thus are the stimuli and response present together in cases of analogic synthesis, and, consequently, there no longer appears to be any good reason for not regarding instances of analogic synthesis to be like cases of strict conditioning *in this respect*; nor does there any longer appear to be a good reason for saying that *because* a language contains sentences learned by analogic synthesis it cannot be characterized as a fabric of sentences variously associated to one another and to nonverbal stimuli by the mechanism of conditioned response.

On the other hand, there is, obviously, more to be told to this story of how a child could produce a new sentence by analogic synthesis than Quine has told, even if we include his account given in *The Roots of Reference*. There is, for example, the as yet unwritten chapter concerning the innate structure, whatever it is, that accounts for the child's ability to recognize grammatical similarities and analogies and to wield transformation rules such as the substitutional transformation rule that we supposed was instrumental in forming 'My hand hurts' by substituting 'hand' for 'foot' in 'My foot hurts'. Even so, we may presume that conditioning is a *necessary* mechanism of all language learning even if not a *sufficient* mechanism, for even in the domain of analogic synthesis language learning must be stimulated by example and shaped by reinforcement on the part of the other members of the speech community.

Where does all of this leave us with respect to the *first* of Chomsky's three inconsistency charges? Recall that Quine-II has been quoted as proclaiming that ostension is learning by simple induction, the mechanism of such learning is conditioning, and this method is notoriously incapable of carrying us far in language learning. In short, he claimed that conditioning is insufficient to explain language learning. Chomsky maintained that this proclamation is inconsistent with Quine-I's characterization of a language as a fabric of sentences associated by the mechanism of conditioned response *and* with the "three" methods of sentence learning discussed by Quine-I.

I have spent a great deal of space unsnarling the tangles in this misinterpretation of Quine-I's remarks on methods of sentence learning. I pointed out along the way that this misinterpretation was at the bottom of the claims (a) that Quine-I was committed to the view that a language is both a *finite* set of sentences and an *infinite* set of sentences, and (b) that if Quine-I's characterization of a language is accepted, then his account of sentence learning must be rejected and vice versa. It should now be clear that this same misinterpretation is also at the bottom of the second half of the present inconsistency charge, namely, (c) that if conditioning is insufficient to explain language learning (Quine-II), then sentences are not learned by the "three" methods discussed by Quine-I, and, therefore, I shall ignore it. However, this still leaves the first half of the *first* inconsistency charge to be dealt with, namely, (d) if conditioning is insufficient to explain language learning (Quine-II), then a language is not a fabric of sentences associated by the mechanism of conditioned response as Quine-I alleged.

The answer to this charge lies with the distinction made earlier between saying that conditioning is a *necessary* mechanism of all language learning and saying that conditioning is a *sufficient* mechanism of all language learning. Denying the latter does not deny the former, and it is on the basis of the former that Quine-I claims that a language is a fabric of sentences variously associated to one another and to non-verbal stimuli by the mechanism of conditioned response. Even in cases of analogic synthesis there is a stimulus and response, but the innate mechanism linking the two is something additional to quality space. So, the characterization of a language in question was not intended by Quine-I to be the complete story of the innate mechanism responsible for language learning. Indeed, if it were the complete story, he could have omitted from *Word and Object* any consideration of indeterminacy of translation and analytical hypotheses, for then all of language would have been learnable solely on the basis of induction. Quine himself has pointed out that the recognition that conditioning is insufficient to explain language learning is of a piece with his doctrine of indeterminacy of translation (*see* LP, 58). Consequently, if we construe Quine-I's characterization of a language in the "sufficient" sense, then we should be prepared to admit that Quine-II's claim that conditioning is insufficient to explain language learning *is* inconsistent with it. On the other hand, if we give Quine-I's characterization the "necessary" interpretation, then Quine-II's claim is *not* inconsistent with it. My preference for the latter interpretation is that it is consistent with the rest of *Word and Object*, whereas the former is not.

Recall, now, Chomsky's *second* charge concerning Quine's alleged inconsistency, namely, that if generative grammar is the essential defining characteristic of human language, then, again, the earlier account of language can be dismissed, since a generative grammar cannot be described as a fabric of sentences and stimuli associated by conditioning. Quine-II does indeed acknowledge that "it is generally appreciated that generative grammar is what mainly distinguishes language from subhuman communication systems" (RC, 304). But it is not clear to me why this admission is inconsistent with Quine-I's characterization of a language as a fabric of sentences variously associated to one another and to nonverbal stimuli by the mechanism of conditioned response, at least when this characterization is properly understood. On the other hand, if one were to construe Quine-I's characterization as the claim that it is only unstructured whole sentences that are associated with one another and with nonverbal stimuli, then I can see the inconsistency. But such an interpretation of Quine-I's characterization would be a misinterpretation, derived in part, perhaps, from a misunderstanding of Quine-I's remarks on methods of sentence learning.

Chomsky's final charge concerning Quine's alleged inconsistency pertains to innate mechanisms of language learning: "If innate mechanisms of arbitrary complexity are permissible, so long as conjectures are eventually made sense of in terms of external observations, then there is no reason to assign any special place to dimensional structures such as a 'quality space,' nor to structures determined by differential conditioning and extinction tests." [14]

Quine-I introduced the notion of quality space in connection with his lengthy discussion of the child's *earliest phase* of language learning, ostensive learning (cf. WO, 80–90). The mechanism of this early phase of learning is direct conditioning. Since the child is amenable to such training, he must have an innate ability to weight qualitative differences unequally; he must be able to notice more similarities between some stimulations than between others. Otherwise a dozen reinforcements of his response 'Red' on occasions where red things are salient would no more encourage the same response to a thirteenth red thing than to a blue one.

Quine-II has claimed that even though the qualitative spacing of stimulations must be recognized as an innate structure needed in accounting for any learning, and, hence, in particular, language learning, unquestionably much additional innate structure is needed, too, to account for language learning:

> The qualitative spacing of stimulations is as readily verifiable in other animals, after all, as in man; so the language-readiness of the human infant must depend upon further endowments. It will be interesting to find out more and more, if we can, about what this additional innate structure is like and how it works. Such discoveries would illuminate not only language but learning processes generally. (LP, 57)

This duality of types of innate structures needed for language learning advocated by Quine-II is consistent with Quine-I's view of the duality of methods of language learning: ostension and analogic synthesis. Learning by ostension is learning by simple induction over observed similarities, and the mechanism of such learning is, according to Quine, conditioning. For conditioning to be possible there must be innate, prelinguistic quality space (or spaces), or, in the technical language of his later writings, innate standards of perceptual similarity. Learning by analogic synthesis, on the other hand, is learning by anal-

14. Chomsky, *Reflections on Language*, pp. 199–200.

ogies and requires further innate endowments. The innate mechanisms of such learning are little understood but nonetheless necessary for language learning.

Consequently, if Chomsky's third change is taken to mean that Quine-II's position is somehow broader in its admission of innate mechanisms of language learning than is Quine-I's and, therefore, supersedes it or is inconsistent with it, then the charge is false. For in *Word and Object*, as already noted, Quine does give innate quality space a central role to play in his discussion of language learning, but *not* an *exclusive* role. Quality space is discussed only in connection with the earliest phase of language learning. Immediately after that discussion of ostensive learning Quine goes on to discuss more advanced phases of language learning without mentioning quality space.

I think it is fair to conclude that the position of Quine-I and the position of Quine-II regarding the matters of methods of sentence learning, characterizing a language, and innate mechanisms of language are not inconsistent with each other, at least not in the ways Chomsky alleges. But what are we to make of the second half of Chomsky's major charge, namely, that Quine-II has almost completely abandoned the behaviorism of Quine-I?

§4.4   *Has Quine-II abandoned the behaviorism of Quine-I?*

It is worth recalling that Quine recognizes three levels of explanation of human behavior generally (including verbal behavior): the mentalistic level, the behavioristic level, and the physiological level. The least satisfactory of these is mentalism, the most satisfactory is physiology; but in language theory we are, for the present, best advised to opt for behaviorism. In a way, then, behaviorism is for Quine a kind of methodological halfway house situated between the obscurantism of mentalism and the promise of neurophysiology. Furthermore, so far as language theory is concerned, Quine sees no alternative to this kind of behavioristic approach:

> even those who have not embraced behaviorism as a philosophy are obliged to adhere to behavioristic method within certain scientific pursuits; and language theory is such a pursuit. A scientist of language is, insofar, a behaviorist ex officio. Whatever the best eventual theory regarding the inner mechanism of language may turn out to be, it is bound to conform to the behavioral character of language learning: the dependence of verbal behavior on observation of verbal behavior. A language is mastered

through social emulation and social feedback, and these controls ignore any idiosyncrasy in an individual's imagery or associations that is not discovered in his behavior. (PPLT, 4)

Quine has claimed to be "as behavioristic as anyone in his right mind
could be" (RH, 296). The humor of this claim derives from its para-
doxical air, what with it being a pledge of allegiance to behaviorism
expressed in the form of a mentalistic colloquialism. But the paradox is
more than humorous; it is also didactic, for it reminds us that Quine's
brand of behaviorism incorporates two vestiges of the mentalism that
characterized the empiricism of Locke, Berkeley, and Hume, namely,
reliance upon the method of introspection and utilization of mentalistic
terms. These appear in Quine's externalized empiricism, however, as
mere vestiges, not as vital organs.

These two vestiges linger in Quine's general learning theory and
language theory. Quine's general theory of learning necessarily incorporates many terms having mentalistic overtones (e.g., 'salience',
'traces', 'pleasure', etc.) as well as certain mentalistic-sounding principles (e.g., the reciprocal enlivening effects of activated traces, etc.),
many of which were arrived at via introspection. Further mentalistic
terms such as 'induction', 'abstraction', 'generalization', 'covergence
of images' are scattered throughout Quine's discussion of language
learning. Without the aid of these terms, no theory of learning at all
could be stated at this time.

"But what kind of behaviorism is this," one might ask, "which
countenances introspection and mentalistic terms?" First, while
Quine's brand of behaviorism does condone introspection, "it con-
dones it as a means of arriving at conjectures or conclusions *only* insofar as these can eventually be made sense of in terms of external observation" (LP, 58; *my emphasis*). Second, when Quine uses mentalistic
terms in stating his theories of learning, he is not using these terms to
posit the existence of any irreducibly mentalistic objects. Rather, he
uses them to refer to "hypothetical states of the nervous system" (RH,
296), the exact nature and functioning of which system neurophysiology may someday reveal. To hasten the arrival of that day, Quine urges
that the criteria for the application of such mentalistic terms be stated
in behavioral terms whenever possible. In this spirit does Quine attempt to provide a behavioral specification of 'perceptual similarity' in
The Roots of Reference.

Preliminaries aside, let us now respond to the second charge leveled against Quine in *Reflections on Language*, namely, that Quine-II has almost completely abandoned the behaviorism of Quine-I. Presumably, this charge is prompted by Quine-II's admission that as yet unknown innate structure, over and above quality space, is needed to account for language learning, and, further, it may turn out that the processes involved are very unlike the classical process of reinforcement and extinction of responses. This position of Quine-II is indeed inconsistent with the interpretation of Quine-I that claims quality space and conditioning are sufficient for explaining all of language learning. But, as we have seen, this interpretation is a misinterpretation. Of the two methods of language learning discussed in *Word and Object*, ostension and analogic synthesis, only ostension was assumed to approximate the classical process of reinforcement and extinction of responses. The complete nature of the processes underlying analogic synthesis was as much an open question for Quine in 1960 as it was for Quine in 1969 (and is for Quine in 1981—despite his *speculations* in *The Roots of Reference*). Consequently, if Quine has almost completely abandoned behaviorism, he did so not in 1969 but as early as 1960 or before.

Contrary to the allegation, Quine's theory of language learning remains behavioristic, even if not behavioristic along the lines that Chomsky interpreted Quine-I to be. Quine has never maintained, as Chomsky alleges of Quine-I, that quality space and conditioning are by themselves *sufficient* for explaining all of language learning. But Quine has and does maintain that quality space and conditioning do go a long way toward explaining how observation sentences are learned. And Quine has and does maintain that language theory should be developed within a behavioristic framework.

Quine's behaviorism is, then, at once both substantive and heuristic. His behaviorism is *substantive* insofar as he claims that an early phase of language learning, namely, the learning of (some) observation sentences, approximates the classical process of reinforcement and extinction of responses and, further, that the dimensions of the innate structure which the process of conditioning presupposes, namely, quality space, can, in principle, be determined by differential conditioning and extinction tests.

His behaviorism is *heuristic* (or methodological) insofar as he admonishes us to conjecture about meanings, the rules of language, and the mechanisms of language learning only insofar as our conjectures can, eventually, be made sense of in terms of external observation.

This is the force of Quine's dictum that language (or mind) should be studied in the same empirical spirit that animates natural science (OR, 26).

Chomsky has been critical of both aspects of Quine's behaviorism. On the substantive side, in response to Quine's claim that some observation sentences are learned by conditioning, Chomsky writes:

> it seems that in Quine's . . . view, the mechanisms (namely, conditioning) that account for learning of observation terms are . . . qualitatively different from those involved in other aspects of language learning. However, I see no reason to suppose that there is any fundamental difference in this regard. . . . [C]onsider what is perhaps the most "elementary" notion we have, the notion "physical object," which, I suppose, plays a role in the most elementary processess of learning through ostension, induction, or conditioning. But the notion "physical object" seems to be quite complex. At the very least, some notion of spatiotemporal contiguity seems to be involved. . . . But even spatiotemporal contiguity does not suffice as a general condition. One wing of an airplane is an object, but its left half, though equally continuous, is not. Clearly some *Gestalt* property or some notion of function is playing a role. Furthermore, scattered entities can be taken to be single physical objects under some conditions: consider a picket fence with breaks, or a Calder mobile. The latter is a "thing," whereas a collection of leaves on a tree is not. The reason, apparently, is that the mobile is created by an act of human will. If this is correct, then beliefs about human will and action and intention play a crucial role in determining even the most simple and elementary of concepts. Whether such factors are involved at early levels of maturation, I do not know, but it is clearly an empirical issue and dogmatic assumptions are out of place. It may be that a schematism of considerable complexity and abstractness is brought to bear in learning processes that might be regarded as very "elementary," whatever sense can be made of this notion; very little sense, I am suggesting.[15]

Prior to discussing this critical passage of Chomsky's, it should be pointed out that Chomsky uses the term 'physical object' in this con-

15. Chomsky, *Reflections on Language*, pp. 202–3.

text where Quine would use the term 'body'. Quine reserves the term 'physical object' for use in discussions of the more esoteric business of conscious ontologizing. Consequently, to avoid confusion, I shall translate 'physical object' in the above quotation as 'body'.

The central claim that Chomsky appears to be making in the above passage is that Quine is being dogmatic in differentiating, on qualitative grounds, the mechanisms (i.e., conditioning) underlying that fragment of language learned by ostension, namely, (some) observation sentences, from the mechanisms (largely unknown) involved in learning sentences by analogic synthesis. Apparently Chomsky understands this qualitative difference to be based upon an unargued assumption attributed to Quine that learning language by conditioning is, somehow, a "simpler" matter than learning language by the mechanisms of analogic synthesis. To show that this unargued assumption is doubtful, Chomsky argues that learning by ostension, induction, or conditioning involves the notion of body and, further, that the notion of body clearly involves some notion of function, or some notion of human agency, or some Gestalt property, all of which are rather "complex" notions. Consequently, there is good reason, Chomsky thinks, to doubt the assumption that learning language by conditioning is qualitatively different, in the sense of being "simpler," from learning language by the mechanisms of analogic synthesis.

Chomsky's argument implicitly assumes that Quine's conception of learning by conditioning excludes such data as Gestalt properties, function or purpose, and human agency from the field of possible data that serve as stimuli for such learning. Elsewhere Chomsky has made this implicit assumption into an explicit charge that Quine dogmatically restricts the scope of quality space to dimensions which have some simple physical correlates such as hue or brightness.[16] Quine has responded to this misinterpretation of his position by drawing attention to the fact that "the denizens of quality spaces are expressly stimulations . . . , any and all, with no prior imposition of dimensions" (RC, 306–7).

Further evidence that Quine's conception of learning by conditioning has been misunderstood can be found in *The Roots of Reference*. There Quine sums up his discussion of the similarity basis underlying the ostensive learning of the observation sentence 'Mama':

16. Chomsky, "Quine's Empirical Assumptions," p. 55.

The similarity basis of 'Mama' was rather a long story. Each view of her is a continuous patch? Not quite; there was the little matter of eclipse and parallax. Each view of her is similarly shaped? No indeed, but there is the continuity of deformation. This rather tortuous sort of similarity is the unifying principle not only of Mama but of Fido and indeed of bodies generally. For all its tortuousness, it is apparently a sort of similarity that we are innately predisposed to appreciate. The well-known Gestalt effect is basic: the readiness to recognize a simple and unified figure, ignoring interruptions of outline. A similar readiness to recognize the persistence of an object in uniform motion, despite temporal interruption, is reported in early infancy: the baby will see an object pass behind a screen and show surprise when it does not duly emerge at the other side. It is no wonder that bodies, bodily identity and bodily persistence, are the mainstay of ontology. Bodies, for the common man, are basically what there are; and even for the esoteric ontologist bodies are the point of departure. Man is a body-minded animal, among body-minded animals. Man and other animals are body-minded by natural selection; for body-mindedness has evident survival value in town and jungle. (RR, 54; *note omitted*)

It is impossible, I would think, to reconcile these passages from Quine's writings with Chomsky's implicit assumption, or his explicit charge, that Quine's notion of learning by conditioning disallows such data as Gestalt properties, etc., from being considered among the data serving as stimuli for such learning. This being the case, there is no evident justification for the claim that Quine dogmatically differentiates the mechanisms of ostensive learning from those of analogic synthesis along the qualitative lines suggested by Chomsky.

Chomsky has also leveled criticism against the second claim associated with the substantive aspect of Quine's behaviorism, namely, the claim that a subject's quality space can, in principle, be determined by differential conditioning and extinction tests. Chomsky writes:

A scientist investigating human cognitive structures might construct an abstract quality space as part of the full integrated system, but I see no reason to suppose [1] that it has a more primitive character than other components of the system, or [2] that it can be determined in isolation, or [3] that a reasonable hypothesis about a quality space is less infected by theoretical considerations with their "indeterminacies" than other components of innate cognitive structure, or [4] that relevant experiments for determining dimensionality can be selected in isolation from the general theory of innate cognitive structure. Thus both the commitment to a particular class of experiments (conditioning and extinction) and the commitment to an isolable quality space with some privileged character seem to me highly questionable.[17]

Chomsky's first observation concerning the "more primitive character" of quality space can be ignored since he apparently has in mind the same misunderstanding of Quine's position previously discussed in connection with the qualitative differentiation of the innate structures underlying conditioning (viz., quality space) and the innate structures (whatever they are) presumed to underlie analogic synthesis. Observations [2] and [4] together amount to the claim that there is no good reason to think that quality space is isolable from whatever other cognitive structures are possessed by humans; thus the commitment to a particular class of experiments, namely, differential conditioning and extinction tests, is highly questionable. It seems to me that the issue here is illusory. It arises from taking the expression 'quality' in 'quality space' too narrowly.

Recall the passage quoted earlier where Chomsky was shown to think (erroneously) that in *Word and Object* Quine was restricting the dimensions of quality space to those which have some simple physical correlates such as hue or brightness. If one were to understand the nature of quality space in this way, i.e., atomistically, then perhaps there would be no reason to suppose that quality space is isolable from other cognitive structures possessed by humans. But once this misinterpretation of Quine's view is given up, there seems to be little or no difficulty with the notion of an isolable quality space determined experimentally. For example, recall the hypothetical experiments cited by Quine in *The Roots of Reference* (Chap. 1), where the subject was encouraged to the point of habituation to depress a lever when confronted with the presentation of a circular stripe upon a screen, and was discouraged to the point of habituation from depressing the lever when confronted with the presentation of four dots placed on the screen in a semicircular fashion. On a subsequent occasion the subject was presented with a

17. Chomsky, *Reflections on Language*, p. 202.

circular arrangement of eight dots on the screen. If the subject depressed the lever he was said to regard the circular arrangement of dots to be perceptually more similar to the circular stripe than to the semicircular arrangement of four dots. If the subject failed to depress the lever then the opposite was true. To be sure, there are, as Quine pointed out, some theoretical problems with this technique. There is the problem of interference from within, that is, internal states of the organism could, undetectably in a single experiment, either prompt or inhibit the conditioned response, thereby invalidating the experiment. There is also the problem of changing standards of perceptual similarity, and the problem, due to the theoretical imprecision of the notion of intersubjective receptual similarity, of correlating findings intersubjectively. However, Quine does suggest ways of reducing the practical significance of these problems substantially (RR, Chap. 1).

The important thing to keep in mind in connection with quality space, and the thing Chomsky has apparently overlooked, is that "the denizens of quality spaces are expressly stimulations . . . , any and all, with no prior imposition of dimensions" (RC, 306–7). The isolation of *this kind* of quality space does not appear to be excessively problematic:

> Any irrelevant features of the stimulations will in principle disappear of themselves in the course of the experimental determination of the quality space. A little advance guessing of relevant dimensions could be handy in practice to economize on experiments, but this need not concern us. In principle the final dimensionality of someone's quality space, if wanted, would be settled only after all the simply ordinal comparisons of distance had been got by the differential conditioning and extinction tests. (RC, 307)

Chomsky's third observation, [3], to the effect that he sees no reason to suppose that a *reasonable* hypothesis about a quality space is less infected by theoretical considerations with their indeterminacies than (are hypotheses about) other components of innate cognitive structures, arises, apparently, from Quine's claim that hypotheses about the dimensions of quality space can be confirmed or refuted, subject only to the ordinary uncertainties of induction, by means of conditioning and extinction experiments (whereas hypotheses about cognitive mechanisms which are not discoverable, in principle, in a subject's behavior are not merely inductively uncertain but are, in principle, behaviorally indeterminate). Chomsky would, apparently, agree with Quine's position only insofar as those hypotheses concerning quality space were restricted to some *unreasonable* lot.

The criteria of Chomsky's term 'reasonable' are left obscure in the context in which it occurs, but perhaps what he means by 'reasonable' can be captured intuitively by the phrase 'significant and informative'. If this is so, then what Chomsky intends is that significant and informative hypotheses about quality space are sufficiently theoretical that they are not stable in behavioral (or observational) terms. Surely, however, this is not a matter for dogmatic pronouncements. Whether a given hypothesis about quality space stated in behavioral terms is significant and informative is clearly an empirical question.

Nevertheless, it might be the case, and more than likely is the case, that *more significant* and *more informative* hypotheses about the mechanisms of language learning transcend those about quality space altogether, but there is nothing about this that Quine would find uncongenial. Quine implicitly admits as much when he says:

> it has long been recognized that our innate endowments for language learning go yet further than the mere spacing of qualities. Otherwise we should expect other animals to learn language; and also, as Chomsky has lately stressed, we should expect our own learning to take longer than it does. Two generations ago, the supplementary innate endowment that got the main credit was an instinct for mimicry. One generation ago, a babbling instinct moved to first place; the infant babbles at random and the parent reinforces these utterances selectively. Currently, the babbling instinct is losing favor and the instinct for mimicry is back in the ascendency. I expect that both of these innate aids are there, and also of course the innate spacing of qualities, and also *some further innate apparatus which is not yet identified*. (PPLT, 5; *my emphasis*)

Clearly, we have gradually moved away from considering the strictly substantive aspect of Quine's behaviorism to a consideration of its heuristic aspect. A question of some importance for determining the nature of this heuristic aspect is: What, precisely, is Quine's methodological attitude toward conjectures about this *further innate apparatus* underlying language learning? The following quotation from Quine provides a particularly lucid answer:

dispositions to behavior are for me . . . neural mechanisms. As of now they are hypothetical mechanism, and our behavioral ticketing of them is only a partial description by a superficial, conditionally observable manifestation. Further mechanisms may be yet more remotely theoretical, deep in the DNA; and I am just as receptive to such conjectures, regarding the mechanisms of language, as I am to the physicists' conjectures regarding elementary particles. I ask only that the positing of such "intervening variables" be motivated by an earnest quest for an eventual explanatory model, integrated with our overall physical system of the world. Such a prospect or project, and not mere affection for time-worn mentalistic myths, should be the motivation.

The distinctive and vital role of behaviorism, for me, is in the partial explication of our terms; not in their causal explanation, nor even, usually, in any full definition. The important methodological principle is just that mentalistic explication is no substitute. In the extreme case where a theoretical element utterly devoid of observable manifestations is posited for the sake of some theoretical integration that it promises, I still say let us give it a try, recognizing what we are doing. But let us scorn any purported justification of the posit in irreducibly mentalistic terms. (W. V. Quine, 1977; personal communication)

As I noted earlier, Quine sees no acceptable alternative to this kind of behavioristic approach to language theory, since, according to him, language is learned by social emulation and social feedback, and these controls ignore any idiosyncrasy in an individual's imagery or associations that are not behaviorally detectable. Presumably, then, when we conjecture about the further innate apparatus underlying language learning, which is not yet identified, we have no choice but to keep within the guidelines prescribed by the heuristic aspect of Quine's behaviorism if we intend to be scientific about it (at least in Quine's sense of 'scientific').

§4.5   *Summary and conclusions*

Quine's behaviorism has both a substantive aspect and a heuristic (or methodological) aspect. Two of his substantive behavioristic claims are that the learning of some observation sentences approximates the classical process of reinforcement and extinction of responses, that the dimensions of the innate structure which the process of conditioning presupposes, namely, quality space, can, in principle, be determined by differential conditioning and extinction tests. A third substantive claim is, of course, the NB thesis itself: "Language is a social art which we all acquire on the evidence solely of other people's overt behavior under publicly recognizable circumstances" (OR, 26). This claim is, no doubt, the most fundamental of Quine's substantive behavioristic claims, and it is easy to see how it gives rise to the heuristic aspect of his behaviorism: From the fact (or assumption) that language is a social art it quite naturally follows that language is accessible to the intersubjective techniques of inquiry characteristic of natural science generally.

In the introduction to this book I remarked that Quine's commitment to behaviorism may very well prove to be his Achilles' heel. Nevertheless, I think we may fairly conclude that while Quine's naturalistic-behavioristic theory of language, especially that part pertaining to language acquisition, is in a sense incomplete, it has not been refuted. Whatever that outcome, it is certain that the prospects for the survival of empiricism (as a philosophy) have been greatly enhanced by Quine's work, and future proponents of empiricism will, therefore, owe a great debt to the philosophy of W. V. Quine.

References

Ayer, Alfred Jules. *Language, Truth and Logic*. 2d ed. London: Victor Gollancz, 1946.

Berkeley, George. *Principles, Dialogues, and Correspondence*. Edited by Colin Murray Turbayne. Indianapolis: Bobbs-Merrill, 1965.

Carnap, Rudolf. *Der logische Aufbau der Welt*. Berlin, 1928.

———. *Meaning and Necessity*. Chicago: University of Chicago Press, 1947.

———. "Physicalism." In *Dictionary of Philosophy*, edited by Dagobert D. Runes, p. 235. Totowa, N.J.: Littlefield, Adams and Company, 1977.

Chomsky, Noam. *Aspects of the Theory of Syntax*. Cambridge, Mass.: M.I.T. Press, 1965.

———. "Knowledge of Language." *The London Times Literary Supplement* (1968), pp. 523–25.

———. *Language and Mind*. Enlarged edition. New York: Harcourt Brace Jovanovich, Inc., 1968.

———. "Quine's Empirical Assumptions." In *Words and Objections, Essays on the Work of W. V. Quine*, edited by D. Davidson and J. Hintikka, pp. 53–68. Dordrecht-Holland: D. Reidel Publishing Company, 1969.

———. *Reflections on Language*. New York: Pantheon Books, Random House, Inc., 1975.

Chisholm, R. M. *Perceiving: A Philosophical Study*. Ithaca: Cornell, 1957.

Cohen, R. S., et al. *Essays in Memory of Imre Lakatos*. Dordrecht-Holland: D. Reidel Publishing Company, 1976.

Craig, William. "Replacement of Auxiliary Expressions." *Philosophical Review* 65 (1956): 38–55.

Davidson, D., and Hintikka, J., eds. *Words and Objections, Essays on the Work of W. V. Quine*. Dordrecht-Holland: D. Reidel Publishing Company, 1969.

Descartes, René. *The Philosophical Works of Descartes*. Translated by Elizabeth S. Haldane and G. R. T. Ross. 2 vols. Cambridge: Cambridge University Press, 1973 (Vol. I), 1970 (Vol. 2).

Dewey, J. *Experience and Nature*. La Salle, Ill.: Open Court, 1925, 1958.

Duhem, Pierre. *La théorie physique: Son objet et sa structure*. Paris, 1906.

207

Eddington, A. S. *The Nature of the Physical World*. Cambridge, England, 1928.

Frege, Gottlob. *The Foundations of Arithmetic*. New York: Philosophical Library; Oxford: Blackwell, 1950.

Goodman, Nelson. *Fact, Fiction, and Forecast*. New York: Bobbs-Merrill, 1955.

Guttenplan, Samuel, ed. *Mind and Language*. Oxford: Clarendon Press, 1975.

————, and Tamny, Martin. *Logic: A Comprehensive Introduction*. New York: Basic Books Incorporated, 1971.

Harman, Gilbert, ed. *On Noam Chomsky: Critical Essays*. Garden City, N.Y.: Anchor Press/Doubleday, 1974.

————. "An Introduction to 'Translation and Meaning', Chapter Two of *Word and Object*." In *Words and Objections, Essays on the Work of W. V. Quine*, edited by D. Davidson and J. Hintikka, pp. 14–26. Dordrecht-Holland: D. Reidel Publishing Company, 1969.

Hume, David. *A Treatise of Human Nature*. Edited by L. A. Selby-Bigge. Oxford: Clarendon Press, 1968.

Jourdain, P. E. B. *The Philosophy of Mr. B*rtr*nd R*ss*ll*. Chicago and London, 1918.

Kuratowski, Kazimierz. "Sur la notion de l'ordre dans la théorie des ensembles." *Fundamenta Mathematicae* 2 (1921): 161–71.

Leiber, Justin. *Noam Chomsky: A Philosophical Overview*. New York: St. Martin's Press, 1975.

Leibniz, G. W. *Opera Philosophica*. Edited by J. E. Erdmann. 2 vols. Berlin, 1840.

Lewis, C. I. *A Survey of Symbolic Logic*. New York: Dover Publications, Inc., 1960.

Lewis, C. I., and Langford, C. H. *Symbolic Logic*, 2d edition. New York: Dover Publications, Inc., 1959.

Lieb, Irwin C. "Feature Review of *Word and Object*." *International Philosophical Quarterly* (February 1962): 92–109.

Locke, John. *An Essay Concerning Human Understanding*. Collated and annotated by Alexander Campbell Fraser. 2 vols. New York: Dover Publications, Inc., 1959.

Lowinger, Armand. *The Methodology of Pierre Duhem*. New York: Columbia University Press, 1941.

Magee, Bryan, ed. *Modern British Philosophy*. New York: St. Martin's Press, 1971.

Mill, John Stuart. *A System of Logic*. New York, 1867.

Neurath, Otto. "Protokollsätze." *Erkenntnis* 3 (1932): 204–14.

Orenstein, Alex. *Willard Van Orman Quine*. Boston: Twayne Publishers, 1977.

Quine, W. V. *A System of Logistic*. Cambridge: Harvard University Press, 1934.

————. *Elementary Logic*. Boston: Ginn, 1941. Revised edition: Harvard University Press, 1966. Paperback: Harper and Row, 1965.

————. "Epistemology Naturalized." In *Ontological Relativity and Other Essays*, pp. 69–90. New York: Columbia University Press, 1969.

————. "Facts of the Matter." In *Essays on the Philosophy of W. V. Quine*, edited by Robert S. Shahan and Chris Swoyer, pp. 155–69. Norman: University of Oklahoma Press, 1979.

————. *From a Logical Point of View*. Cambridge, Mass.: Harvard University Press, 1953. Revised edition: 1961. Paperback: Harper and Row, 1963.

————. "Identity, Ostension, and Hypostasis." In *From a Logical Point of View*, pp. 65–79. New York: Harper and Row, 1963.

————. "Intensions Revisited." *Midwest Studies in Philosophy* 2 (1977): 5–11.

————. "Linguistics and Philosophy." In *The Ways of Paradox and Other Essays*, revised and enlarged edition, pp. 56–58. Cambridge, Mass.: Harvard University Press, 1976.

————. "Methodological Reflections on Current Linguistic Theory." In *On Noam Chomsky: Critical Essays*, edited by Gilbert Harman, pp. 104–17. Garden City, N.Y.: Anchor Press/Doubleday, 1974.

————. *Methods of Logic*. New York: Holt, 1950. Revised edition: New York: Holt, 1959; London: Routledge, 1962. 3d edition, revised and enlarged: Holt, 1972; Routledge, 1974.

————. "Mind and Verbal Dispositions." In *Mind and Language*, edited by Samuel Guttenplan, pp. 83–95. Oxford: Clarendon Press, 1975.

————. *Mathematical Logic*. New York: Norton, 1940. Emended 2d printing: Harvard University Press, 1947. Revised edition: 1951. Paperback: Harper and Row, 1962.

————. "On Empirically Equivalent Systems of the World." *Erkenntnis* 9 (1975): 313–28.

————. "On Mental Entities." In *The Ways of Paradox and Other Essays*, revised and enlarged edition, pp. 221–27. Cambridge, Mass.: Harvard University Press, 1976.

————. "On the Reasons for Indeterminacy of Translation." *The Journal of Philosophy* 67 (1970): 179–83.

————. "Ontological Relativity." In *Ontological Relativity and Other Essays*, pp. 26–68. New York: Columbia University Press, 1969.

————. *Ontological Relativity and Other Essays*. New York: Columbia University Press, 1969. Paperback: 1977.

————. "On What There Is." In *From a Logical Point of View*, pp. 1–19. New York: Harper and Row, 1963.

————. "Philosophical Progress in Language Theory." *Metaphilosophy* 1 (1970): 2–19.

————. *Philosophy of Logic*. Englewood Cliffs, N.J.: Prentice-Hall, Inc., 1970. Paperback: 1970.

————. "Posits and Reality." In *The Ways of Paradox and Other Essays*, revised and enlarged edition, pp. 246–54. Cambridge, Mass.: Harvard University Press, 1967.

————. "Quantifiers and Propositional Attitudes." In *The Ways of Paradox and Other Essays*, revised and enlarged edition, pp. 185–96. Cambridge, Mass.: Harvard University Press, 1976.

————. "Reference and Modality." In *From a Logical Point of View*, pp. 139–59. New York: Harper and Row, 1963.

————. "Reply to Chomsky." In *Words and Objections, Essays on the Work of W. V. Quine*, edited by D. Davidson and J. Hintikka, pp. 302–11. Dordrecht-Holland: D. Reidel Publishing Company, 1969.

————. "Reply to Harman." In *Words and Objections, Essays on the Work of W. V. Quine*, edited by D. Davidson and J. Hintikka, pp. 295–97. Dordrecht-Holland: D. Reidel Publishing Company, 1969.

————. "Reply to Professor Marcus." In *The Ways of Paradox and Other Essays*, revised and enlarged edition, pp. 177–84. Cambridge, Mass.: Harvard University Press, 1976.

————. "Reply to Smart." In *Words and Objections, Essays on the Work of W. V. Quine*, edited by D. Davidson and J. Hintikka, pp. 292–94. Dordrecht-Holland: D. Reidel Publishing Company, 1969.

————. *Selected Logic Papers*. New York: Random House, Inc., 1966. Paperback: 1968.

————. *Set Theory and Its Logic*. Cambridge, Mass.: Harvard University Press, 1963. Revised edition: 1969. Paperback: 1971.

————. "The Limits of Knowledge." In *The Ways of Paradox and Other Essays*, revised and enlarged edition, pp. 59–67. Cambridge, Mass.: Harvard University Press, 1976.

―――. "The Nature of Natural Knowledge." In *Mind and Language*, edited by Samuel Guttenplan, pp. 67–81. Oxford: Clarendon Press, 1975.

―――. *The Roots of Reference*. La Salle, Ill.: Open Court, 1974.

―――. "The Scope and Language of Science." In *The Ways of Paradox and Other Essays*, revised and enlarged edition, pp. 228–45. Cambridge, Mass.: Harvard University Press, 1976.

―――. *The Ways of Paradox and Other Essays*. New York: Random House, Inc., 1966. Paperback: 1968. Revised and enlarged edition: Harvard University Press, 1976. Paperback: 1976.

―――. "Two Dogmas of Empiricism." In *From a Logical Point of View*, pp. 20–46. New York: Harper and Row, 1963.

―――. "Use and Its Place in Meaning." *Erkenntnis* 13 (1978): 1–8.

―――. "Whither Physical Objects." In *Essays in Memory of Imre Lakatos*. Edited by R. S. Cohen et al., pp. 497–504. Dordrecht-Holland: D. Reidel Publishing Company, 1976.

―――. *Word and Object*. Cambridge, Mass.: The M.I.T. Press, 1960. Paperback: 1964.

―――, and Ullian, J. S. *The Web of Belief*. New York: Random House, Inc., 1970. Paperback: 1970. 2d edition: 1978; paperback: 1978.

Shahan, Robert S., and Swoyer, Chris, eds. *Essays on the Philosophy of W. V. Quine*. Norman: University of Oklahoma Press, 1978.

Sheffer, H. M. "A set of five independent postulates for Boolean algebras." *Transactions of the American Mathematical Society* 14 (1913): 481–488.

Skinner, B. F. *About Behaviorism*. New York: Alfred A. Knopf, 1974.

Smart, J. J. C. "Quine's Philosophy of Science." In *Words and Objections, Essays on the Work of W. V. Quine*, edited by D. Davidson and J. Hintikka. Dordrecht-Holland: D. Reidel Publishing Company, 1969.

Whitehead, A. N., and Russell, Bertrand. *Principia Mathematica*. Vol. 1. Cambridge, England, 1910; 2d ed., 1925.

Wiener, Norbert. "Simplification of the Logic of Relations." *Proceedings of the Cambridge Philosophical Society* 17 (1912–14): 387–90.

Wittgenstein, Ludwig. *Philosophical Investigations*. Translated by G. E. M. Anscombe. Oxford: Basil Blackwell, 1968.

Ziff, Paul. "A Response to Stimulus Meaning." *The Philosophical Review* 79 (January 1970): 63–74.

Index

The Philosophy of W. V. Quine
An Expository Essay

Roger F. Gibson, Jr.

with a foreword by W. V. Quine

How we acquire our theory of the world is
for W. V. Quine the central question of
epistemology. Roger Gibson sets forth
Quine's philosophy as a systematic attempt
to answer this question; his analysis
challenges those who might view Quine's
doctrines and theses as multifarious and
disparate.

Gibson first explores Quine's unique
brand of empiricism as well as Quine's views
on perception, learning, and English grammar. He then turns to an examination of
Quine's naturalistic-behavioristic conception of language learning and linguistic
meaning, maintaining that this conception of
language provides a framework within which
Quine formulates his discursive philosophy
—his answer to the central question of
epistemology. Ever faithful to Quine's own
language, Gibson meticulously examines
this philosophy, revealing its systematic
unity and making accessible the many difficult Quinian notions. The essay concludes
with a defense of Quine's philosophy of
language against the criticisms of Noam
Chomsky.

Gibson maintains throughout that Quine is
a central figure in the modern history of empiricism. Quine's enlightened empiricism, he
argues, is a post-positivist attempt to articulate a conceptually sound empiricism